Texas & Southwestern Lore

Edited by

J. Frank Dobie

Publications of The Texas Folklore Society Number VI

University of North Texas Press
Denton, Texas

Copyright © 2000 by The Texas Folklore Society
All rights Reserved

Copyright © 1927 by The Texas Folklore Society
Second Printing 1982
Southern Methodist University Press

Printed in the United States of America

Permissions:
University of North Texas Press
P. O. Box 311336
Denton, Texas 76203
(940) 565-2142 FAX (940) 565-4590

Library of Congress Cataloging in Publication Data

Dobie, James Frank, 1888–1964 ed.

Texas and southwestern lore, edited by J. Frank Dobie . . . Austin, Tex. Published by the Texas folklore society, 1927. 259 p. (music) 24 cm. (Publications of the Texas folklore society, no. VI)

"Proceedings of the twelfth annual session (1926) of the Texas folklore society" : p. [239]-240

1. Folklore—Texas 2. Cowboys—Songs and Music 3. Ballads, American 4. Folksongs, American—Texas I. Title II. Series
(contents)
GR1 • T4 no. 6   A 33-1131
ISBN 0-98-74-044-x (cloth)
ISBN 1-57441-104-7 (paper)

CONTENTS

I

The Editor's Prerogative.. 5
Folk-Lore of the Texas-Mexican Vaquero........*Jovita González* 7
Tales and Rhymes of a Texas Household.............................
....*Bertha McKee Dobie* 23
Lore of the Llano Estacado.................................*J. Evetts Haley* 72
Names in the Old Cheyenne and Arapahoe Territory............
....*Della I. Young* 90
Nicknames in Texas Oil Fields................*Hartman Dignowity* 98
The Devil's Grotto..*Mody C. Boatright* 102
Myths of the Tejas Indians...................*Mattie Austin Hatcher* 107
A Note on Four Negro Words....................*Robert Adger Law* 119

II

Ballads and Songs of the Frontier Folk............*J. Frank Dobie* 121
Songs the Cowboys Sing................................*John R. Craddock* 184
Songs of the Open Range..*Ina Sires* 192
"The Texas Cowboy"..*Arbie Moore* 196
Cowboy Songs Again..*J. Evetts Haley* 198
The Ballad of "Davy Crockett"..............................*Julia Beazley* 205
"Annie Breen from Old Kaintuck"........*George E. Hastings* 207
Songs and Ballads—Grave and Gay................*L. W. Payne, Jr.* 209
Proceedings of the Texas Folk-Lore Society, 1926..................... 239
Contributors 241
Index 243

THE EDITOR'S PREROGATIVE

"I am amazed at the work your organization is doing in gathering so much material, strictly in its line." Thus writes Carl Sandburg, who, after strumming folk tunes all over America and writing a folk history of Abraham Lincoln, is about to come forth with a book to be called *The American Songbag*. I must confess that I am becoming somewhat "amazed" myself. The supply of folk-lore in Texas and the Southwest seems inexhaustible; the growing interest in the subject is indeed heartening.

The West Texas Historical and Scientific Society, which is "staked" to Sul Ross State Teachers College at Alpine and of which Victor J. Smith, erstwhile president of the Texas Folk-Lore Society and all the while one of its best working and best contributing members, is "wagon boss," has issued a bulletin containing as much Big Bend folk-lore as history. The Panhandle-Plains Historical Society, the "bed ground" of which is Canyon, is through its field secretary, J. Evetts Haley, collecting the folk-lore as well as the history of the Staked Plains. East Texas, so long hiding in the cane brakes, is, with Miss Martha Emmons "loose-herding" the folk-lorists around Nacogdoches, getting ready to "trail out." This issue of the *Publications* contains the announcement of a new book of cowboy songs by Miss Ina Sires, of Dallas. The other day a young lady from Fort Worth stepped into the office of Dr. L. W. Payne, Jr.,—Nestor of Texas folk-lorists—with a book-sized manuscript of original negro songs. (For the cream of it watch next year's *Publications*.) A little before that two "prospectors" from Kansas with a "minometer"—a costly instrument for meting the path to buried treasure, if not meeting it—came to my home seeking confidential information on the seventy-five jack loads of Spanish bullion hidden on Dagger Hollow. I could tell a tale, not foreign to the Texas Folk-Lore Society, as to how the Kansans came thus questing "authentic tidings of invisible things." Almost weekly a new Texas legend is added to the store that will in time be issued as a second volume of *Legends of Texas*. Yet, as usual, the cry goes out not only for more legends but for more folk material of all kinds.

By next San Jacinto Day the membership of the Texas Folk-Lore Society will number five hundred. Increasing orders for the *Publications* are coming from all over the nation. In short, banal and contemptible though *boosting* is, "everything is lovely and the goose is hanging high."

And what, some people are asking, is to be done with all this collected folk-lore? For one thing, a number of intelligent people read it and enjoy it and are instructed by it as they read and enjoy and are instructed by history. This folklore is a part of our social history, as legitimate in its way as the best authenticated state papers. But will someone appear to weave it into fine ballads and novels, sift it and translate it into representative literature? The Texas Poetry Society is offering a prize each year for the best poem of "The Texan Class," and it is noteworthy that many of the poems entered make use of the findings of the Texas Folk-Lore Society. Miss Dorothy Scarborough, a past president of the Society, has woven an astonishing amount of folk material into her novel, *The Wind*. Like Hamlet's ghost, "methinks I scent the morning air." It is a fresh air and wonderfully bracing; it has life in it; it is sweet to the nostrils. May it bring rain!

I wish to express thanks to Miss Anne Garrison, of the University Conservatory of Music, Austin, for going over all the music printed in the pages that follow. Bertha McKee Dobie, my wife, has helped with editing and proof reading and I am hoping that she will make the index, as she did last year.

University of Texas, Austin, Texas,
Cinco de Mayo, 1927.

FOLK-LORE OF THE TEXAS-MEXICAN VAQUERO

By Jovita González

It is hardly conceivable that in this era of publicity and in this Texas, where every phase of ranching has been more or less popularized, there should exist unknown to the vast majority of Texans and other Americans an extraordinary type of range men. Such, nevertheless, is a fact. Moreover, this distinct and unfamiliar man of the range has been in Texas for nearly two centuries. Texas born and Texas bred, he is considered even by many of those who know him—superficially—as an undesirable alien. He is a product of the state, and loves Texas as his country; yet to Anglo-Americans of a few years' stay in the state he is an outcast. On one side, he descends from the first Americans, the Indians; on the other, his ancestry can be traced to the Spanish adventurer and conquistador. From the mingling of these two races a unique type has resulted, possessing not only salient racial characteristics of both but also certain peculiar traits created by the natural environment and surroundings in which he lives. This composite type is the vaquero of the Texas-Mexican frontier.[1]

First, his inherited traits will be considered. From his Indian ancestor he has inherited a love for freedom and the open prairie, a dislike for law and restraint, a plaintive melancholy that permeates all his actions, and a fatalistic tendency that makes him see the hand of fate guiding and mastering all his efforts. *"Suerte y Mortaja del cielo bajan"* ("Fortune and Death come from above") seems to be his motto in life. When misfortune assails him, the only answer to his problem is a shrug of the shoulder and a *"Si es mi suerte que le voy á hacer?"* ("It is fate: what can I do about it?")

From the Spaniard comes a courteous attitude toward women (especially before he is married), a daring spirit of

---

[1] The vaquero is not the aristocratic, landed proprietor of the borderland, but the wandering cowboy whose only possessions are his horse, an unlimited store of legends and traditions, and the love for his **Chata**, by which name the Spanish-American cowboy, whether Mexican vaquero or Argentinean gaucho, calls his sweetheart.

adventure, and a deep rooted love for beauty, particularly music and singing. From the same source he has also inherited a sincere religious feeling, which, mingled with pagan superstitions and beliefs, has added flavor and color to the legends and other forms of folk-lore of the borderland.

Living far from all contact with civilization, he is naturally suspicious of all innovations and newcomers. Every new invention introduced is a check to his freedom. An old vaquero told me once of what to him was paradise: the open prairies with no fences to hinder the roaming of the cattle and the wanderings of the cowboys. *"Cuando vino el alambre, vino el hambre."* ("With the coming of wire hunger came.") In spite of his pessimism, the vaquero is a poet at heart. He sees the beauty of the sage-brush in bloom; the singing of the mocking bird on clear moonlight nights invites him to sing—not songs of joy and happiness but plaintive melodies of unrequited love and tragedies. Like all people who live in close touch with Nature, he understands all the creatures of the woods and interprets them in his fanciful way. I am giving a few calls of birds as the vaquero understands them.

The turtle dove was once an Indian maid. She was in love with a shepherd lad, but he wandered away with his flock and soon found another love. The lovesick girl mourned and wept many moons for her faithless lover. The Great Spirit took pity on her and changed her to a turtle dove. She could not forget him and as a dove she still calls to him:

Cu-Cu	Coo-Coo
Cu-Cu	Coo-Coo
¿Qué quieres, pastor?	What do you want, shepherd lad?
Comer comas, comer comas,[2]	I want to eat comas, eat comas,
Adiós, pastor,	Good-bye, shepherd lad,
Adiós, pastor.	Good-bye, shepherd lad.

The dove known as the Spanish dove, vain creature that she is, tells every one with a toss of her head, *"Fea tú, fea tú,"* ("You're ugly, you're ugly"). The killdee (or killdeer) is a very cold-natured bird and is forever complaining of the cold. At dusk his cry can be heard,

¡Que frío, que frío!	How cold I am! How cold!
Tápame con la capa de tu tío	Cover me with your uncle's cape
Y tírame al río.	And throw me into the river.

---

[2]Berry growing on a shrub-like tree. The berry resembles the small purple wild grape in size and color.

As has already been stated, the vaquero is at heart a religious man; all the wonders of Nature he attributes to a supernatural power. All goodness and beauty come from the Virgin Mary and are part of her. A beautiful sunset is her smile; the blue sky is the blue of her mantle; the rainbow is formed by the tears that she sheds for sinners.

The folk-lore of the Mexican vaquero has the combined charm of the Andalusian lore as told by Fernán Caballero and the quaintness and simplicity of the Indian myth. To understand it is to understand the spirit and the soul of the Mexican people. With the hope that the true character of the Mexican vaquero will be better understood these legends are introduced.

One of the greatest hardships against which the vaquero has to contend is the drought. It is the enemy that blights all his hopes and frustrates all his plans. This is the theme of the story of *El Cenizo*.

EL CENIZO

It had been an unusually hard winter, cold and dry. But then coyotes had in the fall announced it would be so, for their fur had been heavy and thick, and they had stayed close to the ranches, not daring to go to the hills. All vegetation had been killed by *el hielo prieto* (the black frost), and even the cactus, the always reliable food for the cattle, had wilted.

Spring came, and with it new hope. But whatever young, green things sprang up died for need of water. The mesquites were mere ghosts; the huisaches, shameful of not bearing their sweet-smelling velvety blooms, hid their leaves. All the waterholes had dried up, and death and starvation ruled the prairie. The buzzard was lord of the plains, and as it flew over the trees was a constant reminder of death. The cattle, once so plentiful and fat, had diminished to a few, and those that remained looked at the world with sad, death-like eyes.

"¿*Por qué no llueve, Dios mío?*" ("Why do you not make it rain, my Lord?") the vaquero said, looking up at the sky. And with a sigh of resignation he added, "*Así es la suerte.*" ("That's luck.")

There was just one possible way of salvation, and that was prayer, prayer to the Virgin. The cowmen gathered together and reverently knelt on the plain to beg for help. As the last prayer of the rosary was said, a soft breeze, a *lagueño*,[3] blew from the east. Soon drops began to fall; all night the rain fell like a benediction.

Filled with new hope, the people rose early the next day to see the blessing that had fallen over the land. And indeed it was a beautiful blessing. For as far as the eye could see, the plain was covered with silvery shrubs, sparkling with raindrops and covered with flowers, pink, lavender, and white.

It was a gift of the Virgin, and because the day was Ash Wednesday the shrub was called *el cenizo*.[4] The interpretation given by the vaquero is charming, to say the least; the gray of the leaves signifies the Passion of Christ; the white flowers, the purity of the mother; and the pink, the new dawn for the cowmen and the resurrection of life.

The Mocking Bird

An equally interesting story tells how the mocking bird got the white feathers of its wings. There was a time when all the creatures of Nature talked a common language. This language was Spanish. *El zenzontle,* the mocking bird, had the sweetest voice of all. The other birds stopped their flight to listen to him; the Indian lover ceased his words of love; even the talkative *arroyo* hushed. He foretold the spring, and when the days grew short and his song was no longer heard, the north winds came. Although he was not a foolish bird, *el zenzontle* was getting conceited.

"I am great, indeed," he said to his mate. "All Nature obeys me. When I sing, the blossoms hid in the trees come forth; the prairie flowers put on their gayest garments at my call and the birds begin to mate; even man, the all wise,

---

[3]A breeze from the Gulf.

[4]**Ceniza** means **ashes**. The shrub is common all over Southwest Texas, and is known to country people of that section only by the Mexican name, **cenizo** or **ceniza** (pronounced **cenisa**), a name probably derived from the ashen color of the leaves. The botanical term is **Leucophyllum texanum**. Nurseries are popularizing it as a shrub for landscape planting—and it certainly has a great deal more character than the ligustrum! In the more arid parts of Texas it blooms after every summer rain; it is evergreen—or, more accurately, everashen. Mexicans make a medicinal tea of it.—Editor.

heeds my voice and dances with joy, for the happy season draws near."

"Hush, you are foolish and conceited like all men," replied his wife. "They listen and wait for the voice of God, and when He calls, even you sing."

He did not answer his wife, for you must remember he was not so foolish after all, but in his heart he knew that he was right.

That night after kissing his wife goodnight, he said to her, "Tomorrow I will give a concert to the flowers, and you shall see them sway and dance when they hear me."

"*Con el favor de Dios,*" she replied. ("If God wills it.")

"Whether God wills it or not I shall sing," he replied angrily. "Have I not told you that the flowers obey me and not God?"

Early next morning *el zenzontle* could be seen perched on the highest limb of a huisache. He cleared his throat, coughed, and opened his bill to sing, but no sound came. For down with the force of a cyclone swooped a hawk and grabbed with his steel-like claws the slender body of the singer.

"*Con el favor de Dios, con el favor de Dios,*" he cried in distress, while he thought of his wise little wife. As he was being carried up in the air, he realized his foolishness and repented of it, and said, "O God, it is you who make the flowers bloom and the birds sing, not I." As he thought thus, he felt himself slipping and falling, falling, falling. He fell on a ploughed field, and what a fall it was. A white dove who had her nest near by picked him up and comforted him.

"My wings," he mourned, looking at them, "how tattered and torn they look! Whatever shall I tell my wife?"

The dove took pity on him, and plucking three of her white feathers, mended his wings.

As a reminder of his foolish pride, the mocking bird to this day has the white feathers of the dove. And it is said by those who know that he never begins to sing without saying, "*con el favor de Dios.*"

El Cardo Santo (The Thistle)

One time there were two *compadres*[5] who, although they were good friends, always contradicted each other. And this was because one, whom we shall call Juan, always saw the good and beautiful side of life, and the other, Antonio, always took pleasure in seeing the unpleasant and ugly side of things.

As the two were out in the *potrero* (pasture) one day, Juan said, "Don't you think, *compadre,* that the mesquites look pretty today? The bloom is heavy and that means abundant food for the pigs this winter."

"Humph," growled Antonio, "how can you call them beautiful when their thorns are so sharp you can't touch them without killing yourself in the attempt?"

The two continued their way, Juan seeing the beauty of cactus and the *pitahaya*[6] (or *pitalla*) in bloom, smelling the fragrance of the huisache and the *uña de gato* (catsclaw), while Antonio saw only the thorns and wastefulness of Nature in creating things that a person could not pluck and gather at his will.

"And the priest says that God knows what he does. The idea of plants having thorns!" he grumbled.

"Hush, *compadre*," replied Juan, "the Virgin will punish you."

"What else can I expect when this world is upside down?" continued Antonio.

The rest of the day they rode in silence. At evening, having come to a *laguna,* they decided to camp for the night. Antonio found fault with everything, first with the night because it was dark, and then when the moon came up, because the brightness kept him from going to sleep.

Finally he went to sleep. Soon he was dreaming, but even the dream displeased him, for in it he saw a great radiance,

---

[5]The godfather of a child is the **compadre** of the child's father. Although there is no blood relationship, the tie is very dear. **Compadre** also means simply **friend**—a common usage.

[6]A cactus growing on the dry rocky soil of the border land. It bears a purple-red flower and a palatable fruit similar in taste to the strawberry. The soldiers of Fort Ringgold, Rio Grande City, call it Mexican **strawberry**. The cactus itself is used to make candy There is a candy **shop** on Alamo Plaza, San Antonio, where **pitalla** candy is made.

something like a cloud of light, approaching. In the midst of the cloud he saw a lady, holding an armful of lavender and pink flowers. The presence spoke to him with a voice that sounded like the singing of all the spring birds.

"Antonio," it said, "I have heard your words of displeasure and because I love the vaqueros, I have brought you a thornless flower that you can pluck, and fondle, and love."

With these words the lady disappeared, leaving Antonio stunned at what he had seen and heard. When he awoke, there, growing beside him, was a thistle-like flower which he called *cardo Santo,* for it was a holy gift of the Virgin.

The Guadalupana Vine

In south Texas there is a vine used for medicinal purposes known as the Guadalupana vine. It bears small gourd-like fruit. The seeds have a bright red covering, which on being removed show the image of our Lady of Guadalupe. Everybody is acquainted with the story of the apparition of our Lady of Guadalupe in Mexico. The story of the vine in itself is equally as interesting.

Two vaqueros were going to the nearest town for provisions. One of them was riding a very spirited *potro*. On coming to a creek the horse was frightened, and in spite of all that the rider could do the bronco threw him on the rocky banks. The other, terrified by the accident, did not know how to help his companion, who was slowly bleeding to death. As he sat there, a lovely lady came to him. She was dressed in blue, and he noticed that her mantle was sprinkled with stars. What astonished him more was to see that she floated, her feet not touching the ground. But he attributed this phenomenon to his bewildered condition. She approached, holding a small red fruit in her hand.

"Try this, my son," the lady said; "dip it in mescal and put it on the wound."

"But it will burn," stammered the surprised vaquero. The lovely lady smiled, shook her head, and whispered, *"No arde, no arde."* ("It will not burn.")

The vaquero did as he was told, and, strange as it may seem, his companion was cured immediately. The vaqueros consider this a miracle of the Virgin, and to verify this story they point to the fact that the Virgin left her image engraved on all the seed.[7]

Legends of Ghosts and Treasures

Another class of legends and traditions is equally fascinating, the stories of ghosts and treasure. It is a well known fact that many treasures were buried in Southern Texas and Northern Mexico during the last years of Spanish dominion. Other treasures were hid by the settlers when Indian raids were expected. Stories about such hidden wealth are without number. Wherever a treasure is buried, there is sure to be a ghost or a number of ghosts watching over it. They make their presence known by apparitions, moans, groans, clanking of chains, and clashing of swords.

Nothing so delights the vaquero as to sit around a camp fire and tell tales of ghosts, while the flames form weird and fantastic figures and shapes. On one such occasion I heard the story of the Chimeneas Ranch (Chimney Ranch), which is in Maverick County. I shall try to tell it as it was told to me.

It was a cold drizzly afternoon in November. A man in a khaki hunting suit, gun on shoulder, plodded wearily through the gray chaparral. Undoubtedly he was lost, for once in a while he stopped and looked around as if wishing to guide himself by some sign of Nature. A faint cry sounded in the distance. The hunter stopped, listened attentively, and answered by a loud "Hullo."

Nearer and nearer the cry came. *"Arre, arre, cabras,"* the hunter made out the cry to be. Not far off, half-hidden by *uña de gato* (catsclaw) and mesquites, he distinguished a herd of goats. Then a brown shaggy dog trotted into view. On seeing the hunter, the dog gave a bark, followed by a howl of warning.

"Calla, Lobo, calla," came the cry of the approaching *pastor* (shepherd).

He was a little old man, comical in his ugliness. His wrinkled brown face contrasted with the white of his hair. His toothless grin and his snappy, bright black eyes gave him

---

[7]On the border, the Mexican housewife puts up jars of the Guadalupana fruit in mescal. The people use no other remedy for cuts and wounds.

the appearance of a jack-o'-lantern. The brim of a straw hat jauntily set on his head resembled the halo of a saint. The remains of a Prince Albert coat, gaudily patched, protected him from the rain and cold. Instead of shoes he wore *guaraches* (sandals) of rawhide.

Seeing the hunter, he drew near, "halo" in hand, and, making a bow, said, "Excuse my Lobo, señor. He never sees anybody but your most humble servant, and considers everyone else an enemy of the flock. *Calla*, Lobo, *calla*, the señor is a friend." The dog probably understood, for he wagged his tail in sign of friendship.

"Can I be of any help to you, señor?" the *pastor* added.

"I am lost," the stranger said. "I left camp this morning and got turned around following a wounded deer. I am hungry and cold; a cup of coffee and a fire to dry myself will be all I need. Could you guide me to a ranch house where I can spend the night?"

"The nearest one is some miles off," the *pastor* replied, "but if the señor wishes to share the humble home of a poor man, he is most welcome."

The man nodded in silent assent and prepared to follow.

"This way, señor."

Night was swiftly descending; and what had been an evening mist was changing to rain. At a turn of the trail they were following, silhouetted against the darkness of the chaparral, was faintly discerned a white mass. As the two approached, the stranger discovered it to be a white stone house semi-hidden by shrubs and *nopal* (prickly pear).

"Didn't you tell me there were no ranch houses near here?" asked the hunter. "What do you call that?"

"Oh, señor," replied the *pastor*, "hush! Do not ask me, and *por la Virgen Santa*, do not go in."

"If you want to stay out in the rain, you are perfectly welcome, but as for me I am going in," and forthwith the brusque hunter made a motion towards the house.

"Señor, señor, but you'll come to harm."

"But what is wrong with the house?"

"It is accursed, señor," and the *pastor* crossed himself reverently. "The spirits of the dead live there."

"That sounds interesting," the stranger said with a smile

of incredulity. "Have your way about it. I will not go in, but you'll have to tell me the story of that house."

"The ghosts do not like the living to speak of them. It molests them, señor, and I do not like to do it, but to keep you from harm I will gladly do that and more. Now, *vámonos,* señor."

Soon they came to a thatch-roofed *jacal* built at the foot of a large mesquite.

"This is your home *a sus órdenes,* señor. Let me build a fire and you will be as comfortable as a king."

As the fire blazed, the stranger said to the goat herder, "I want to hear that story now, *amigo.*"

"*Bien,* it is a long story, señor. That house we passed was built by an old Spanish family, los Vegas by name, many years ago when the Spaniards ruled the land. They built the house well and strong, out of solid rock. In time of danger it was used as a fort, for you can still see the loop-holes on the walls. Some dreadful calamity must have befallen los Vegas, for they disappeared as mysteriously as they came. Some say they were carried away by the Indians; others, that they were killed by enemies, probably Spaniards. Their blood stains the floors yet. Because there is a fireplace in nearly every room the house has come to be called Las Chimeneas.

"The spirits of los Vegas wander at night. They look for the gold they buried. The American cowboys here call it Mexican superstition, but I swear to you that strange things do happen there, señor.

"One evening at sundown, as I was returning home with my flock, I heard voices inside of the house. Thinking that some of my friends were there, I stopped. They were talking of something that I did not quite understand, of a duel fought with swords, a murder, a proposed vengeance, and of money buried under a certain tree. Then I realized that I had been listening to the voices of the dead. I hurriedly gathered my flock and left.

"Just then José, that worthless fiddler, caught up with me and said meaningly, 'You'll soon be rich, won't you, *tío?*'

"'No,' I answered, 'there is not much money in herding goats.'

"'Don't be so sly, *tío.* What about the legacy of los Vegas?'

"He had also heard, the scoundrel. *Bien,* señor, the next day, taking a pick, I went to the place where I thought the money would be. But I was too late. José had been there before. Queer things happen there, señor.

"My wife, Juanita—may her soul rest in peace!—saw an apparition once. She was outside of this very *jacal* watering her flowers. She felt a presence near her; looking up, she saw a beautiful Spanish lady, all dressed in black. She wore a dress like the one *mi señora's* grandmother wore when she was presented to the viceroy in Mexico. She smiled at Juanita. My wife asked her what she wanted, but her only reply was a smile; and she faded away. Juanita never forgot that lovely face and smile; she was haunted by it day and night, and like her she faded away. I buried her on the hill top; from here I can see her grave and say an *Ave* for the repose of her soul. Believe me or not, it is the truth.

"That you may believe, I am going to tell you what happened to some American cowboys. They were regular daredevils, feared neither the dead nor the living. They boasted that they would spend a whole night at Las Chimeneas. Everybody was anxious, of course, to see what the outcome of it would be. They made their preparations in true cowboy fashion. Got their six-shooters in readiness, took enough tobacco to last them a week, and provided themselves with a deck of cards to play poker.

"All went well until midnight. That is the hour when the spirits of the dead wander about. All of a sudden the light went out. Footsteps of someone wearing spurs were heard coming into the room. Of course they said it was the wind— as if the wind could wear spurs. One of them got up, lit the lamp, and the game went on. Again they heard footsteps, and this time they heard the clashing of swords as of combatants fighting a duel. What else happened that night I never knew. Of one thing I am certain. By 4 o'clock that morning the cowboys were camping a mile from the house. Another thing I have noticed is that they do not make fun of me any more, and when I mention Las Chimeneas, they talk of something else or look at each other with a look of alarm.

"It is time to go to bed, señor. I hope the ghosts will not molest you. You sleep inside; the rain has stopped; and I will keep watch until the hour of danger is past. *Hasta mañana*, señor, may the Virgin protect you from all evil spirits."

The War of Independence in Mexico was followed by an exodus of the rich Spanish families who refused to pay allegiance to the newly created empire. Some left by way of Vera Cruz; others came northward towards the frontier. Many reached their destination; others with their wealth were lost, either killed by the Indians or dying from exposure. What became of the treasures they carried with them is a question that has occupied the minds of many fortune hunters.

I have heard three stories in regard to these treasures of the exiles. Two are concerning the treasure that is supposedly buried at or near old Las Escobas Ranch (*escoba* means *broomweed*), in Starr County.

About the year 1820 a family of wealthy Spaniards came to Ciudad Mier, now in Tamaulipas. They were coming from the interior; the men were well armed and rode pack mules. These were loaded with little chests covered with canvas cloth. They came into the town at nightfall and hurriedly looked for guides that would take them to New Orleans. So great was their hurry that they did not even stop to give the women and children a rest. They crossed the river and came into the province of Texas. But here they met with disaster; their mules could go no farther; two died from fatigue and another broke a leg. After much deliberation, they decided to go on with the women and children and later come back for the gold. The guides were blindfolded and taken to a distant thicket while the treasure was buried in a safe place.

On the return trip, the guides, knowing that they would be immensely rich if they acquired the gold, killed their masters. They came to Las Escobas to look for the buried money, but, search as they might, the exact spot was never found.

Three miles from this ranch is another, Las Víboras (Ranch of the Snakes), where also a treasure was buried. Several years ago, two boys while digging a hole found an ebony tablet buried at the foot of a tree. On it were carved as near as I can remember these ciphers: X. - - X. - -. As the season in which the tablet was found was very busy, no one paid much attention to it. Later I was told what might be a possible solution.

During the Spanish occupation of Texas a body of soldiers was sent to escort the money that was to pay the garrison at San Antonio. In those days the Comanches were the terror of the border land; they pillaged the ranch houses and murdered the settlers. A band of Indians attacked the soldiers, who, unaware, were taking their siesta. A brave resistance was made by the Spaniards, but to no avail, for by evening the last of the guard was killed. Not knowing what to do with money, the Indians buried it somewhere near Las Escobas or Las Víboras.

On what used to be *el camino real,* in what is now Jim Hogg County, is another old Spanish ranch, El Blanco. The place has always been thought to be haunted. Ghosts and spirits in different forms are supposed to haunt a buried treasure. Every vaquero when asked about the ghost of El Blanco will give his own version. The following was told me by one named Martiniano.

It was after midnight. Martiniano, the vaquero, was returning from a dance. He was happy. No evil thought disturbed his mind, and he whistled to himself as he remembered the pleasures of the *baile.* All of a sudden his horse reared and snorted as if frightened. And a good reason the poor beast had to be so terrified, for there in the middle of the road stood a woman dressed in white, her hair hanging down her back. Giving a sudden leap, she grabbed the reins of the horse. Martiniano, as can be imagined, was greatly frightened, but he had enough presence of mind to ask, "*¿Eres de este mundo ó del otro?*" ("Are you from this world or the other?")

"*Del otro*" ("From the other"), the ghost replied. For a while, which seemed an eternity to the vaquero, the ghost and the horse struggled. Finally, taking courage, the vaquero took out his pistol and shot once, twice, but the ghost held firmer grasp on the reins. About this time the moon came out from behind a cloud, and Martiniano saw the fleshless face of the ghost. As soon as he saw her face to face, the spirit dropped the reins and faded away.

Another vaquero told me that on passing by the ranch at night his horse began to limp, but he kept going and then, after having traveled all night, at dawn he found himself at the same place from which he had started the night before. Another told me of being attacked by a monster turkey gobbler, and of wrestling all night with it.

The love for music that characterizes all people of Spanish origin is developed to a great extent in the vaquero. However, the vaquero as a distinct type has not created music of his own. He plays the guitar with mastery, and to its accompaniment sings songs which have been introduced from old Mexico. The theme, as a rule, is of love, of war, of Nature, of the home, and not seldom of animal life. Some of the songs have the vivacious *sal* of the Spaniard, the quick wit of the Andalusian, while others, especially those treating of love, have a certain sadness peculiar to the Mexican peon.

One of the most popular songs that I have heard is "Las Mañanitas de San Juan." On early, misty spring mornings I have heard the vaqueros singing it while saddling their horses.

LAS MAÑANITAS DE SAN JUAN

Que bonitas mañanitas,	What beautiful mornings,
como que quiere llover;	as if it might rain;
parecen las mañanitas	they are just like the mornings
en que te empecé á querer.	when I began to love you.
Despierta, mi bien, despierta,	Awake, my beloved, awake,
mira que ya amaneció;	see it is already dawn;
ya los pajarillos cantan,	the birds are already singing,
la luna ya se metió.	and the moon has gone to rest.

In speaking of the vaquero songs, the fact should be mentioned that the *horse* as a theme is used extensively. The vaquero has no more faithful friend, no more constant companion in his lonely wanderings in the *potrero* than his horse. When he goes courting, the horse shares the same spirit of joy and adventure, and in case of an elopement, which is not uncommon, the horse, although a third party, is never a crowd. The horse is the theme of the ballad, "Mi Querida Nicolasa," given below.

Mi Querida Nicolasa

Ay, mi querida Nicolasa,	My beloved Nicolasa,
si te vinieras conmigo,	if you would come with me,
te llevaría hasta mi casa,	I would take you to my home
en ancas de mi rosillo.	riding my red roan horse.
Mi machete y mi petate,	My knife and my sombrero,
mi rosillo y mis espuelas,	my *rosillo*, and my spurs
¡ay! me han de dar tu linda mano,	will help me to make you mine,
Chatita, aunque no quieras.	Chatita, against your will.
Que cosa pa' mí tan buena,	What a blessed thing for me
esperar en el potrero,	to await in the *potrero*,
abrazar á mi morena	and to embrace my dark beauty
detracito de un maguey.	behind a maguey plant.
Despues ya con su chamaco,	Afterwards with her baby,
mi querida Nicolasa	my beloved Nicolasa
componiendo sus macetas	will arrange her flower pots
pa'que esté chula su casa.	to beautify her home.

The second ballad is an elegy, if it may so be called, in which the vaquero mourns the death of his horse.

Mi Caballo Bayo

Ya no vuelve a su palenque	Never again to his corral will return
mi fiel caballo, no vuelve, no;	my loyal horse, never return;
ya no relincha de gozo,	he will not neigh with pleasure
como cuando alguien lo acarició.	when someone caresses him.
Maldita la suerte perra	Cursed be the evil fate
que de repente me lo llevó.	that took him suddenly away.
¡Ay! mi pobre caballo bayo,	Oh, my poor dun horse,
cuanto he llorado	how I cried
cuando él murió.	when he died!

The story of the complete ballad is very touching and shows the mutual affection between master and horse. The vaquero is notified of the sickness of his horse; he goes to the *potrero* to see him. With almost human intelligence, the horse looks at his master as if to say, "Can't you relieve my pain?" Making a last effort, he tries to neigh a farewell, but with a groan he dies as his master says, *"Bayo, te lleve Dios."* ("God take your soul.")

There is only one type of song that is typically of the vaquero, and that is the *tragedia*. It is his song, which he sings while at work, and it is the most enjoyed of all his songs. He has made it his very own. As preposterous as the idea may seem, the *tragedia* in many respects resembles the epics of Mediaeval France and Spain, *La Chanson de Roland* and *El Cantar de Mío Cid,* not in quality of literature, of course, but in origin and theme. Like that of the *chansons de geste,* the action of the *tragedia* centers around some character whose deeds have made him, by popular assent, a hero. The author or authors are unknown, and verse after verse is added to suit the imagination of composer or singer. As time goes on, other exploits are attributed to the hero, until by the time of its completion the *tragedia* may contain as many as fifty verses of disconnected events, all dealing with the same subject. One of the best known is that treating of the famous border bandit Cortina.

Though the words of the *tragedia* frequently appear in the form of broadsides, the music is never printed; and, despite broadsides, the transmission of additions to *tragedias* is by word of mouth. Hence, many variations, both in music and words, are heard. When singing with the guitar accompaniment, the player picks the chords to suit his mood and fancy.[8]

A literature around the vaquero, or cowboy, of the pampas, known as the "gaucho" literature, has developed in South America, particularly Argentina, within the last century. Those who are familiar with it will notice the similarity in content to the vaquero stories, though we can not say in form, since no vaquero literature has been produced. Nevertheless, in interest and originality, the stories and character of the vaquero rival the stories and character of the gaucho. The material only awaits the touch to make of it a new type of Texas literature.

---

[8]For a good example of the **tragedia,** with ample discussion, see "A Mexican Popular Ballad," by W. A. Whatley in **Publications** of the Texas Folk-Lore Society, No. IV, 1925; also see "Versos of the Texas Vaquero," by J. Frank Dobie, in the same issue.

TALES AND RHYMES OF A TEXAS HOUSEHOLD

Edited by Bertha McKee Dobie

On the second of January, 1846, a young private named Charles Russell was honorably discharged at Corpus Christi from General Taylor's army. A New Yorker by birth, he had at eighteen enlisted in the United States Army for a period of five years. He was eager to see his mother after so long a time, and planned to take a sailing boat to Galveston on the very day of his discharge and from Galveston to ship to New York City. He and four northern comrades arrived at the landing in time to watch the boat dwindle on the bay. The boat plied regularly between Corpus Christi and Galveston, but would not be back for another trip until three weeks later.

The boys were so impatient to be off that they bought mustang ponies, "saddle-broke," for ten or twelve dollars apiece and rigging for a few more dollars and set out on the next day around the bay shore to Galveston. They rode up the Nueces River until they came to San Patricio, where they crossed and turned northeast. On the third day of their journey they reached historic old Goliad, or La Bahia, on the San Antonio River. The river was at too high a stage to admit of fording it, but the young men saw a ferry boat tied to the opposite bank. They called to the ferryman and he pulled over and brought them across.

Now this ferryman was George Claver Brightman, who, after frontier experiences as a journeyman cabinet maker in Indiana, then for two years in Florida at the time of the Seminole War, and again in Indiana, had come to Texas and had lived in the new town of Goliad, across the river from century old La Bahia, for something like a year when the five young men hallooed to be set on the east bank.

It was almost noon, and hospitality was the custom of the country. Mr. Brightman said, "Well, boys, you'd better 'light and rest your horses and we'll fix you up some dinner."

So the five young men tied their horses to the ferryman's fence, which was constructed of sapling pickets interwoven with bear grass, and, having fed their horses, went in to dinner. A young woman, Mr. Brightman's daughter, waited on them very pleasantly at the table.

Whether Emeline Brightman was the lotos flower that caused the home-returning soldiers to forget their journey or whether they had had enough of riding horseback or were too out of pocket to go on, is not known. But certain it is that not one of them sailed from Galveston on the appointed day. Young Russell lingered in Goliad for a year and then married the girl who had served him at table on the day of his arrival. "And this accounts," their son wrote me eighty years later, "for a man named L. B. Russell, sitting here pounding out the remnants of a history that he should know much better than he does. Suppose the young men had caught that boat. Then L. B. Russell would not have been himself but somebody else, the Lord only knows who."

More than a year ago the man who is himself sent from Comanche, Texas, to the Texas Folk-Lore Society a considerable body of stories and verses, written in a firm hand on the reverse side of old insurance record sheets. They are tales, a ballad, and some nursery jingles with which Emeline Brightman Russell entertained her children back in the 1850's, and which, when she was more than eighty years old, she wrote at the suggestion of Mr. L. B. Russell, who felt "that it was a pity for so much folk-lore to die with her." She died in 1910. Mr. Russell kept the manuscripts until a chance mention of the Texas Folk-Lore Society determined their disposal.

The marriage of Charles Russell and Emeline Brightman on February 25, 1847, was the first marriage recorded at the court house in Goliad after Texas became a state. Their home, which was their own without mortgage, had saplings for studs, hewn logs for sills, clapboards for weatherboarding, and trodden earth for floor. It presented the contrasts of many a western frontier home. Mrs. Russell had had a fair education, which included elementary Latin. Mr. Russell during his service in the army had read and studied to such good purpose that at old Point Comfort he taught a post school. He understood surveying and read law. Besides textbooks, the library in the dirt-floored house consisted of about a hundred volumes, among them the works of Shakespeare, Byron, Scott, Dryden, and Pope, *Pilgrim's Progress*, *Don*

Quixote, Gil Blas, Rasselas, Gulliver's Travels, Locke's *Essay concerning Human Understanding,* Watts' *Improvement of the Mind,* and Brande's encyclopedic *Dictionary of Science, Literature, and Art.*

In this home and in the one established six years later at Helena, which was only a day's journey from Goliad when *Studebaker* meant a wagon, Mrs. Russell, after the strenuous day of a frontierswoman was over and the children were ready for bed, said and sang and acted the tales that her mothers before her had in turn related. "We folk-lorists," remarked Andrew Lang, "trace our descent in the old way, through the mother." That the descent of these folk tales was maternal is indicated by a note that Mrs. Russell attached to a phrase occurring in one of them, "The Lord send plenty." "My mother," she explains, "always had us say, 'The dear send plenty,' as she was afraid it was a sacrilege to use the Lord's name in stories." This delightfully cautious lady was born Nancy Moore in South Carolina of a family that must have been in that province and state for at least two generations, since Mrs. Russell, in her manuscript, refers an alphabetic jingle "to the old Dilworth spelling book, South Carolina, between 1750 and 1780." (Mr. Russell can remember seeing this old spelling book among his mother's keepsakes.) Now the name Nancy Moore has an Irish sound, but Nancy's mother's name was Elizabeth Baker. The tales themselves are proof that they were handed down not from Irish but from English and Scottish folk.

For Mrs. Russell the folk tales were an oral inheritance. But years after she told them to her children in the straggling Texas towns of Goliad and Helena, Joseph Jacobs collected most of them from various printed and oral sources into two volumes, *English Fairy Tales* (1890) and *More English Fairy Tales* (1894), and earned the right to be considered "the English Grimm." Some of Mrs. Russell's variants are printed here because they are fuller and livelier than those found elsewhere; others, because the details show interesting variations. For many people the social interest of these antique tales told in a single Texas frontier home must be greater than the interest attaching to any variation in form. It may not be amiss to remark that, although like Mopsa in the play we all incline to believe that what we have seen in print is true, Mrs. Russell's versions are as likely as those in Jacobs' collections to have had a folk range.

Variations in the details of oral narratives are common. The teller remembers the run of the story and supplies forgotten particulars from a mode of life familiar to her hearers or herself. Mrs. Russell had a remarkable memory. Most of the characters and occupations in her tales are those usual to English and European folk-lore. But occasionally they are drawn from the life of another and later world. A rail-splitter takes the place of the woodcutter of Grimm's tales. He doubtless was drawn from Indiana, where Mrs. Russell passed her childhood. For the "shoemaker" (dog) in the well-known English tale "How Jack Went to Seek His Fortune" is substituted a "vendor of o'clo'," who may have been reminiscent of a brief residence of the Brightman family in New Orleans. The man boiling soap, whom the johnny-cake met in his flight, suggests the ash hoppers of pioneer America, great black kettles filled with boiling lye and fat from the hog-killing, and skimmings of yellow soap. At any rate, I have never encountered a soap boiler in English or European folk tales. Jacobs includes "Johnny-Cake" in *English Fairy Tales,* and it had no doubt an English prototype—as it had a Scotch prototype in "The Wee Bannock"—but if ever a johnny-cake was baked in England it was mixed by an American hand.

> Come on an' take some Johnny cake,
> . . . .
> For that and Independence make
> A full blood Yankee Doodle.

So runs an old song made upon the entrance of Texas into the Union.

A few turns of expression are confined to the United States. "Oh, just a little piece out yonder," answers the johnny-cake when asked where he is going. The unfortunate boy who is sent to mill receives "a powerful whipping." The robber in "How Jack Went to Seek His Fortune" runs "across lots." "Rooster" is American for "cock," as an Englishman named Flint wrote home in 1822; and in the United States a bin for storing corn is called a "crib." "Gal" is good Texan.

Mrs. Russell must have been an entrancing story teller and have possessed a lively sense of the dramatic. Her grandchildren remember her as a white-haired old lady, with a curl bobbing on each side of her face. When she sat, she habitually turned her feet in an exaggerated pigeon toe to keep the children who crowded about her from stepping on them. Even then, when she was old, she acted out all the stories, as she talked "in a long Texas drawl." But her son makes a distinction: "She always talked slowly, with not exactly a drawl but with a good deal of hesitancy and some interval between words." Of her dramatic manner he writes thus: "Take, for instance, the story of the old cat spinning in the oven and the little mouse whose tail the cat 'jumped' at and bit off. When mother came to that 'jumped,' she would go through the motion of springing like a cat, and emphasize the word with capital letters, so to speak. And when she repeated the lingo,

>Away he went trittety trot;
>The faster he went the sooner he got,

she would make a song out of it, resembling somewhat the old-time hardshell preacher's sing-song sermon. All this singing and action captured us as children."

Her children and her children's children begged often for one "story" that was all action and in which the narrator's right hand served for stage and characters. The persons of the dialogue are an old lady, her little maid, and a friar. The old lady is represented by the thumb, the maid by the little finger, and the friar by the middle finger of a hand held vertically. The only property is a door formed by joining the first and third fingers at the tips. The friar is outside the door. Each speech is accompanied by a movement of the impersonating finger.

An old lady sat rocking by the fire (*movement of thumb toward inside of hand and back, repeated while these words are spoken*) and her little maid was standing by (*similar movement of little finger*) when they heard a knock, knock, knocking at the door. (*Quick, repeated tapping of middle finger against the joined tips of first and third fingers.*)

Little Maid: Some one is at the door, ma'am. Some one is at the door. (*Agitated movement of the little finger toward "old lady"; so whenever the maid speaks.*)

Old Lady: See who it is; pray, see who it is. (*Calm and regular movement of thumb; so whenever the old lady speaks.*)

Little Maid: Who is it, sir? Who is it, sir?

Friar: A friar, ma'am; a friar, ma'am. (*Tapping of middle finger against joined tips of first and third fingers; so in friar's next speech.*)

Little Maid: It's a friar, ma'am; it's a friar, ma'am.

Old Lady: Pray, what does he want? Pray, what does he want?

Little Maid: What do you want, sir? What do you want, sir?

Friar: To get warm, ma'am; to get warm, ma'am.

Little Maid: He wants to get warm, ma'am; he wants to get warm.

Old Lady: Then let him come in. Pray, let him come in.

Little Maid: Come in, kind sir. Come in.

Friar: Thank you, dame.[1]

(*The friar comes through the door: the middle finger is passed between joined fingers to inside of hand.*)

Two of Mrs. Russell's grandchildren have told me that she could bring the friar into the parlor without unhinging the door. If anyone things that this is easy to do, let him try it for himself.

Even better than the English tales the Russell children liked stories of pioneer life, of their own life one and two generations removed. From their front door step in Helena they could see deer feeding on the hills half a mile away. And now and then they heard of Indian raids a little farther to the west. Their mother told them of how her family had settled, soon after they came to Texas, on a farm along the Guadalupe River, and of how shortly afterward they and other families fled when General Woll, at the head of a Mexican army, invaded San Antonio. During that year and the following she had taken her turn with her brothers in

---

[1]For another version of the friar pantomime see Chambers, Robert, **Popular Rhymes of Scotland,** London, 1870, "Katherine Nipsy," pp. 116-117.

guarding the home against both Mexican and Indian raiders. Two frontier incidents came through the South Carolina lady who would not take the Lord's name in vain, Nancy Moore Brightman, Mrs. Russell's mother. They are printed below under the titles "The Crane's Drumstick" and "Uncle Billy and the Buck." Unlike the English tales, which, through generations of telling, move with swift and economical precision, these stories were somewhat incoherent and have been reshaped.

A welcome visitor in the Russell home, where he sometimes stayed for weeks, was John C. Duval,[2] who, many years before he put the romantic narrative into a book, *Early Times in Texas*, told the never-tiring children about his escape from the Goliad massacre: how the man in front of him was killed by the Mexicans' first fire and, in falling, knocked him down; how he lay on the ground until the Mexicans, in hot pursuit of the Texans remaining alive, passed over him; how then he made his way to the river, crossed it swimming, and was about to pull himself up the steep bank by a mustang grape vine when a ball from a Mexican *escopeta* cut the vine in two just above his head; and how he then swam on down the river until he found a place where the bank came more gradually to the water, and clambered out. For the young children Mr. Duval spun "fairy" tales, chiefly out of his own imagination, so Mr. Russell believes. One of them appears below as "The Cricket's Supper."

The Russell children never wanted for entertainment. Though their mother was their chief dependence, their father occasionally took time off from his duties as a busy land title lawyer and sang ballads. The song they liked best was "The Poor Little Fisherman Boy So Far Away from Home,"[3] so mournful that they would cry when they heard it, and, before their tears were dry, would beg to hear it again.

---

[2]An interesting sketch of J. C. Duval is "John Crittenden Duval," by William Corner, in Texas State Historical Association **Quarterly**, Vol. I, pp 47-67.

[3]Tolman and Eddy, "Traditional Texts and Tunes," **Journal of American Folk-Lore,** Vol. 35, pp. 366-367, give a full version.

Down in the Lowlands a poor boy did wander,
Down in the Lowlands this poor boy did roam;
And by his friends neglected,
He seemed much dejected,
This poor little fisherman boy,
    So far away from home.

"O, where is your father, and where is your mother?"
They asked the little fisherman boy so far away from home.
"My mother died on her pillow,
My father's on the billow,"
Replied the little fisherman boy,
    So far away from home.

Sometimes he told them tales. A variant of "How Jack Went to Seek His Fortune," learned from a New England aunt, is printed herewith.

I. THE ENGLISH FOLK TALES

THE JOHNNY-CAKE

[A version of "The Johnny-Cake" was printed in the *Journal of American Folk-Lore,* Vol. 2, (1889), pp. 60-63, and was followed by a variant in a later number of the same volume, pp. 217-218. Jacobs used the first version in *English Fairy Tales,* pp. 155-158, 247. The unlikeness in particulars to Mrs. Russell's version is indicated by the johnny-cake's words to the fox, who forthwith devours him:

"I've outrun an old man, and an old woman, and a little boy, and two well-diggers, and two ditch-diggers, and a bear, and a wolf, and I can outrun you too-o-o."

The second version is a mere fragment, but is like Mrs. Russell's in that the johnny-cake calls out, "I can turn myself." He does not, however, turn himself but jumps out of the oven and runs away. In Mrs. Russell's alone is the end of the johnny-cake followed by a narrative of the pursuit by the old man and the old woman. In one Scotch variant of "The Wee Bannock" the pursuers are the center of interest. Chambers printed three variants of "The Wee Bannock" in *Popular Rhymes of Scotland,* pp. 82-87 (edition of 1870). The first of these, Jacobs, having reduced the Scotch words to English, included in *More English Fairy Tales,* pp. 66-70, 227. In volume 3 of the JAFL, pp. 291-292, appeared "The Little Cakeen." A variant called "The Gingerbread Boy," published in *St. Nicholas* for May, 1875, has become the basis of stories in popular children's books.]

It is necessary in explanation to the little ones of the present generation to say how the johnny-cake was baked in the time when Grandma was a little girl.[4] People would have an oak or hickory board, much like the middle of a barrel head, about six inches across. On this board they would pat out cornmeal dough about an inch thick, and then spread cream all over it with a knife and make it smooth, and put the board down on the hearth before a bed of coals or hot fire and bake the edges first. Then, when the dough was baked about the edges, they would set the board up straight with a flat iron behind it to hold it up. When the lower side was brown, they would turn the upper side down so that the johnny-cake might bake an even brown. When it was browned just right, they would take it up on the table and run a case knife under it to loosen it from the board. Next they turned the board upside down on a clean table; then they slipped the johnny-cake, brown side down, back on to the board, after smoothing it again with cream, and set it up again in front of the iron, turning it once and baking it until it was a nice brown. And there never was sweeter bread to eat with butter or milk than this.

---

[4]Mrs. Russell was thinking of her grandchildren when she wrote the story. The explanation was not a part of the tale she had told to her own children. It is to be observed that the explanation of the process and the incidents of the tale do not fit. The name of the American cornmeal cake was substituted for some Old World baking, but no further attempt at adaptation was made.

Well, once there was an old man and an old woman who lived by themselves in a little log cabin in the woods. One morning they got up and put on a johnny-cake to bake. After a while the old man says, "Old woman, it is time to turn that johnny-cake."

And it says in a squeaking voice, "I can turn myself over," and over it flopped.

After a while the old man again says, "Old woman, that side of the johnny-cake is done, and it is ready to turn."

The johnny-cake says in the same squeaking voice, "I can turn myself over," and over it flopped.

After a while the old man says, "Old woman, that johnny-cake is done; you had better take it up."

The johnny-cake squeaked out, "I can take myself up." So it *flew* upon the table, flippity-flop, and out of the door flippity-flop, and the old man and the old woman went after it hippity-hop. But it could fly faster than they could run and soon got out of sight.

So it went flippity-flop till it came to some men thrashing out wheat, and they asked it, "Where are you going?"

It says, "Oh, just a little piece out yonder," and away it went flippity-flop till it came to a man boiling soap.

He says, "Where are you going?"

It says, "Oh, just a little piece out yonder," and away it went flippity-flop till it came to a miller grinding corn.

The miller says to it, "Where are you going?"

It says (squeaking), "Oh, just a little piece out yonder," and away it went flippity-flop till it came to a wolf.

And the wolf says, "Where are you going?"

It says, "Oh, just a little piece out yonder."

And the wolf says, "I'm deaf; I can't hear you; come a little closer."

So it went a little closer and says, "Oh, just a little piece out yonder."

The wolf says, "I can't hear you yet; come a little closer."

It went a little closer and says, "Oh, just a little piece out yonder."

And the wolf says, "I'm very deaf; come right close up to me."

And it came close up to the wolf and says, "Oh, just a little piece out yonder," and the wolf jumped at it and caught it and ate it up.

So the old man and old woman went after it hippity-hop till they came to the men thrashing out wheat, when they asked, "Have you seen a johnny-cake going by here flippity-flop?"

"Yes."

"What did it say?"

"It said, 'Oh, I'm going just a little piece out yonder.'"

Then away they went hippity-hop after it till they came to the soap boiler. They asked, "Did you see a johnny-cake go by here flippity-flop?"

He says, "Yes, and I asked, 'Where are you going?' It says, 'Oh, just a little piece out yonder.'"

And away went the old man and old woman hippity-hop, hippity-hop till they came to the miller grinding his corn, and they said, "Have you seen a johnny-cake go by here flippity-flop?"

The miller says, "Yes; I asked it, 'Where are you going?' It says, 'Oh, just a little piece out yonder.'"

And away went the old man and old woman after it hippity-hop, hippity-hop till they came to the wolf. They said to the wolf, "Did you see a johnny-cake going by here flippity-flop, flippity-flop?"

He says, "Yes. I asked it, 'Where are you going?' and it says, 'Oh, just a little piece out yonder.'"

And away went the old man and old woman after it, hippity-hop, hippity-hop, on and on into the woods, but they never saw anyone else who had seen their johnny-cake. So they were very tired and went back home hippity-hop, hippity-hop.

HOW JACK WENT TO SEEK HIS FORTUNE

[The first version printed below is Mrs. Russell's and is marked in the manuscript E. C. R.; the second is Mr. Russell's and is marked C. A. R.

In the *Journal of American Folk-Lore*, Vol. 1 (1888), pp. 227-234, were printed, with copious comparative notes, three versions. Two of these versions, one of which Jacobs (having deleted "a malodorous and un-English skunk") included in

English Fairy Tales, pp. 24-27, 231, follow the general course of Mrs. Russell's narrative. Her version is given a place here because of its greater fullness and its vivacious dialogue.

Jack is an English character, but the fortune-seeking animals are cosmopolitan. Their story is told in Grimm under the title "The Town Musicians of Bremen" ("Die Bremer Stadtmusikanten"). See Bolte und Polívka, *Anmerkungen zu den Kinder-U. Hausmärchen der Brüder Grimm,* No. 27. In Bremen to this day are made and sold donkeys, cats, and roosters, of terra cotta, wood, brass, and pewter—emblems of the ancient folk tale. They are used as paper weights throughout Germany.

The words with which a tale of fortunate outcome concludes may indicate both the temper of the teller and the spirit of her times. The *Journal of American Folk-Lore,* Vol. 38 (1925), pp. 340-374, contains a collection of tales, chiefly variants of old English folk tales, from the Blue Ridge Mountains. The characteristic ending of these tales is, "And when I left there Jack was plumb rich." Mrs. Russell's fortunate conclusion, twice occurring, "They ever after lived in peace and plenty," is the utterance of a woman who had known fighting and narrow circumstances—a woman of the frontier.

Mr. Russell's version I have not seen elsewhere. There is, however, some similarity in the means by which the robbers are frightened away in this tale—an overturning mill hopper —and that by which they are sent scampering in "Mr. Vinegar" (Jacobs), "Hereinafterthis" (Jacobs), and "Frederick and Catherine" (Grimm)—a door dropped from a tree. Though the pronoun I is used throughout, Mr. L. B. Russell says that he always knew the story as "Jack Going to Seek His Fortune." It is to be noted that the style is not a transmitted folk style like that of Mrs. Russell's English tales.]

A

Once upon a time Jack took a notion to go and seek his fortune. So he went to the barnyard and told the old rooster that he must take care of all the hens and chickens while he was gone. The rooster says, "Where you goin', Jack?"

"Goin' to seek my fortune."

"May I go too?"

Tales and Rhymes of a Texas Household 35

"Jump in the cart behind."

He went to the old gander and said, "You must take care of all the geese and goslings while I am gone."

The gander says, "Where you goin', Jack?"

"Goin' to seek my fortune."

"May I go too?"

"Jump in the cart behind."

He went to the sheepfold and told the old ram that he must take care of all the ewes and lambs while he was gone.

The ram says, "Where you goin', Jack?"

"Goin' to seek my fortune."

"May I go too?"

"Jump in the cart behind."

He went to the bull and told him to take care of all the cows and calves while he was gone.

The bull says, "Where you goin', Jack?"

"Goin' to seek my fortune."

"May I go too?"

"Jump in the cart behind."

He went to the old tom-cat and said, "You must take care of the old cat and all the kittens while I am gone."

The tom-cat says, "Where you goin', Jack?"

"Goin' to seek my fortune."

"May I go too?"

He says to his old dog, "You must take care of all the dogs and puppies while I am gone."

"Where you goin', Jack?"

"Goin' to seek my fortune."

"May I go too?"

"Jump in the cart behind."

So when he got all his animals together, with his cart load and all, he started with his cavalcade and traveled and traveled and traveled till night was about to overtake them, and he found no place where they could stop for the night.

Bime-by, as it was getting dark, he came to a deserted place which was said to be haunted. But he thought he would stop there. So he put the bull outside the gate and told him he must defend it and not let anything come in. He put the ram inside of the gate and told him that he must knock or butt anything over that entered inside the gate. He put the gander on the outside of the door and told him to whip and pinch anything that came to the door. He put the cat in the chimney corner (the favorite place of cats), and told him to bite and scratch anything which attempted to come there. He put the rooster up on the top of the chimney and told him to keep strict watch and give the alarm at any disturbance by crowing just as loud and hard as he could. He put the dog under the bed and told him to tear anyone to pieces who came there. And last of all, Jack put himself in bed. They soon all went to sleep (as much as animals sleep), as they had traveled all day and were tired.

After a while a man came to the gate to go in, and the bull hooked him. He jumped inside the gate, and the old sheep butted him over. He jumped up and ran for the door, and the gander caught him by the nose with his bill and flopped him with his wings. He ran inside the house to the fireplace (intending to make a light), and the cat scratched and clawed him so bad that he tried to run under the bed, and the dog bit him. He tried to get on the bed and Jack hit him in the face and head with his fists. And all this time the old rooster was cackling and crowing with all his might and main where he was perched on top of the chimney. And the man ran out of the door and made his escape as quickly as possible.

The house was a robbers' den, and the robbers had sent one of their number to report if some money they had there were all right. He went back to them and reported that the whole place was full of witches and that he would never go back for all the money and valuables that they ever had. He said, "When I was going to the gate, one of the witches of the old Satan stuck me with his pitchfork but did not hold me." (That was the bull.) "I ran in at the gate, and a witch that was a blacksmith knocked me down with his sledge hammer." (That was the ram.) "I ran to the door, and a shoemaker witch grabbed me by the nose with his pinchers and nearly whipped me to death with his leather apron." (That was the gander.) "I ran into the house to the fireplace" (intending to make a light), "and an old woman sitting in the corner carding with a pair of cards struck me in the face with both cards at a time and came near putting out my eyes." (That was the cat.) "I ran to the bed to get under it, and a witch who must have been a vendor of o' clo'" (old clothes) "tried to tear off my clothes." (That was the dog.) "I thought I would jump on the bed, and a fist fighter struck me on the head and face." (That was Jack.) "The blow staggered me and I ran out of the door. All this time an old witch on top of the house was hollowing as loud as he could, 'Hand him up to me! Hand him up to me!' I ran across lots, got over the fence, and here I am in this pitiful plight, which shows you the truth of my adventure."

Early in the morning Jack arose and thought he would investigate the premises. He found bags of money, silver and gold, and valuable jewels where the robbers had hid the spoil till they could come and get it and divide it among them. Jack did not hesitate long what to do. He soon had them all in his cart, and started off home with his trusty animals, who had helped him so much when he went to seek his fortune. They ever after lived in peace and plenty.

B

When I was a little boy, my father died and my mother was poor. So one day I started out to seek my fortune. In those days there were no railroads, and if you were not able to own a horse to ride you had to walk wherever you wanted to go. It was a beautiful morning; and when I got out of the village to where the great forest trees were musical with the songs of birds, it seemed a happy world to me, though we had always been poor in the world's goods.

Somewhere about noon, I began to be warm and weary and sat under the shade of a tree to rest and eat my lunch, which I had stowed away in my pocket. After eating lunch and having a good rest in the cool shade, I arose and started on, without knowing whither to go. The houses got farther and farther apart. I began to think I would not get any place to stay all night, when at last, a while before sundown, I came to a house and stopped and went in. No one was there but a little girl about my size. I told her I wanted to stay all night. She said I could not, but I said, "I will."

She says, "No, you can't unless you can beat me jumping."

Well, I thought that was easy enough, and consented. We went to the door to jump off the steps. After a parley on the subject, it was agreed that I should jump first. So I gave the biggest jump that I could, so as to beat her, and she slammed the door shut, and I was out of the house, as she wanted. There was no other chance but for me to go on; so I went on, and the woods were getting dark. And I began to be afraid of wild animals, and hardly knew what was best to do. About dusk, I came to an old deserted mill. Well, I thought I might find a hiding place in it, to protect me from the wild animals; and after looking about, I crawled up in the hopper of the mill, which was away over and above the floor. I cuddled down in the hopper and, being tired and hungry, soon went to sleep.

Some time in the night I awoke and heard the sound of men's voices. I was very anxious and afraid; so I raised partly up and listened. I could tell that they were close by. I very cautiously raised up so as to peep over the top, but could not see and hear sufficiently. So I stretched up a little higher and saw two or three men, but to my horror, all of a sudden, over went the hopper with me in it, bangety bang, right in their midst. I thought that was the last of poor me, but when I crawled out of the hopper I could see no one. In their flight they had left bags of money. They were robbers and had come there to divide their spoil. They thought the rattle-banging of the hopper was caused by officers who would catch them, and so ran away as fast as their heels could carry them. I took up the bags of money and made my way back home with them, and that was the good luck I had when I went to seek my fortune.

THE LITTLE LONG TAIL

[The accumulative story "The Little Long Tail" occurs in Jacobs' *English Fairy Tales*, pp. 188-189, 249, where it is reprinted from Halliwell's *Nursery Rhymes and Tales*, pp. 154-155, as "The Cat and the Mouse." A fuller version, one very much like Mrs. Russell's, is given in "Notes and Queries," *Journal of American Folk-Lore*, Vol. 13 (1900), p. 229. In

Vol. 18 (1905) of the JAFL, p. 34, n. 3, Newell appends a considerable bibliography on "The Cat and the Mouse" to his article "The Passover Song of the Kid." An abbreviated version is printed as "Little Long Tail" in Jane Hoxie's *Kindergarten Story Book* (1906). Mrs. Russell's opening with the old cat spinning in the oven does not occur in other versions that have been examined, but it does occur in Chambers' quite different story in *Popular Rhymes of Scotland,* 1870 ed., pp. 53-54:

> The cattie sits in the kiln-ring,
> Spinning, spinning.

Mrs. Russell's version is given a place here less because it shows a slight variation in details than because it contains a refrain which adds much to the liveliness of the recital and because it, unlike other versions, has a surprise ending. In a note to another tale, p 232, Jacobs remarks that the surprise ending is a frequent device in English folk tales; but in his version of this one, "cat gave mouse her own tail again."]

Once there was an old cat spinning in the oven, and a poor little mouse came creeping along, and the old cat *jumped* at it and bit off its tail, and the little mouse says to the cat, "Pray, give me my little long tail again."

The cat says, "Go to the cow and get me some milk."

> And away he went trittety trot;
> The faster he went the sooner he got.

He says, "P-r-a-y" (drawled out), "cow, give me some milk. I give cat milk; cat give me my little long t-a-i-l again."

The cow says, "Go to the barn and get me some hay."

> And away he went trittety trot;
> The faster he went the sooner he got.

He says, "P-r-a-y, barn, give me hay; I give cow hay; cow give me milk; I give cat milk; cat give me my little long t-a-i-l again."

The barn says, "Go to the smith and get me the key."

> And away he went trittety trot;
> The faster he went the sooner he got.

He says, "P-r-a-y, smith, give me key; I give barn key; barn give me hay; I give cow hay; cow give me milk; I give cat milk; cat give me my little long t-a-i-l again."

The smith says, "Go to the pit and get me some coal."

> And away he went trittety trot;
> The faster he went the sooner he got.

He says, "P-r-a-y, pit, give me coal; I give smith coal; smith give me key; I give barn key; barn give me hay; I give cow hay; cow give me milk; I give cat milk; cat give me my little long t-a-i-l again."

The pit says, "Go to the eagle and get me a feather."

> And away he went trittety trot;
> The faster he went the sooner he got.

He says, "P-r-a-y, eagle, give me feather; I give pit feather; pit give me coal; I give smith coal; smith give me key; I give barn key; barn give me hay; I give cow hay; cow give me milk; I give cat milk; cat give me my little long t-a-i-l again."

The eagle says, "Go to the sow and get me a pig."

> And away he went trittety trot;
> The faster he went the sooner he got.

And he says, "P-r-a-y, sow, give me pig; I give eagle pig; eagle give me feather; I give pit feather; pit give me coal; I give smith coal; smith give me key; I give barn key; barn give me hay; I give cow hay; cow give me milk; I give cat milk; cat give me my little long t-a-i-l again."

The old sow says, "Go to the crib and get me some corn."

> And away he went trittety trot;
> The faster he went the sooner he got.

He says, "P-r-a-y, crib, give me corn; I give sow corn; sow give me pig; I give eagle pig; eagle give me feather; I give pit feather; pit give me coal; I give smith coal; smith give me key; I give barn key; barn give me hay; I give cow hay; cow give me milk; I give cat milk; cat give me my little long t-a-i-l again."

The crib says, "Jump in the crack and help yourself."

So he jumped in the crack and got some corn, and took it to the old sow and got the pig, and took the pig to the eagle and got the feather, and took the feather to the pit and got the coal, and took the coal to the smith and got the key, and took the key to the barn and got the hay, and took the hay to the cow and got the milk, and took the milk to the old cat, and the cat licked and lapped and swallowed, and licked till it was all gone, and then she *jumped* at the little mouse and ate it up.

THE SILVER TOE

[Miss Ruth Kennedy, of Austin, says that as a child in Harrison, Arkansas, she had a chum who told a variant of "The Silver Toe." It was the most shiver-producing tale of all the tales they knew. An old woman cut a head of cabbage from the garden, but, when she went to cook it, found that she had no meat to boil it with. So she went back to the garden to find some meat. She found some and cut off a piece and boiled it with the cabbage, and she and the old man ate it for dinner That night something came and knocked at the door and said in a deep, slow voice, "Give-me-my-great-toe. Give-me-my-great-toe." This version, like Mrs. Russell's, had a "Red Riding Hood" ending.

"The Silver Toe" may be compared with two tales in Jacobs' *English Fairy Tales*: "Teeny-Tiny," in which a woman takes a bone from a churchyard to make soup and is visited at night by the owner, pp. 57-58, 233; and "The Golden Arm," in which a man severs from his dead wife's body her golden arm and is visited on the following night by her ghost, which demands its missing member, pp. 138-139, 246. In "How to Tell a Story," Mark Twain tells "The Golden Arm" as a "negro ghost story" that he had used on the lecture platform.]

Once upon a time there was an old man and old woman working in their garden, digging potatoes. And the old woman found a silver toe. She took it in the house and put it under her pillow at the head of the bed. So that night something came and knocked at the door and said in a gruff, unearthly voice very slowly, "Give-me-my-silver-toe. Give-me-my-silver-toe. Give-me-my-silver-toe."

At last the old woman raised up mad and cross and says, "I've got no silver toe for you."

The coarse voice repeated slowly, "Give-me-my-silver-toe" (drawled out long).

The old woman again says, "I've got no silver toe for you."

It kept on saying, "Give-me-my-silver-toe. Give-me-my-silver-toe."

The old man says in a whisper, "You had better give him his silver toe."

But the old woman jumped up mad and opened the door a little bit, and there was something the like of which she had never seen in her life. She says, "What's them great long ears for?"

"To hear with."

"What's that great long hair for?"

"To sweep my grandmother's hall."

"What's that great long nose for?"

"To smell with."

"What's them great long nails for?"

"To scratch my grandmother's pots."

"What's them great big eyes for?"

"To see with."

"What's them great big teeth for?"

"To bite you, to bite you, to bite you."

THE BAD GAL AND THE GOOD GAL

["The Bad Gal and the Good Gal" in part resembles Perrault's "Toads and Diamonds" ("Les Fées") and in part Jacobs' "The Three Heads of the Well" (*English Fairy Tales,* pp. 222-227, 253), reprinted from Halliwell's *Nursery Rhymes and Tales,* pp. 158-161. Both are named in Bolte und Polívka as parallels of "Frau Holle," No. 24. Perrault's *Contes de Ma Mère L'Oye* was first translated into English in 1729; and "Toads and Diamonds," together with "Little Red Riding Hood," "Sleeping Beauty," "Cinderella," and "Blue Beard," was quickly appropriated by the English folk. A variant of "The Three Heads of the Well" occurs in Chambers' *Popular Rhymes of Scotland,* 1870 ed., pp. 105-107, as "The Wal at the Warld's End." Chambers says, p. 48, that this tale is mentioned in

The Complaynt of Scotland, a pamphlet published in 1548. Jacobs notes the use of the story in Peele's *The Old Wives' Tale.* For a discussion of this use see "Peele's Use of Folk-Lore in *The Old Wives' Tale,*" by Sarah Clapp, in *Studies in English,* University of Texas, No. 6, pp. 146-156.

An instance of the power of folk-tales to travel from one people to another and in the journey to undergo strange transformations and accretions is "The Story of Spióla," a variant of "Toads and Diamonds" found among the Thompson Indians. See *Journal of American Folk-Lore,* Vol. 29 (1916), pp. 301-307.]

Once there was an old woman who had two girls. They were called "the bad gal and good gal." One was very sweet and amiable, and the other was very cruel, ill-tempered, and mean.

One morning the good gal started to a celebrated spring some distance from her home, whose waters had a strange effect on those who took a wash and bath in them.

The first thing she came to in a narrow lane was some large, savage horses fighting. They were pawing and cutting each other all to pieces, and she did not know how she might pass them. After studying a minute, she says in a good, kind manner, "Part, horses, and let me through." And they parted and let her through.

She went on a piece farther, and came to two bulls fighting very savage. She says, "Part, bulls, and let me through." And they parted and let her through.

She went on a little farther and came to two old buck sheep fighting. She says, "Part, sheep, and let me through." So they parted and let her through.

She went on then till she came to a gate that was very heavy and hard to open. She says in a soft tone, "Open, gate, and let me through." So the gate opened and let her through.[5]

She went on and came to the spring. She was washing and bathing and feeling very happy when all of a sudden up came a little thing[6] and says, "Wash me and comb me and

---

[5]In "The Three Heads of the Well," the only obstruction is a "thick, thorny hedge."

[6]A "head" in Jacobs' tale.

lay me down softly." And she washed it and combed it and laid it down softly.

Up came another little thing and says, "Wash me and comb me and lay me down softly." She washed it and combed it and laid it down softly.

Up came another little thing and says, "Pretty you are, and ten times prettier you shall be."

Up came another little thing and says, "Every time you comb, you shall comb out gold and silver."

Up came another little thing and says, "Every time you spit you shall spit a diamond."

So she went back home combing out gold and silver, spitting diamonds, and growing prettier and more lovely all the time.[7]

The bad gal, seeing her sister's good fortune in her visit to the spring, thought she would go and try the effects it would have on her. One morning she put out and soon came to the narrow lane where the horses were fighting, and she says in a rough, savage voice, "Part, horses, and let me through." And they parted and let her in the middle, when they ran together and kicked her and hurt her considerably.

She went on and came to the two bulls fighting, and she says in as rough a voice as before, "Part, bulls, and let me through." They parted, and when she came between them they rushed together and she barely missed being killed by their horns.

So she went on till she came to the sheep fighting. She says in an angry voice, "Part, sheep, and let me through." So they parted and let her in the middle and then they butted her and butted her very much.

So she went on till she got to the gate, and she says in a more cross manner than ever, "Open, gate, and let me through." So it opened, and, as she passed, it slammed to and almost knocked her heel off.

So she went on to the spring and went to washing and bathing. And after a while up came a little thing and says,

---

[7] In Perrault's tale the reward for kindness is the gift of casting from the mouth with each word spoken either a flower or precious stone. Here the three rewards and punishments follow Chambers' version.

"Wash me and comb me and lay me down softly"; and slap! she took it on its poor little head and killed it.

And up came another little thing and says, "Wash me and comb me and lay me down softly." Slap! she took it on its poor little head and killed it.

Up came another little thing and says, "Ugly you are and ten times uglier you shall be."

Up came another little thing and says, "Every time you comb, you shall comb out a peck of nits and lice."

Up came another little thing and says, "Every time you spit, you shall spit a toad."

So she went on home, combing out nits and lice, spitting toads, and getting uglier all the time.[8]

NOR'WEST WIND AND JACK

["Nor'west Wind and Jack" has had a wide currency. In Asbjörnsen (Dasent's translation) it is "The Lad Who Went to the North Wind"; in Grimm, "The Wishing Table, the Gold Ass, and the Cudgel" ("Tischchen, Goldesel, Knüppel"); in Jacobs, "The Ass, the Table, and the Stick." See Bolte und Polívka, No. 36. The tale is still told and is still in the making among American folk. The *Journal of American Folk-Lore*, Vol. 38 (1925), pp. 363-365, contains a variant in racy dialect from the Southern Blue Ridge. It is also to be found under the title "Tablecloth, Donkey, and Club" in "Tales from Maryland and Pennsylvania," JAFL, Vol. 30, pp. 210-212, which see for further findings.]

Once an old woman had a little home and had one apple tree. She had a son Jack. One night the Nor'west Wind blew down the old woman's apple tree. She bade her son Jack to go to the Nor'west Wind, and stick his hat in the hole from which the Nor'west Wind blew down her apple tree.

So Jack went and came to the Nor'west Wind, and said, "I am going to stop up the hole that you blow your breath out of."

The Nor'west Wind begged Jack not to do that, but he said his mother gave orders to him to be sure and stop up the hole for blowing down her apple tree. The Nor'west Wind says,

---

[8]In Perrault's tale the punishment for ungracious behavior is that with each word spoken either a viper or a toad shall leave the mouth.

"If you will not do it, I will give you a colt that will when you say, 'Shake, colt, shake,' shake down everything you want or wish for."

So Jack took the colt and started home. He had to stop at a tavern that night, and before going to bed he says to the innkeeper, "Don't you say, 'Shake, colt, shake,' to my colt tonight."

The innkeeper says, "No," and Jack went to bed.

In the morning Jack went on home to his mother and told her that the Nor'west Wind had given him a colt that when she said, "Shake, colt, shake," would shake down everything in the world she would wish for. So the old woman tried him and said, "Shake, colt, shake," and he didn't do a thing. Then she was more mad than ever. She told Jack to go right straight back and stop up the hole of the Nor'west Wind with his hat.

So Jack went and came to the Nor'west Wind and said, "Your colt was no good and I'm going to stop up the hole that you blow your breath out of."

"Oh, please don't," says the Nor'west Wind. "If you won't do it, I'll give you a napkin and when you say, 'Spread, napkin, spread, it will spread out with all the dainties you can imagine, everything good to eat."

Well, Jack took it and started on home, and he had to stop at the tavern he had stopped at before. So he says to the innkeeper, "Don't you say, 'Spread, napkin, spread,' to my napkin tonight."

The innkeeper says, "No, I won't."

So Jack went to bed, and in the morning he took his napkin and went home. He told his mother that all she had to do was to say, "Spread, napkin, spread," and it would be spread with everything nice to eat that she could imagine. So she says, "Spread, napkin, spread," and not a thing did the napkin do.

So this time she was very angry and told Jack the Nor'west Wind was just fooling them, and that he should go right straight back and stick his hat in the hole where the Nor'west Wind blew his breath out.

So the Nor'west Wind begged once more. He says, "I'll give you a pot which will fight all your battles if you will let me off just one more time. When any one says, 'Thump, pot, thump,' it will jump up on to their head and thump them till you tell it to stop."

Well, Jack took the pot and started on home, and had to stop at the same tavern, and before going to bed, he says to the innkeeper, "Don't you say, 'Thump, pot, thump,' to my pot tonight.

The innkeeper says, "Oh, no, certainly not."

So in the dead hours of the night Jack was awakened from his sleep by a dreadful noise like some one being murdered. He hurried to see what it was, and found his pot thumping the innkeeper nearly to death. And he was calling Jack to take it off. Jack says, "You rascal, that's the way you have stolen my colt and put another colt in its place, and stolen my napkin and put another napkin in its place, and now I'll let the pot beat you to death if you don't deliver to me my colt and napkin."

So Jack made him have the colt and napkin brought before he would stop the pot from thumping him. In the morning he took his colt, his napkin, and his pot home to his mother. And all they had to do was to say, "Shake, colt, shake," or "Spread, napkin, spread," to get everything in the world they wanted or wished for. And Jack had his pot to fight his battles, and the poor old Nor'west Wind got rid of Jack's importunities and has the hole open to blow down apple trees to this day.

THE CRICKET'S SUPPER

[Repetitive stories in which the characters range from an insect or small animal to a man are numerous, but I have not elsewhere seen this particular combination. Below this story in Mrs. Russell's manuscript is written, "J. C. D.'s [John C. Duval's] story."]

One afternoon a little cricket came out of his hiding place to find something to eat, and all of a sudden, pow! came a lizard and caught him. The cricket says, "Oh, please let me go just this time, and I'll never come here any more."

"Oh, no, I can't do that. I have some young lizards at home, and they are very fond of crickets, and I promised to bring them one for their supper."

Pang! went a frog onto the lizard and says, "Oh, I've got you now, have I?"

"Oh, please let me go this one time, and I'll never come out here any more."

"Oh, no, I can't do that; I have a nest of little frogs at home, and they are very fond of lizards, and I promised to bring them home one for their supper."

Pang! went a snake onto the frog, and says, "Oh, I've got you now, have I?"

"Oh, please let me go, and I'll never come back here any more."

"Oh, I can't do that. I have some little snakes at home, and they are very fond of frogs, and I promised to bring them one home for their supper."

Down came an eagle onto the snake and says, "Oh, I've got you now, have I?"

The snake says, "Oh, please let me go this time, and I'll never come back any more."

"Oh, I can't do that. I have a nest of young eagles at home, and they are very fond of snakes, and I promised to bring them one home for their supper."

Bang! went a gun, and down came the eagle, and down came the snake, and down came the frog, and down came the lizard, and down came the cricket, which ran to his hole; and the lizard ran to *his* hole, and the frog ran to *his* hole, and the snake ran to *his* hole, and the man with the gun took the eagle to *his* hole (or home), and that ended all of their suppers.

II. THE INCIDENTS OF PIONEER LIFE

UNCLE BILLY AND THE BUCK

[Concerning the victim in the following incident, Mr. L. B. Russell writes thus: "Uncle Billy Moore was my maternal grandmother's brother, and came to Texas at an early day, though not with the Brightman family. At least, I never heard my mother mention him as having been with them when they left Indiana in the spring of 1842, taking a flatboat on the Ohio and proceeding thence down to New Orleans. Uncle Billy lived in Goliad County, and I knew him in my early childhood. He was a considerable poet but was withal, as I get it from tradition, a rather dangerous man. From some of his poetical essays that I have seen, I judge that he had a good deal of pepper and vinegar for those whom he disliked. His favorite method of getting even with them was to write an original song about them and sing it for the amusement of his neighbors."

Mrs. Russell's grandchildren made a game of this story. Need it be said that the coveted rôle was that of the buck?]

In the forests that surrounded the clearings where early settlers of Indiana planted their corn and wheat, lived wild animals of many kinds. Those that were good to eat, such as bear and deer, the settlers called game, and those that sometimes crossed over into the cleared land and carried away a hog or a chicken they called varments. Among the varments were catamounts, panthers, wildcats, and wolves. In such a country a man's best friends were his rifle and his hunting dog.

When Uncle Billy Moore was a young man he had a large, brindle hunting dog named Tige (or Tiger), which he used to say he would put up against any man's dog in Indiana. Tige could laugh and smoke a pipe—that is, hold it between his teeth as if he was smoking. Then one day something happened that made Uncle Billy think more of Tige than ever.

But before I tell you the story, I want to tell you what kind of gun Uncle Billy had and how it was loaded. It was called a flintlock rifle because a spark produced by striking flint on steel ignited the charge. When Uncle Billy went hunting, he carried rifle balls, extra flints for the lock, a gun screw-driver, tinder horn and steel to strike fire, and other things too, most likely, in a shotpouch made of coonskin. The shotpouch was suspended on a strap about two inches wide, which went over the left shoulder and down under the right arm. To this strap was also attached a scabbard, in which Uncle Billy kept a sharp butcher knife for skinning and cutting up the game that he killed. The powder for his gun he carried in a horn, which was worked down so smooth and clear that he could see through it and tell how much powder he had. The powder horn was slung on the same strap with the shotpouch and the scabbard.

Now, a man had to know how much powder he was pouring into his gun, and so he took along little measures called chargers, some of which were made of the point of a horn and others of a bear's tooth, polished very bright. There were chargers for heavy loads and for light loads, and they hung one above the other on a cord to the right side of the strap. From the strap, in front of the right arm, hung a buckskin string full of patches. When I say "patches," perhaps you think of the mending basket or of squares cut for piecing quilts. But the patches that Uncle Billy strung on his buckskin string were not for mending or for making quilts. They were pieces of domestic three-quarters of an inch square with the corners cut off, and they were used to make the bullet fit tight in the gun barrel. When Uncle Billy wanted to load his gun, he first put in a charge of powder, then laid a patch over the muzzle of the gun, and put the ball on that. Then he pushed the patch and ball down the barrel of the gun with the ramrod. The patches were easily slipped off the buckskin string but would not come off of themselves. A waterproof leather cap fitted over the gun lock, so as to keep it, load and all, dry. When a hunter was ready to fire he knocked the cap off with a light flip of his finger, and it hung by a buckskin string out of the way below the lock until it was wanted again.

One morning Uncle Billy took down his hunting paraphernalia and called, "Come, Tige, let's go and see if we can't get an old buck today." Tige understood the words, or perhaps he merely remembered what always occurred when Uncle Billy took down his rifle and shotpouch, with all its attachments. Anyway, he was so pleased that he almost laughed. They took one of the trails that led into the deep forest, where grew gigantic trees—walnut, beech, oak, sugar maple, yellow poplar, or American tulip tree, ash, elm, hackberry, and buckeye—and such smaller growth as dogwood, redbud, boxelder, water beech, mulberry, and paw-paw. You must know that in those days a hunter in the forest traveled very slowly, as he had to peer into the brush on all sides and into the trees. Tige walked along step by step at Uncle

Billy's heels, for he was too well trained to run ahead or out on either side of the trail. Tige always waited for his master's command when the two went hunting.

They walked and poked around in the trails until Uncle Billy began to get tired and to think that it was not a good day for hunting. Then all of a sudden his eyes fell upon a great big old buck looking at him. The buck's horns stretched away up higher than a man could reach. Uncle Billy jerked "old Betsy" (his rifle) up to his shoulder and took sight, and bang went the gun, and down came the buck.

After kicking and flouncing about for a moment, the buck jumped up and ran toward Uncle Billy. Uncle Billy saw him coming and aimed to jump behind a tree, but was not quick enough. The buck caught him between the horns, which were so broad that they straddled the tree, and jammed him against the trunk. He scrubbed Uncle Billy up with all his force against the tree and then down and up and down again. Then Uncle Billy collected his wits and said, "Take him, Tige!"

Tige was only waiting for those words. At one bound he seized the buck by the nose and threw him a somerset and held him fast until Uncle Billy could draw his big butcher knife and slit the buck's throat. Uncle Billy said, "Bless old Tige, he has saved my life, good old dog!" He skinned the buck, which was so large that he could carry only a quarter home. He hung up the other three quarters and the hide on the limb of a tree to keep them from wolves and other varments. After he had had dinner he came back with a horse for the head, horns, hide, and flesh. You may be sure that Tige had all the venison that he could eat that day.

THE CRANE'S DRUMSTICK

The Georgia and Carolina Indians were not subdued when the colonies made peace with Great Britain, but for many years came down at intervals upon lonely farmhouses, killing and foraging.

Early one morning some Indians surprised a family named Huffman, who lived in South Carolina east of the Wateree River, and killed the father, mother, and all the children except one boy and a half grown girl. The boy ran away fast and hid in a hollow log near the house, so that the Indians did not find him. They took the girl away with them, and as much provender as they could carry. They made a straight shoot for the woods to the west and forced the girl to walk and half run to keep up with them. Whenever they came to a stream they would push her in and make her wade it, though sometimes the water was nearly to her chin.

Along in the afternoon one of the Indians killed a crane, and they all stopped long enough to broil and eat it. They gave a drumstick to the child. But she felt too tired and sad and frightened to eat. So she just held the drumstick tight in her hand.

Then they started on again. They walked all day through the forest, keeping free of the clearings. When night came, they stopped and made camp. As they had been on a raid all the night before, the Indians were very tired. They ate what they had and went to sleep early. The girl lay down, with the crane's leg in her hand, on a blanket that one of the braves spread out for her, and pretended to go to sleep. But after a while, she raised up easy and listened and looked and moved around a little and watched the Indians to see if they stirred. When she was sure that they were all fast asleep, she lifted up her dress so that the dead leaves would not rattle, and softly picked her way out.

Once beyond hearing, she began to run. The moon shone and she could see well enough. She did not know which way to go, but ran through bush and briar in the direction that she thought was right. Morning came and she kept on. She was afraid that if she stopped, the Indians would come and find her. She crossed a creek that looked like one she had waded the day before. About noon or a little later she came to a stubblefield. Beyond it was a river and on the other side a ferry boat. She recognized the Wateree crossing two miles from her home. A man came down to the ferry, and she called to him. But he ran back, fearing Indians. Then she stepped into the water and waded down the edge a few rods to where some gall bushes made a deep thicket.

Not long after she had hidden herself, she saw two of her Indian captors come right on her tracks to the edge of the stream where she had waded in. She looked at them through the bushes and her poor heart quaked. But they looked across the river, spoke a few words to each other, and turned back.

The girl watched to see if anyone came to get water or to cross on the ferry. She grew hungry, crouched there quiet in the gall bushes; and, seeing that she had carried the crane's drumstick in her hand since it was given to her the afternoon before, ate it and took heart. After what seemed to her a very long time, someone came down. She ran out where she could be seen and cried, "For the love of God, come over and take me across."

So she was ferried over the river. And the brother who had concealed himself in the hollow log came, and each rejoiced that the other had escaped from the hands of the Indians.

III. Manuscript Tales Not Here Printed

(1) "The Vinegar Bottle" is the Grimm brothers' "The Juniper [or Almond] Tree" ("Van den Machandelboom"), and Jacobs' "The Rose Tree" (*English Fairy Tales*, pp. 15-19, 230). See Bolte und Polívka, No. 47. As "The Rose Tree" it was contributed by S. Baring-Gould to *Notes and Queries*, 3rd Ser., Vol. 8, pp. 82-84. St. Swithin added a note on pp. 135-136. Reference is made in "Antiquities of Nursery Literature," *Quarterly Review*, Vol 21 (1819), p. 97, to a tale collected by Dr. Leyden similar to "The Grim White Woman" of Matthew Gregory Lewis, in which a bird whistles,

". . . . Pew—wew—pew—wew,
My minny me slew."

This is the refrain that occurs in Chambers' version (*Popular Rhymes of Scotland*, 1870 ed., pp. 49-51) called "The Milk-White Doo."

Corrupted snatches of the tale survive among American negroes, and have been recorded from North Carolina, South Carolina, and Louisiana. See *Journal of American Folk-Lore*, Vol. 30, pp. 196-197; Vol. 32, p. 364 ("The Murderous Mother"); Vol. 34, p. 17 ("The Murderous Mother"). See also "The Singing Bones," *Louisiana Folk Tales*, by Alcée Fortier, p. 61. In the tale from North Carolina the rabbit that the woman tasted all away has undergone a characteristic metamorphosis into a 'possum.

The residence in a vinegar bottle, which occurs in Mrs. Russell's version, is probably due to confusion with another English folk tale, given as "Mr. Vinegar" in Jacobs' *English Fairy Tales*, pp. 28-32, 231. The only other variations of interest are the repetitive "leetle old" and the circumstances of killing the child. The introduction, which shows these variations, follows.

"Once there was a leetle old man and a leetle old woman and leetle old boy and leetle old girl lived in a vinegar bottle, and one morning the leetle old man went out hunting and killed a leetle old rabbit and brought it in and told the leetle old woman to cook it for his dinner while he went out to his work. So the leetle old woman put it on to cook, and she tasted it to see if it were done, and she kept tasting and tasting till she tasted it all away. Then the thought came to her (after it was too late), What in the world should she do when the leetle old man came home for his dinner? So she called the leetle old boy out to the wood-pile to pick up some chips, and before he knew what she was going to do she chopped his head off and cooked him for the leetle old man's dinner."

(2) "The Peck and a Half" is "Stupid's Cries" in Jacobs' *More English Fairy Tales,* pp. 195-197, 242. The only considerable variations are in the beginning and the ending. In the latter version the boy is sent by his mother to buy "a sheep's head and pluck," and after many misadventures is thrown into prison and sentenced to die. In Mrs. Russell's variant he is sent to a mill to buy "a peck and a half of meal," and after the same misadventures is thrown into the millhopper by the miller whom his foolish words have angered and is ground to meal. Perhaps the proverb "Don't send a boy to mill"—a proverb that Jim Ferguson used in the race for governor of Texas against Dan Moody in 1926—originated from this tale.

Jacobs took the story for his collection from *Folk-Lore Record, Vol.* 3, p. 153, where it appears as "Stupid's Mistaken Cries." This version is reprinted for comparison with an American variant, known as "The Forgetful Boy," in the *Journal of American Folk-Lore*, Vol. 3, pp. 292-295.

(3) "Count Li—without" is Jacobs' "Mr. Fox," *English Fairy Tales*, pp. 148-151, 247, which it closely resembles. A European variant was told by the Grimm brothers under the title of "The Robber Bridegroom" ("Der Räuberbräutigam"). For further parallels see Bolte und Polívka, No. 40. See also "Old Foster," in "Mountain White Folk-Lore," *Journal of American Folk-Lore*, Vol. 38, pp. 360-361.

(4) The only interest attaching to the manuscript version of "The Old Woman and Her Pig" is the evidence of Scotch origin and of oral transmission in the repetitive, "The poor old woman won't get home tonight to eat her bonnie bushy berries." The familiar version from Halliwell's *Nursery Rhymes and Tales*, pp. 114-115, reprinted in Jacobs' *English Fairy Tales*, pp. 20-23, has nothing like it. But Chambers' variant, in which a kid takes the place of the pig, *Popular Rhymes of Scotland*, pp. 57-59, is entitled "The Wife and Her Bush of Berries," and has as repetitive, "Till I pu' my bonny buss o' berries."

(5) The manuscripts also include the variant of "The Old Woman and Her Pig" called "Kid Won't Go," almost identical in form with that recorded by Newell, as an unpublished variant from New England, in "The Passover Song of the Kid," *Journal of American Folk-Lore*, Vol. 18, pp. 33-48. In connection with the religious significance of the folk tale among German Jews, of which Mr. Newell treats in this article, a contribution made by Thomas Ratcliffe to *Notes and Queries*, 10th Ser., Vol. 3, pp. 74-75, acquires interest. Mr. Ratcliffe says, "The most interesting bit in the story, as told in Derbyshire to me and the other children, was that the man [a man in white who set the balkers to moving] was Christ Himself."

(6) "Old Blackbeard the Robber and Murderer" is an inferior variant of "Blue Beard." The only item of peculiar interest in Mrs. Russell's version is that the widow of Blackbeard, having been aided by the hostler in getting word of her plight to her friends, after a decent interval, marries him. The sister Anne of Perrault's tale has fallen out of the story.

(7) "Simon" is the simple nursery tale of warning to the boy who goes fishing on Sunday. It is reported in contracted form from the negroes of Guilford County, North Carolina,

JAFL, Vol. 30, p. 185.

(8) "Monkeys and Redcaps" and (9) "The Young Lion" are not old English folk tales.

IV. THE TURKISH FACTOR

"The Turkish Factor," commonly known as "The Factor's Garland" and sometimes as "The Turkey Factor," had a long and extensive popularity. In *Notices of Fugitive Tracts and Chap-books Printed at Aldermary Churchyard, Bow Churchyard, etc.,* Percy Society, Vol. 29 (1849), p. 46, Halliwell says: "In a late reprint of this garland by Fordyce of Newcastle, we are told that it was formerly in great circulation in this part of the country." The eight editions (nine copies) listed in the *British Museum Catalogue of Printed Books* were printed at Newcastle, Edinburgh, Worcester, Glasgow, and Dublin. Eight broadside and chapbook editions (ten copies) are recorded in the *Catalogue of English and American Chap-Books and Broadside Ballads in Harvard College Library* (1905), Nos. 809-815 and 2420. In this catalogue W. C. Lane, the compiler, says that the garland appears in *A Collection of Old Ballads*, London, 1723 [1725?], III, 221. Halliwell mentions its being in a collection of songs printed at London in 1738.

One strain of the rather complicated plot is known as *The Thankful Dead Man*, and this Max Hippe has traced from its first extant form in the Hebrew apocryphal book of *Tobit* across the whole of Europe (Herrig's *Archiv*, Vol. 81, pp. 141-183, "Untersuchungen zu der mittelenglischen Romanze von Sir Amadas"). The earliest known version of *The Thankful Dead Man* in English is the metrical romance Sir Amadas, which was probably composed in the fourteenth century. The combination of *The Thankful Dead Man* with other plot strains has been exhaustively examined by G. H. Gerould, of Princeton University, in *The Grateful Dead, The History of a Folk Story*, which was published in 1908 by the Folk-Lore Society. Professor Gerould reviews "The Factor's Garland" as one of many combinations of the themes of *The Grateful Dead* and *The Ransomed Woman*, page 110.

Halliwell records Ritson's assertion that "The Factor's

Garland" was based on the romance *Oliver of Castylle,* a translation (1518) by Wynkyn de Worde of a French prose romance. Professor Gerould, in the work cited, pp. 92-93, gives an analysis of Oliver, from which it is apparent that "The Factor's Garland" bears far less resemblance to that romance than to several European folk versions of *The Thankful Dead Man.*

"The Turkish Factor" has once before been collected from oral tradition in the United States. A student in the University of the South took down "The Turkish Factor," together with nine other ballads, from a North Carolina woman. These ballads formed the basis of a paper, "Certain Songs and Ballads Heard and Collected in Eastern North Carolina," read by Professor John Bell Henneman, of the University of the South, before the Modern Language Association in 1906. See *Publications of the Modern Language Association,* 1907, Vol. 22, p. xvi.

In *Notes and Queries,* 1st Ser., Vol. 3, pp. 49-50, Edward F. Rimbault scores Frederick Sheldon for having stood "godfather" to and so "baptized and remodeled"—in the words of Sheldon's own confession—some of the broadside ballads included in *The Minstrelsy of the English Border.* He quotes for comparison the opening stanza of Sheldon's "The Merchant's Garland" and of "The Factor's Garland." See Professor Kittredge's reference below.

Professor George Lyman Kittredge, of Harvard University, kindly sent photostats of two American broadsides, of an English chapbook copy, and of the copy in *A Collection of Old Ballads.* He also supplied these additional references: a broadside copy of about 1814 printed by N. Coverly at Boston, acquired by Harvard College Library in 1915; a Wrentham (Mass.) chapbook, "printed for Joseph Ward," 1812; Buchan's *Scarce Ancient Ballads,* 1819, pp. 29-37; Greig's *Folk-Song of the North-East* [Scotland], No. CXX; Sheldon, Frederick, *The Minstrelsy of the English Border,* 1847, pp. 274-290, "a faked rifacimento," says Professor Kittredge; a text sent to Child by an American contributor but rejected by him (see Child MSS. in Harvard College Library); Ebsworth, *Roxburghe Ballads,* VIII, 183 ("List of Roxburghe Collection Garlands"); a letter from Sir Walter Scott to G. Ellis, Oct.

17, 1805 (Lockhart's *Life,* 1st edition, II, 74), in which Scott connects *Sir Amadas* with "a vulgar ballad called the Factor's Garland"; Brown, F. C., *Ballad Literature in North Carolina,* p. 10; and Ford, W. C., *Massachusetts Broadsides* (published by the Massachusetts Historical Society), Nos. 3092-3096.

Mr. Russell writes thus of his mother's ballad: "While I could not say positively that my mother never saw it in print, it is my opinion that she learned it by rote from her mother. I have heard her go over the thing from start to finish several times, though its length precluded frequent repetitions." Mr. Russell's opinion that his mother learned the ballad from oral communication is borne out by certain ear corruptions. The opening words, "I'll tell you a ditty," substituted for "Behold, here's a ditty," are clear indication that Mrs. Russell did not sing the ballad, probably had never heard it sung. Yet without doubt it had been sung earlier in its history. Halliwell quotes from Fordyce, who "recollects some old persons who sang the garland from beginning to end." In *A Collection of Old Ballads,* "The Wand'ring Lady" is named as the tune to which "The Factor's Garland" was sung; and in an American broadside, "Paul Jones' Victory."

Rhyme-words of Mrs. Russell's ballad preserve the archaisms in form and pronunciation of the original broadside or chapbook. Thus *weign* is the past participle of *weigh,* rhyming with *main* (stanza 23); *joined* rhymes with *designed* (stanza 25) and with *find* (stanza 45); and for the noun *convoy* occurs *convey* (stanza 28). The long archaic use of *duties* in the sense of *debts* (stanza 4) may also be noted.

Stanzas and lines not in Mrs. Russell's copy occur in *A Collection of Old Ballads* as follows: a descriptive stanza after stanza 6; two lines after the first two lines of 23; two lines after the first two lines of 26; two lines after the last two lines of 41; two lines after the first two lines of 42; and a stanza after 53. Thus Mrs. Russell's version is sixteen lines short. There are a few shiftings of lines. Of more interest are lines apparently improvised (as they do not occur in any of the four copies examined) to fill memory gaps. Five couplets that occur in four printed copies with little variation are here set down from *A Collection of Old Ballads* as (a), each followed as (b) by the corresponding couplet in Mrs. Russell's form of the ballad.

(a) And into that Country his course was to steer,
   Which by his Maid's Father was gov'rned we hear.

(b) He gave his housekeeper for to understand
   That he was going Factor unto such a land.

(a) Next morning as soon as Day light did peep,
   He waked this young Princess out of her Sleep.

(b) Early next morning the Captain arose
   And down to this young Princess' cabin he goes.

(a) To hear this sad News her Eyes they did flow,
   He said noble Lady now since it is so . . .

(b) He says, "Noble Lady, and since it is so,
   I knew it would grieve you when I let you know."

(a) Where he so long tarry'd he then did relate,
   And by what means he came to her Father's Gate.

(b) The Factor being saved from a terrible fate,
   Where he'd so long tarried he soon did relate.

(a) With a grimly look then this Old Man appears,
   Which made the Court tremble, and fill'd 'em with fears.

(b) The grandparents kissed him with sighs and with tears,
   And embraced him farewell both with sorrows and fears.

1 I'll tell you a ditty, a truth and no jest,
  Concerning a young gentleman in the east,
  Who by his great gaming came to poverty,
  And afterward went many voyages to sea.

2 He was well educated, and one of great wit;
  Three merchants in London they all thought it fit
  To make him their Captain and Factor also;
  So for them a voyage he to Turkey did go.

3 As going along in Turkey, one day there he found
  A poor dead man's carcass lying on the ground;
  He asked the reason why there it did lie,
  And one of the natives made him this reply:

4 "This man was a Christian, sir, when he drew breath,
   But his duties being not paid, he lies above earth."
   "O what were his duties?" the Factor he cried.
   "O fifty good pounds, sir," the Turks they replied.

5 "O fifty good pounds is a great sum indeed,
   But to see him lie here makes my poor heart to bleed."
   And so by the Factor the money was paid,
   And under the ground the dead body was laid.

6 On going a little farther, by chance he did spy
   A beautiful creature, just going to die,
   A young waiting maiden, who strangled must be
   For nothing but striking a Turkish lady.

7 He asked what her crime was, for to end the strife,
   Saying, "What will you take for this young creature's life?"
   The Turks they replied, "A hundred pound";
   And that for her pardon he freely paid down.

8 He says, "Noble lady, you may not be free
   In trusting a stranger, especially me,
   But since I have purchased your pardon, will ye
   Be willing to go into England with me?"

9 "I thank you, kind sir, that has freed me from death;
   I'm bound to pray for you as long as I've breath.
   And, if you are willing, to England we'll go;
   I'll bear respect to you till death I do show."[9]

10 He took her to England and, as it is said,
   He set up housekeeping, and made her his maid
   For to wait upon him; and he found her so just,
   The keys of his riches he did her intrust.

11 At length this young Factor was hired once more,
   To cross the proud seas, where the billows do roar;
   He gave his housekeeper for to understand
   That he was going Factor unto such a land.

12 It being a hot country, this man did prepare;
   He got him light clothes in that country to wear;
   He bought him a garment, and as it was told,
   His servant maid flowered with silver and gold.

13 She says, "Noble sir, as I understand
   That you are going Factor unto such a land,

---

[9]The printed copies examined have, with slight differences in wording,
   And due respect to you until death I will show.

And as its the custom a present to bring,
Pray, sir, let this fine flowered garment be seen."

14 He says, "To that Emperor's court I must go,
And the meaning of your words I'm longing to know."
She says, "I won't tell you; there's a reason, you'll find."
"Well, then," says the Factor, "I'll fulfill your mind."

15 He sailed till he came to the desired port,
And as he went up to the Emperor's Court,
And it being a custom of old in that place,
To present some "noble gift" to his Majesty's Grace.

16 The gift was accepted, and as he stood by,
On this fine flowered garment the Prince cast an eye,
Which made him to color and thus he did say,
"Friend, who flowered your robe? Come tell me, I pray."

17 "Please you, my last voyage it was to Turkey;
I saw a young creature who strangled must be.
And I for her pardon paid a hundred pound,
And brought her home with me to fair London Town.

18 "She is my housekeeper while I'm in this land,
And of my being coming she did understand.
She flowered this robe, and give great charge to me,
To let it be seen by your good Majesty."

19 The Prince says, "Behold! the robe that I wear
Is of the same flower and spot, I declare.
Your maid draught[10] them both, and she's my daughter dear;
I have not heard from her, till now, this three year.

20 "I was to pay a visit to a young neighbor Prince,
I sent her in a ship and have ne'er seen her since.
I doubted the seas they had proven her grave,
Till I heard she was taken in Turkey a slave.

21 "For the loss of my dear child, whom I thought was dead,
A well full of tears in my court has been shed.
The old Princess, her mother, and she could not rest,
For groans they drew millions of sighs from her breast.

22 "Your ship shall be richly loaded with speed,
And I'll send a ship for her convoy indeed,
And all for the love that you saved my child's life,
Bring her alive to me, I'll make her your wife.

---

[10]"Wrought" in the printed copies.

23 "And if you do not live to bring her to me,
   Whoever brings her here, their bride she shall be."
   The ship was soon loaded and anchors were weign,[11]
   And so with the convoy came over the main.

24 To fair London city and home he did go,
   He gave this young creature these tidings to know.
   He says, "Noble lady, I've good news to tell,
   The old Princess, your mother, and Father's both well.

25 "And that your dear parents these things have designed,
   That in the bonds of marriage we both shall be joined;
   Perhaps, noble lady, you may not be free
   To marry a poor man, especially me."

26 "Sir, were you a beggar, I would be your wife
   Because, when just dying, you saved my life;
   And now I will tell you, I'm well pleased, I vow;
   I am glad my dear parents these things will allow.

27 "Come, sell off your goods that you have now in store,
   And give all the money you have to the poor,
   And let us be traveling over the main,
   For I long for to see my dear parents again."

28 Oh, this was soon done, and they sailed away
   In the ship that her father sent for her convey.
   But mark what was acted on the ocean wide
   To deprive the Factor of his noble bride.

29 One night as the Factor did lay in sleep,
   The captain that convoyed them over the deep,
   Being under full sail, overboard did him throw,
   Saying, "Now I shall have this young creature, I know."

30 Ah! and there being a small island at hand,
   The Factor swam to it, as we understand.
   And there we will leave him some for to mourn,
   And then back again to the ship we'll return.

31 Early the next morning the Captain arose,
   And down to this young Princess' cabin he goes,
   Saying, "Noble lady, the Factor's not here;
   He has fallen over and drowned, I do fear."

32 He says, "Noble lady, and since it is so,
   I knew it would grieve you when I let you know.
   There's none here can help it. Don't troubled be,
   For in two or three days more your parents you'll see."

---

[11]"Weighing" in **A Collection of Old Ballads** and in the chapbook copy at hand; "weighed" in broadsides.

33 They sailed till they came to the desired port.
    This Princess went weeping to her father's court,
    Who gladly received her with joy and great mirth,
    Saying, "Where is the man that has freed you from death?"

34 The Captain then answered, "One night in his sleep,
    He fell overboard and was drowned in the deep.
    You said whosoever did your child home bring
    Should have her; I hope you will perform that thing."

35 "Yes, that was my promise," the Emperor replied.
    "What say you, my daughter, will you be his bride?"
    "O yes," says she, "Father, but first if you please,
    For him who saved my life I'll mourn forty days."

36 Then into close mourning this lady she went,
    For the loss of her true love some time to lament.
    And there we will leave her for to mourn a while
    And turn to the Factor, who lies on that isle.

37 On that desert island, the Factor he lay,
    With floods of tears weeping two nights and a day,
    Until all at once there appeared to his view
    A little old man, paddling in a canoe.

38 The Factor called to him, which caused him to stay;
    And as he drew near him, the old man did say,
    "Friend, how came you hither, whose eyes they do flow?"
    He told him his secrets, and where he would go.

39 "On this desert island much longer you lie,
    With grief and great hunger you surely will die."
    Saying, "What will you give me and I'll be your guide?"
    "I've nothing to give you," the Factor replied.

40 "Well, if you will promise and be true to me,
    And give me the first babe that is born to thee,
    At thirty months old, I'll you to that place bring;
    I will not release you without that very thing."

41 The Factor considered; that thing would cause grief,
    But for him without it there was no relief;
    Saying, "Life is sweet, and my life for to save
    Bring me to that place and your will you shall have."

42 She, looking out of her window and seeing him there,
    From grief to great joy transported she were.
    She called him her jewel, her honey, and her dear;
    "Where have you so long tarried? Pray now, let me hear."

43 The Factor being saved from a terrible fate,
    Where he'd so long tarried he soon did relate.
    He says, "I was thrown overboard in my sleep,
    And I think it was the Captain threw me in the deep."

44 The Captain was sent for then with all speed,
    And hearing the Factor had come there indeed,
    To show himself guilty like a cruel knave,
    Leaped into the ocean, which proved his grave.

45 The next day in joy and triumph we may find
    The Princess and Factor in marriage were joined.
    Ah! and in the valley[12] and space of three year,
    They had a young son born and daughter, we hear.

46 The son was the first born, of perfect beauty;
    He was well beloved by the whole family.
    And at thirty months old the man came for his child,
    Who released the Factor on that desert isle.

47 When the Factor did see him, his eyes they did flow,
    He gave this young mother's parents to know
    He was forced to make him that promise or lie
    On that desert island with hunger and die.

48 "Yes, that was my promise, and I'll have my due,
    Here's one babe for me and another for you.
    I will the first born have; come, give him to me."
    And with that the whole family wept bitterly.

49 The babe's mother says, "I am grieved at my heart
    That from our dear darling infant we must part,
    To one who will carry him we know not where,
    Perhaps our dear darling in pieces may tear."

50 The babe's mother kissed it, and down the tears fell
    And having embraced it, she bid him farewell.
    "'Tis all for the sake of my husband and I,
    I part with my first born, though for him I die."

51 The grandparents kissed him with sighs and with tears,
    And embraced him farewell both with sorrows and fears;
    The babe's mother says, "Surely this is no man;
    He will have our darling boy, do what we can."

52 O then to the Factor the old man did say,
    "It's don't you remember, in Turkey one day
    You saw a dead man's body lying on the ground,
    And to have it buried you paid fifty pound?

---

[12]"Compas" in printed copies.

53 "I am the spirit of that dead body,
   I saved your life for your love shown to me;
   You may keep your babe, and the Lord bless you all."
   And soon then he vanished out of the hall.

54 O he left the hall full of joy and great mirth,
   To love one another as long as they'd breath.
   And so by this Factor you may find indeed.
   No mortal can hinder what fate has decreed.

V. THE FOX AND THE HEN

The following lines of homely repartee have eluded my search for an original. Dame Partlet exhibits the sound practical sense that characterizes her in Chaucer's *The Nonne Preestes Tale*.

An old white hen with yellow legs,
Who laid her master many eggs,
Which from her nest the boys had taken
To put in cake or fry with bacon,
Was roosting in an outer hovel,
Where barrel, birdcage, broomstick, shovel,
Tubs, piggin, cornbags, all together,
Were put to keep them from the weather,
When an old fox stole in one night,
When the full moon was shining bright,
Hoping that he his nose might stick in,
That he might carry off a chicken,
Or from a window, ledge, or shelf
Might jump and reach the old hen herself.
The roost, however, was so high
He saw it was in vain to try
By all his jumping to get at her.
"So then," says he, "I think I'll flatter."
And thus says Reynard, smooth and sly,
And thus Dame Partlet made reply:
"Good evening, madam, how do you do?"
"I'm none the better, sir, for you."
"Better you need not, cannot be;
You're always well enough for me."
"Well, if I am then, as you own,
Pray, sir, let well enough alone.
I'm sick and early went to bed
And scarcely can hold up my head."
"Sick, my dear lady; what can ail?
Indeed, you do look very pale.

Too much confinement fades the fair.
A pleasant walk in open air
With pleasant company at night,
When the moon shines, will set all right."
"A walk! the like whoever heard,
A quadruped to woo a bird!"
"And if you tire I'll call a hack,
Or, better, take you on my back,
Nay, my dear lady, never fear
The jealousy of Chanticleer.
He shall not harm a single feather
Of your fair neck while we're together.
Your neck! Aye, now I think upon it,
With your white shawl and scarlet bonnet,
You'll be by all, both far and near,
Mistaken for a cherub, dear."[13]
"Well, Mr. Reynard, are you done?
If so, I think you'd better run.
My master's coming to the hovel;
You see that broomstick and that shovel,
You see that door you came in at.
If you're not off in half a minute,
Instead of hens or even a chicken,
You'll get as you deserve a kicking."
The wily flatterer dropped his chin,
And out he sneaked as he sneaked in.

Moral:

The flatterer seldom gains his ends;
The wise are never without friends.

VI. NURSERY JINGLES

(1) Of all the old English nursery rhymes transported to America by the oral route, perhaps "William a-Trimbletoe" is most general. A part of the rhyme is in Halliwell's *Nursery Rhymes and Tales of England*, No. 293, p. 65. W. W. Newell, in *Songs and Games of American Children*, 1903 ed., p. 203, prints a short version, with the curiously erroneous second line,
Catches his hands, puts them in pens.
H. C. Bolton, in *The Counting-out Rhymes of Children*, gives fifteen versions. See also *Journal of American Folk-Lore*, Vol. 5, p. 119, "Folk Custom and Folk Belief in North Caro-

---

[13]Compare Chauntecleer's compliment to Pertelote in **The Nonne Preestes Tale,**
"For whan I see the beautee of your face,
Ye ben so scarlet-reed about your yen,
It maketh al my drede for to dyen."

lina"; Vol. 26, pp. 141-142, "Songs and Rhymes from the South"; Vol. 31, p. 526, "Some Counting-Out Rhymes in Michigan." Mrs. Russell's version offers several points of difference from other versions that I have seen.

>William a-Trimbletoe,
>He's a good fisherman;
>He catches hens and puts them in pens,
>Some lay eggs, and some lay none,
>White foot, speckled foot, trip and begone.
>Wire, briar, limber lock,
>Three geese in a flock,
>Sit and sing till daylight spring,
>Till comes the Tod with his long rod,
>To chase the Czar, to wig, to war.
>Ellison, dear, come lend me a spear,
>To go in the woods and kill the king's deer.
>>Hetom, petom, potom, pie,
>>Popular, gigama gi.

(2) A version of "William Trimbletoe" from Michigan (cited above) includes two lines that Mrs. Russell ascribes to another rhyme:

>Strike Jack, lick Tom;
>Blow the bellows, old man.

The similar lines appear to be an interpolation in Mrs. Russell's rhyme:

>As I went up the hill today,
>I saw a man dwell.
>He had jewels, he had rings,
>He had many pretty things,
>He had a cat with two tails,
>He had a hammer with three nails.
>Whip Jack, Will, and Tom,
>Blow the bellows, old man.
>He had a little cuddy horse,
>His name was Tabby Gray,
>His head was made of pea pods,
>His tail was made of hay,
>He could travel, he could trot,
>He could carry the mustard pot,
>Until he came to Woodstock.
>"Margaret, Margaret, are you at home?"
>"Yes, morrow [marry?], that I am."

(3) A fragment of "The Beggars of Ratcliffe Fair" survives in the manuscripts:

> As I was going to Strawberry Fair,
> Who do you think that I met there?
> There was Dick and Madam Dickie Dick,
> Buck and Madam Buckie Buck,
> John and Madam Johnniken,
> Tom and Madam Tombolin,
> Ball and Madam Ballywax,
> Bell and Madam Bellicoe,
> Limpin' Joe and Jumpin' Joe,
> Jolly companions every one.

The opening stanza of the rhyme as given by Halliwell, *Nursery Rhymes of England*, [n.d.], pp. 339-341, is this:

As I went to Ratcliffe Fair, there I met with a jolly beggáre ,
Jolly Beggáre, and his name was John, and his wife's name was Jumping Joan,
So there was John and Jumping Joan,
Merry companions every one.

To each succeeding stanza another beggar and his wife are added. The beggars' names are different from those introduced in Mrs. Russell's fragment. "Jumpin' Joe" is no doubt a corruption of the "Jumping Joan" of the old English version. Halliwell remarks that "this singular accumulative tale produces great amusement amongst children when rapidly repeated." In Chambers, *Popular Rhymes of Scotland* (1870 ed.), p. 40, the rhyme is "The Beggars of Coldingham Fair."

(4) The characters Limpin' Joe and Jumpin' Joe reappear in the following jingle, the first two lines of which plainly declare the paternity of college yells:

> Hickey, pickey, zickey, zan,
> Hollabo, crackebo, mulberry pan,
> And when the fat begins to fry,
> Old Limpin' Joe and Jumpin' Joe
> Ain't at home to eat hot puddin' and pie.

This rhyme is given in Halliwell, No. 277, p. 61, in much longer form, as

> One-ery, two-ery,
>   Ziccary zan;
> Hollowbone, crack a bone,
>   Ninery, ten, etc.

Newell, in *Songs and Games of American Children,* p. 198, gives a variant from Georgia.

(5) The next rhyme is a variant of "See, saw, Margery Daw," given in Halliwell, No. 573, p. 108.

> See, saw, saddle the old goose,
> The old hen jumped over the punkin house,
> And called her chickens one by one,
> And left the poor little black-headed one.

(6) The nomony "Robbin [Robin] to Bobbin" has an interesting origin. The following account is quoted in the JAFL, Vol. 6 (1893), pp. 143-144, from "Christmastide in the Isle of Man," *Monthly Packet,* 1868, p. 301: "The day before St. Stephen's Day an unfortunate wren is caught and stoned to death; he is then hung on a bush. The following day three boys, one with a piece of crepe on his cap, and another ornamented with flowers and some wren's feathers, go about from house to house, carrying the bush and singing,

> 'We'll away to the woods,' says Robin the Bobbin."

The note in the JAFL states that the wren was hunted and beaten to death on St. Stephen's Day because the wren is a fairy who, according to ancient tradition, in guise of a beautiful woman once bewitched a host of the best men of the island and then led them all over a cliff to their death in the sea. But Chambers (*Popular Rhymes of Scotland,* 1870 ed., p 38) gives a different explanation: "It is believed to have taken its origin in an effort of the early Christian missionaries to extinguish a reverence for the wren, which had been held by the Druids as the king of birds."

As the custom died out in England and the origin of the song was forgotten, other birds were substituted for the wren: in Derbyshire (*Notes and Queries,* 9th Ser., Vol. 12, p. 503), a crow; in Staffordshire (*Notes and Queries,* 10th Ser., Vol. 1, p. 218), a cock sparrow; and in the West Riding of Yorkshire (*Notes and Queries,* 10th Ser., Vol. 1, p. 172), a green linnet, which was killed to get sixpence to buy some "terbacker."

In the JAFL (*loc. cit.*) twenty-five stanzas are given, most them different from Mrs. Russell's. Louise Pound, in *American Ballads and Songs*, pp. 235-236, prints six stanzas, which are much like the first five stanzas of Mrs. Russell's version. See also Dr. Pound's notes, p. 257; and *Notes and Queries*, 10th Ser., Vol. 1, p. 32.

"Let's go huntin'," says Robbin to Bobbin,
"Let's go huntin'," says Richard to Robbin,
"Let's go huntin'," says John all alone,
"Let's go huntin'," says every one.

"What shall we kill?" says Robbin to Bobbin,
"What shall we kill?" says Richard to Robbin,
"What shall we kill?" says John all alone,
"What shall we kill?" says every one.

"We'll kill a wren," says Robbin to Bobbin,
"We'll kill a wren," says Richard to Robbin,
"We'll kill a wren," says John all alone,
"We'll kill a wren," says every one.

"How'll we get him home?" says Robbin to Bobbin,
"How'll we get him home?" says Richard to Robbin,
"How'll we get him home?" says John all alone,
"How'll we get him home?" says every one.

"We'll hire a cart," says Robbin to Bobbin,
"We'll hire a cart," says Richard to Robbin,
"We'll hire a cart," says John all alone,
"We'll hire a cart," says every one.

"How will we cook him?" says Robbin to Bobbin,
"How will we cook him?" says Richard to Robbin,
"How will we cook him?" says John all alone,
"How will we cook him?" says every one.

"We'll roast him on spit," says Robbin to Bobbin,
"We'll roast him on spit," says Richard to Robbin,
"We'll roast him on spit," says John all alone,
"We'll roast him on spit," says every one.

"Who'll turn spit?" says Robbin to Bobbin,
"Who'll turn spit?" says Richard to Robbin,
"Who'll turn spit?" says John all alone,
"Who'll turn spit?" says every one.

"We'll hire a dog," says Robbin to Bobbin,
"We'll hire a dog," says Richard to Robbin,
"We'll hire a dog," says John all alone,
"We'll hire a dog," says every one.

"How'll we pay him?" says Robbin to Bobbin,
"How'll we pay him?" says Richard to Robbin,
"How'll we pay him?" says John all alone,
"How'll we pay him?" says everyone.

"We'll give him the bones," says Robbin to Bobbin,
"We'll give him the bones," says Richard to Robbin,
"We'll give him the bones," says John all alone,
"We'll give him the bones," says every one.

Of the remaining rhymes in the manuscripts, (7) "If all the waters in the world were made into one water" and (8) "Sing, sing, what shall we sing?" offer little variation from those recorded in Halliwell, No. 636, p. 121, and No. 411, p. 85; (9) a literal rhyme is marked as having been learned from "the old Dilworth spelling book in South Carolina between 1750 and 1780"; and (10) "The Idle Girl" bears no mark of folk origin.

LORE OF THE LLANO ESTACADO

By J. Evetts Haley

West of the one hundredth meridian and to the north of the thirty-first parallel lies the Llano Estacado, the last large area of the state of Texas to be settled. Neither its youth nor the practical-mindedness of its Anglo-American pioneers has been conducive to the development of a wholly distinct and voluminous folk-lore. On the other hand, its geographical location and natural features set it off as a part of the "Great American Desert." As such, what scientific authority lacked in describing its terrors, legend supplied in abundant degree.

The first contribution to Plains folk-lore was the popular myths regarding the extreme aridity of the Llano Estacado. The effect of these stories upon the settlement of the country was noticeable, but they may more logically be considered in connection with that body of legends centering around the naming of the Staked Plains, and will not be given here.

The lore of any country develops along well defined social lines, and the social influences may easily be observed from the historical point of view. A cross-section of the history of the Panhandle-Plains country reveals at least five rather distinct social divisions. Though traces of other influences are to be seen, they are negligible. First, the Indians made the region their home; then Spanish and Mexican hunters and traders became familiar with it; then in the middle and the late seventies the Anglo-American buffalo hunters wrote bloody history with their Sharps rifles; hard on their heels the pioneer cowboy "rode herd" for a few decades; and then came the farming settler to trace the script of civilization in the virgin soil with a sod plow. One after another these social groups left distinct traces that are reflected in the folk-lore of today.

The Indian influence that survives is comparatively small, but it may be observed in the place names of the region. Sometimes a creek, a lake, or a city serves to remind the modern plainsman that this was once the favorite hunting-ground of the "plains children." Captain R. B. Marcy, who explored Red River in 1852, came upon a creek along which were signs of an Indian camp. It was in the country nearly opposite the camps of the Kiowas on the Canadian, and Marcy, supposing that some of that tribe had spent the winter there, called it Kiowa Creek.[1] Marcy was struck by the abundance of prairie dog villages along one fork of the stream, and thought it "probable that the fact of their being so abundant here has suggested the name which the Comanches have applied to this branch of Red River, of 'Ke-che-a-que-ho-no,' or 'Prairie-dog-town River.' "[2] Even today one sometimes hears the translation applied by pioneer plainsmen.

Still noting the Indian influence, we turn to the South Plains country, to observe, in Lynn County, one of the large inland lakes or basins characteristic of the Plains area. Its waters, like those of many similar lakes, are brackish and unfit for use. With sensible directness, the Indians called the lake Tahoka, which means *alkali*,[3] but for personal safety, the word is to be used in the original, not translated, when one speaks to a native of the town called after the lake.

Miami is another town with an Indian name. Its translation is of a more palatable and romantic flavor, as it is said to mean *sweetheart*. The city of Quanah, to the east of the caprock, was named after the noted Comanche chief, Quanah Parker. According to Colonel Charles Goodnight, his were not the discomforts and inconveniences of being born in a smoky and dusty tepee. He came to life in a fragrant bed of wild flowers, on Cache Creek of Indian Territory. His mother, Cynthia Ann Parker, appreciative of the colorful setting, called him Quanah, which is said to mean *perfume*.[4] The name was poetically, not ironically, applied to this Indian, whose wholly uncivilized condition is shown in the fact that he divorced not one of his eleven wives, and, in spite of the thirty-one members of his family, still believed there was "no place like home." Quanah, Texas, should rest proud in her name.

Significant as these direct survivals of Indian lore may be, the Spanish influence is much greater. With one exception— that of the cattle people—the greatest contribution to Plains

---

[1] R. B. Marcy, **Exploration of Red River**, 36.
[2] **Ibid.**, 49.
[3] J. B. Mobely to J. Evetts Haley, August 6, 1926.
[4] Charles Goodnight to J. E. H., November 14, 1926.

lore, it seems to me, is of Spanish origin. At first sight this seems remarkable, when one considers that, of the entire state, this region is today perhaps least touched by Spanish life. But over a century ago, across the Plains from the New Mexican settlements to the west, came Spanish, then Mexican, hunters and traders, poor in worldly goods but rich in legendary lore. They left a definite and enduring impress upon the Planes of Texas, particularly in topographical nomenclature.

The Spanish-speaking men named all the important rivers and creeks from the Conchos to the Canadian. I am told that the Conchos were named for the mussel shells to be found upon their banks. The significance of the name Colorado—Red—is obvious. A whole group of pioneer stories center around the origin of the name Yellowhouse. One fork of the Brazos rises to the west of Lubbock and is called by that name. Near its source is an alkali lake of like designation, an important landmark fifty years ago.[5] The southern part of the XIT Ranch was known as the Yellowhouse Division, the headquarters of which were in the Yellowhouse Canyon. Bordering the lake are some tall bluffs, of yellowish hue, which may be seen at a great distance and which have somewhat the appearance of the walls of a great city, "especially when seen through a good mirage."[6] There were several caves in the face of the bluffs in 1879, when Captain G. W. Arrington, with a party of rangers took refuge in them to escape being frozen to death in a blizzard. It is not unlikely that the caves had something to do with the naming of the place,[7] as these bluffs were known to the Mexicans as Casas Amarillas—Yellow Houses.[8]

A south fork of the Yellowhouse Canyon was called Casa Prieta. The words mean Black House, and the Mexicans so named the canyon on account of an old sod dwelling built on it before the country was settled, probably by some Indian traders.[9] To the north of the Yellowhouse is Agua Corriente

---

[5]Thrall, H. S., **A Pictorial History of Texas,**—44-45.
[6]MS. "Recollections of Charles Goodnight," Panhandle-Plains Historical Society, Canyon, Texas.
[7]MS. G. W. Arrington, "A Scout after Indians," Panhandle-Plains Historical Society.
[8]Goodnight, "Recollections," etc., as cited.
[9]Charles Goodnight to J. E. H., November 13, 1926.

(generally pronounced Agua Curra), or Running Water, which, lower down, is called Blanco Canyon, because of the white dirt along its rim. Yet to the north is the Tule, the Mexican word for a kind of reed or water grass; the Agua Fria, or Cold Water; Cañoncito Blanco, or Little White Canyon; Tierra Blanca, or White Dirt; and the Palo Duro, which is, literally, Hard Pole. It was here that the Indians, away from the timbered regions of Oklahoma and New Mexico, found wild cherry and plum trees—suitable material for arrows. Thus originated the name of the Palo Duro Canyon, of Spanish terminology but Indian application.[10]

Tracing along the edge of the Plains to the north, we find the Agua Dulce, Sweetwater. Bending westward along the Canadian, we come to El Venado Colorado, the Red Deer; Arroyo Piedra, Rock Creek; Arroyo de Gallinas, or Chicken Creek, probably named from the abundance of prairie chickens once to be found along its banks. Yet to the west are the Rios Amarillos, the Yellow Rivers, so called because of the yellowish country through which they flow; Sierrita de la Cruz, Little Mountain of the Cross, which name is applied to both a hill and a creek; and Los Alamocitos, or Little Cottonwoods.[11] Such are some of the names of streams that rise in the Plains country. Others might be mentioned, but the list would grow bulky, especially since some streams were forced to bear two or more names.

Among those thus burdened is a creek flowing out of the eastern Panhandle, which the Mexicans called Alamogordo, literally "fat cottonwood." And if you were unfamiliar with the country and were at a considerable distance from the stream, they would tell you of an immense cottonwood tree growing upon its banks that could be encircled by no less than two lariats.[12] Unfortunately the tree burned to the ground many years ago, thereby depriving the modern visitor of a substantial basis of comparison between the actual size and the imaginary one. Today the stream is called McClellan Creek. It was named by R. B. Marcy in honor of

---

[10]**Ibid.;** also Goodnight, "Recollections."
[11]Charles Goodnight to J. E. H., November 13, 1926.
[12]**Ibid.**

one of his command, Captain George B. McClellan, June 20, 1852. McClellan was thought to be the first white man "to set eyes upon it."[13]

In the same region is the Agua Dulce, or Sweetwater. Some thirsty Mexican traveler who thought no better or sweeter water ever flowed must have bestowed the name. Another Mexican came that way and found some walnuts upon its banks, and thereupon called it Nueces.[14] The first town of the Panhandle sprang to life along the stream and was called Sweetwater by the buffalo hunters and traders.[15] But application for a postoffice in the late seventies brought news that the seat of Nolan County had already appropriated the name. A frontier character named Ben Williams recalled the Comanchean designation of the creek, and suggested as the name Mobeetie, meaning Sweetwater.[16] Thus one small creek in its names shows the influence of those social groups represented by the Mexican, the Indian, and the buffalo hunter. Small wonder that its once deep pools filled with sand and its bold current became lazy and sluggish.

Again, in the name of Tongue River there are three social influences. Even before the frontier forces were withdrawn at the outbreak of the Civil War, the Plains Indians were depredating upon the northwest fringe of settlement, stealing horses and cattle and driving them west. Far out upon the Plains to the northwest of where the city of Amarillo now stands they met the Mexican traders at a spring then called Las Tecovas (perhaps a corruption of *techados*), meaning The Tents. This spring was later the headquarters of the Frying Pan Ranch, of which Henry B. Sanborn was joint owner. Sanborn will be remembered as the man who introduced barbed wire into Texas. In spite of all his unpopularity with some of the old-time cowhands because of that transgression, the spring came to be called after him.

At Las Tecovas, or Sanborn Spring, the trade started. But it was a long drive for the Indians from the northwest frontier of Texas to that rendezvous, and the place of meeting was shifted southeastward to a fork of Pease River, just be-

---

[13]Marcy, **Exploration of Red River**, 40.
[14]Charles Goodnight to J. E. H., November 13, 1926.
[15]Johnnie Long to J. E. H., June 17, 1925.
[16]Marvin Saunders to J. E. H., June 19, 1925.

low the caprock. Here developed the greatest trading ground in the history of Plains cattle theft. For ten years after the close of the Civil War it continued.[17] While Washington theorized, cattlemen were losing their stock, reserving their driest powder for the Indians, and venting their choicest profanity on the politicians.

Nevertheless the Kiowas and Comanches, doubtless sometimes aided by renegade whites, did a profitable business.[18] They found it rare good sport to keep all the horses stolen from the cowmen along the outer edge, and cattle could be stolen much more quickly than they could be raised. Down the trails from Santa Fe and Las Vegas came the New Mexican traders, across the Plains to camp and await the coming of the Indians after "the light of the moon." Some of the traders were poor, and brought but a few burro loads of goods and traded for but a few head of stock. The more prominent ones brought greater quantities in *carretas* (the cumbersome Mexican carts) loaded with calico, trinkets, powder, lead, and even baked bread. In exchange, they secured larger herds.

Indians of various tribes and dialects, Anglo-Americans, and Mexicans gathered at this great exchange ground in the valley of the stream. In order to carry on the barter, the traders or their interpreters were forced to speak several different languages, or *lenguas*—tongues. So the stream came to be known as Las Lenguas; then the name was anglicized, and today the river upon which so many stolen cattle changed hands is known as the Tongue.[19]

Colonel Charles Goodnight told me that he found 600 head of his own cattle in one bunch on Gallinas Creek, New Mexico, in 1867. They had been stolen from near old Fort Belknap and traded to the Mexicans. He went into court at Las Vegas in an attempt to recover them. Not only were his efforts fruitless, but it cost him $75 to get out of court. He left with the "undisputed evidence" that at least 300,000 head of cattle had been stolen from the Texas frontier and sold

---

[17]Charles Goodnight to J. E. H., January 26, 1926; *Ibid.*, November 13, 1926.

[18]See MS., C. V. Hall, "The Early History of Floyd County," Panhandle-Plains Historical Society.

[19]Charles Goodnight to J. E. H., November 13, 1926.

to the New Mexicans during the war,[20] and, also, probably with a firmer conviction of what should be done with cattle thieves.

Further folk history bound up in Spanish names may be illustrated in the account of how Sierrita de la Cruz—Little Mountain of the Cross—got its name. It was a strange anomaly in the ethics of the range when, in 1876, sheepmen with herds numbering about one hundred thousand head, gathered for protection around Goodnight's outfit at Rincón de las Piedras, on the Canadian, just above the state line in New Mexico. But the Indians were bad. Goodnight moved into the Palo Duro in the fall and left the Mexicans behind. They agreed to stay off the Palo Duro range, while he, in turn, agreed to leave the Canadian to them. Only two flocks transgressed the agreement. A cowboy on the Goodnight ranch took the double of his rope and whipped the Mexican herder of one, and it is said on good authority that "he never came back."[21] However humiliating that herder's exit may have been, the men who tended the other flock came to a more tragic end.

Two men, with a Navajo boy as helper, dropped in from New Mexico and turned their flocks along the Palo Duro; that was fifty years ago. Old cowmen, recalling the offensive odor of sheep, assert that Palo Duro waters are yet strongly suggestive of mutton—just another example of "what a whale of a difference a few scents make." In time an outlaw passed that way and killed the two men, intending to steal their property and money. Even old cowboys, extremely tolerant of vigorous measures toward sheep herders, observe that the man who murders one for his property has reached the lowest level of depravity—has indulged in about the worst in the category of crime. The outlaw intended to send the Navajo on a premature trip to the happy hunting ground, and despatched a Mexican boy, who accompanied him, out to shoot the Indian. Whether of faint heart or cold feet, the Mexican weakened, became frightened, and rode the outlaw's horse into Old Tascosa—the capital of the western Panhandle. The fact that the outlaw was forced to shoot the Navajo himself

---

[20]Ibid., February 19, 1927.
[21]Charles Goodnight to J. E. H., on June 24, 1925.

was not so bad, but the humiliating part—something understood by any Western man—was that his horse was taken and he was forced to walk.

The Plains was a dry and lonely country, and soon the outlaw gravitated to Old Tascosa, with its wine, women, and dances. The Mexicans were prepared for him and shot him down. They buried him on a little hill south of the Canadian River. Then with characteristic Latin sentiment they erected a cross above his grave. The name Sierrita de La Cruz—Little Mountain of the Cross—was not illogically applied, and a nearby creek was named after the hill.[22] In spite of the prevailing sandstorms of West Texas, this same hill, old-timers maintain, is still to be seen. For thirty years the longhorn steers looked, with watering mouths, at the luxuriant grama grass which grew along its slopes, but, true to their colors and responsive to their "raisin'," touched not a leaf that was reminiscent of sheep.

Such, then, was the Spanish contribution to Plains lore. Chronologically, the next social influence of importance to touch the area was that represented by the buffalo hunters. Their period was short, as the great slaughter began in the Panhandle in 1874 and was practically done by the close of 1878.[23] At that time the Panhandle and Plains country was almost altogether a man's country. There were very few women. The group of men who engaged in buffalo hunting were rather cosmopolitan and did not compose a folk. Yet around their campfires of buffalo chips stories of the greatest of all hunting ranges passed into a folk-lore that was preserved in part by themselves and in part by the pastoral frontier.

As is generally known, there is a great scarcity of wood in the Plains country, and by the irony of fate the buffalo furnished the fuel over which his own steaks were fried. Not a few stories concern the use of this "prairie coal." L. Gough, of Amarillo, an old cowpuncher on Gunter and Munson's T Anchor Ranch in Randall County, tells this story:

---

[22]Charles Goodnight to J. E. H., November 13, 1926.
[23]See John R. Cook, **The Border and the Buffalo;** also **Life of Billy Dixon.**

"In the spring of 1883 I went down to Gunter and Munson's Grayson County ranch to come back with a herd. The outfit gave me a vacation, and I went down into Lamar County to visit around. One evening I stopped at Sylvester Carter's house, where a couple of cowmen had put up for the night. They asked me about conditions out on the Plains, and one wanted to know what was being done with the buffalo bones. I told them that people were freighting the bones to Wichita Falls, to the railroad, and selling them at $20 a ton. We talked of other features of the Plains country, mentioning the scarcity of wood. During the evening meal Mrs. Carter leaned over, and, with a twinkle in her eye, said:

"'Young man, I've caught you in a story.'

"'All right, Mrs. Carter,' I said, 'what is it?'

"'Well,' she said, 'you were saying there is not a stick of wood upon the Plains for a hundred miles at a stretch. What do they burn?'

"I told her that we burned buffalo chips.

"'Oh,' Mrs. Carter naively replied, 'and that's what makes the bones so high!'"

There were other remarkable things connected with the buffalo range. Upon the frontier, where it has always been considered indelicate as well as hazardous to show too lively an interest in a man's name and past, nicknames have flourished. And it is a marvel of nomenclature that there were only three Joneses on the range in the Panhandle in 1875. One of these, "Buffalo" Jones, is known for his work in helping to preserve the animals with whose name he has been honored. It requires no unusually productive imagination to decide how "Dirty Face" Jones secured his name. "Wrong Wheel" Jones received his from the fact that he could not see how the left-hand wheel of one wagon would fit the right-hand axle of another.[24] Other nicknames familiar upon the range at that time were "Smoky Hill" Thompson, so called because he had long hunted on the Smoky Hill River, in Kansas;[25] "Shorty," whose surname was reputed to be Woodson, "the tallest, slimmest man on the range"; "Powderface" and "Squirrel Eye."[26]

---

[24]Cook, **The Border and the Buffalo,** 159.
[25]**Ibid.,** 202.
[26]**Ibid,** 206.

As great as was the contribution to picturesque diction found in the nicknames of the buffao camps, the contribution made in place names was even greater. It was natural that the unnamed landmarks should receive the attention of the hunters. The results are to be observed from the northern extremities of the Panhandle to the breaks of the Plains on the south.

The highest point in Lubbock County, about five miles northeast of the city, is called Causey Hill after George Causey, an old hunter along the Yellowhouse. Davidson Draw, some fourteen miles to the east, was the site of the dugout of another hunter by the name of Bill Davidson. A party of Indians passed through the country in 1878 and gave Bill such a scare that he hurriedly departed, leaving not only his buffalo guns and skinning knives behind him, but likewise his name.[27]

Far to the east we find Schimerhorn Mountain. During the winter of 1876 Hank Smith, Judge John Schimerhorn, and three others set out from Fort Griffin to Blanco Canyon. They went to locate a ranch for a young Philadelphian, Charles P. Tasker, and an Irish lord by the name of Jamison. Schimerhorn's ambitions ran to other things than the mastery of Blackstone when he undertook to kill a buffalo bull with an old "pepper-box" gun. The bull took offense at the insult, Schimerhorn sought safety in flight and fled to the mountain for refuge, "and the name of the mountain was bestowed in honor of the refugee."[28]

The trader always presses close upon the receding wilderness, and there came to the buffalo range one Pete Snyder, seeking whatever adventure and fortune might be found upon the South Plains. He settled upon Deep Creek in Scurry County, built a house of log framework, covered it with buffalo hides, and opened a trading post for the benefit of the hunters and the pecuniary advantages it offered himself. Thus a "hide town" was started. No sooner had a saloon opened than the tread of the hunter changed to the roaring stampede of civilization, and Snyder, Texas, was born.[29]

---

[27]R. C. Burns to J. E. H., October 29, 1926.
[28]**The Crosbyton Review,** February 29, 1912.
[29]J. W. Woody to J. E. H., October 19, 1926.

Among the adventurous spirits drawn by its stimulating attractions came one from down toward Fort Concho. His covered wagon crept north along the old McKenzie Trail until Pete Snyder's store was almost in sight. He came to the bank of a small "draw." In spite of tradition, a heavy rain had fallen in that part of West Texas, and the "draw" was on a rise. But parching thirst has never recognized the efficacy of water, nor does it stop at physical obstacles. The plainsman drove his wagon into the current, and it and team were swept down. All lodged against a tree, where the horses were drowned. The driver swam to the opposite side, and walked to the store, where he emphatically declared: "That's the hell roarin'st little holler I ever saw." That seemed a popular designation, and today the citizens of Scurry will tell you of Hell Roaring Hollow and the luckless driver.[30]

As Pete Snyder's name is preserved in that of the town, so are the names of others in the natural landmarks. Mooar's Creek, a tributary of the Colorado, and Mooar's Draw, which flows into the Clear Fork, are both named after the noted Mooar brothers, prominent hunters.[31]

If we swing to the northern limits of the Staked Plains we find no less abundant evidence of the buffalo range heritage. Pitcher Creek, which runs into the Canadian from the north, was named for an old trader who kept a store there in 1877.[32] Dixon Creek, from whose subterranean beds oil is now so prodigiously flowing, was named for the noted scout and Indian fighter, Billy Dixon.[33]

Many stories are told of fights between the hunters and Indian parties out from the reservation. A lake in Donley County is said to have been the scene of one of these fights. It was known to the old timers as Worley Lake, but today is called Lelia Lake. In the late seventies, so the story goes, a party of Indians rushed in upon a hunter there by the name of Worley. But with the courage and marksmanship typical of his calling, he offered stubborn resistance and killed several Indians. Then with their characteristic conscientiousness and

---

[30]Ibid.
[31]R. C. Burns to J. E. H., October 29, 1926.
[32]Charles A. Siringo, **A Lone Star Cowboy,** 71.
[33]Charles Goodnight to J. E. H., November 13, 1926.

efficiency, the Federal military officers at Fort Elliott, to the north, sent down a detachment to bring Worley in to answer to the charge of inciting a fight. But the old hunter felt the migratory urge and moved on to a cooler climate. For years the lake near which the fight took place bore his name.[34]

But soon the careless hunters were drifting back along the Rath, the Jones and Plummer, and the old McKenzie trails, leaving the Plains to the advancing cowmen and the greatest of Southwestern pioneers, the Texas cowboy.

The most distinct social group to be found in Plains history is that represented by the cowman; the proudest of his vocation, the happiest in his past. His habits, his means of life, his diction, and his thinking are distinctive. Therefore the cow country possesses a lore of its own, more interesting because more picturesque. It is unusual in its variety. Old cowhands in the Big Bend country will tell you entrancing stories of Judge Roy Bean, self-appointed and self-sufficient "law west of the Pecos," with no less conviction than the pioneer of the North Plains will tell you of a phantom mustang steed. However, but two divisions of this lore, place names, and cowboy stories or legends, will be observed, and these groups overlap to a noticeable degree.

Of course, the cowboy could name only the lesser topographical features of the country, all those of importance having been named before his advent. Frank Mitchell, old time cowboy on the JA and LIT ranches, recalls the incident from which Chisum Canyon, a tributary of the Canadian, received its name. When the Panhandle was young, Jim Chisum, brother of John Chisum of Pecos Valley notoriety, came in and located a herd on the river. Hotel arrangements were unsatisfactory, and he built a dugout in the canyon. His cattle bore the same earmark as his brother's, the widely known "jingle-bob," made by splitting both ears from the base out through the tip. Such a mark caused the lower part of the ears to flop promiscuously, making the cows, it is said, "the craziest to handle" west of the one hundredth meridian. When a cowboy "cut" one of them from a herd, she came out with her ears flopping to the sixteen principal points of the

---

[34]V. C. Crab to J. E. H., June 22, 1925.

compass, her head in the air, her destination somewhere in the distance, and a strong inclination to "take to the tules."[35] What wonder that Chisum's canyon home retaind his name!

At an earlier day, and far to the east, Thomas S. Bugbee turned his herd loose, the first cowman on the Canadian and the second in the Panhandle. He lived in a dugout for two years without experiencing the civilizing influence of a visit from the tax-collector or a prohibition officer. Such things as ad valorem and padlocks were unknown. How he managed to live without such modern comforts is a puzzle to us of this progressive age. However, he lived to mellow years, and Bugbee Canyon is a fitting memorial to this pioneer cowman.[36]

The story of how Deep Lake was stocked with fish may not belong strictly to folk-lore, but it is a part of that body of tales told around western camp-fires. This lake, which seems to have been formed by the sinking of the earth's surface, lies in Hall County. During the buffalo hunting period its banks were precipitous and it had no outlet. The only way of getting to the edge of the water was by a narrow trail, which the Indians had cut out with their tomahawks. Down this trail they would lead their horses to the water's edge, one at a time, and, after they had watered, back them up the trail. There was not room to turn below.

There were no fish in Deep Lake until about 1899, in which year V. C. Crabb, an old buffalo hunter, was punching cattle along Red River. At Ox Bow Crossing one day, he rode up to a little hole of water left by a receding flood. Eight small catfish, trapped within, had about decided that after all this old world is a very small place. Frontier ingenuity came to the cowboy's aid in his desire to propagate the natural resources of the country. He pulled off one boot, filled it with water, and placed the catfish inside. Remounting, he rode several miles with boot in hand, and turned the fish loose in Deep Lake. Now thousands upon thousands swarm its waters.[37]

Some partisan West Texans acquainted with certain pe-

---

[35]H. F. Mitchell to J. E. H., December 1, 1926.
[36]See **Life of Billy Dixon**, 180.
[37]V. C. Crabb to J. E. H., June 22, 1925.

culiar characteristics of a cowboy's boot seem to consider the survival of the fish as positive proof of the hardihood of the catfish raised in the high dry climate of the Plains country. They assert with categorical finality that few catfish, especially the effete specimens grown in the mud of East Texas streams, could ever take such a journey and live to wiggle the tail.

Again the Indian influence appears. In spite of the rapid advance of the pastoral frontier, the Indians gave the cattlemen trouble for many years, and even after 1876 were indulging in raids. The U Ranch, on the North Concho, was the scene of one such late raid. Most of the ranch horses were stolen, and four cowboys and six Texas Rangers took the trail in an effort to recover the animals and mete out a little frontier justice to the Indians. The thieving party separated, and the trail taken by the Texans led toward Midland County. They rode hard for two days and nights, without change of horses and without food, before coming in sight of the Indians. Then they gave chase and gained rapidly. The Indians disappeared over a hill that forms the southern drainage of one of the Plains lakes. Quickly dismounting, they allowed their horses to "lope" off. With knives and tomahawks they dug shallow holes in the loose earth, but sufficient to hide themselves. The cowboys and Rangers spurred their jaded mounts to the top of the hill, only to find the Indians nowhere in sight. A few seconds later they were surprised by a volley from the ground, which cut down three of their horses and one of the Rangers. The ambush was so effective that the leader of the Rangers lost control of his horse, which, fortunately, charged to the rear, and the other Rangers "followed suit." The cowboys, after firing a few rounds of ammunition, decided that horses without life were poor real estate after all and followed the Rangers. The next morning the party returned to the hill, rolled the body of the dead Ranger up in a saddle blanket, dug a shallow grave, and laid him "at ease" to await the final call. Today the duck hunters kick down the mesquite along the banks of the lake in an attempt to secure a shot at the mallards and canvas-backs, with never a thought as to how the body of water received its name. But the cowboy "out on the circle" pulls up at the side of a lonely grave, and as his foaming pony catches his breath and his charge of cows string out for the NA roundup grounds, he pays silent tribute at the grave of Ranger Angling, whose tombstone is a slab of rock and whose monument is a fresh-water lake named in his memory.[38]

The Midland country was not entirely reclaimed for civilization until some time after the final raid of the Indians. While the scattered cow outfits were making "good Indians" out of all they could catch, thereby preparing the way for civilization, a whole flock of sheep herders came in and "squatted" upon portions of the South Plains. Therefore, when the last Indian raid was past the cowboys had to turn their attention to the sheep men. After a struggle the cow interests won out, the herders departed, and culture and civilization followed.

Among the sheep men to settle in the Midland country in the early days was one by the name of Peck. His range lay around a large alkali lake, at one end of which was a spring of brackish water. Large cow outfits settled around him until finally the country became unfit for sheep, and he moved out. The realization that a sheep herder had enjoyed fair health among them must have been almost as bitter to the cowboy's mind as the lake water was to his palate. But whatever the connection, if there was any, the place is known today as Peck's Spring.[39]

The next social group to be represented in the development of the Plains was the farming settler. When the squatters, advancing with irresistible tread and a bunch of brindle cows, reached and desecrated the rolling grazing lands of the Midland country with their sod plows, the cowboys looked upon them with pity. They felt that anyone who tried to make a living in West Texas by farming was a fit object of pity. With the abandon worthy their generous souls they offered some advice to "the man with the hoe." Among those who received this advice were "nesters" putting in fields along the

---

[38]James Cox, **The Cattle Industry of Texas and Adjacent Territory,** 401; Lod Calohan to J. E. H., January 1, 1926. A bit of verse written upon the incident appeared in **Hunter's Magazine,** February, 1912. The name is there spelled **Anglin.**

[39]Leslie Floyd to J. E. H., December 29, 1925.

valley of a large "draw" south of Midland. Now, it mattered not how many years intervened between rains, a shower always brought forth a great assembly of frogs, not the bull variety, but toads, along this "draw." The cowboys commented upon their delicacy as a tabledish, explaining that no warts were to be feared from this western variety. All that the newcomers had to do to catch them was to take a lariat, "build" a loop, and then upon finding a big toad sleepily watching the approach of a gnat, throw the loop. After it had settled down about him the hungry person might approach and pick him up, as he wouldn't jump out of the loop. Some skeptics doubt that toads were ever roped in this way, but Toadloop Draw,[40] long a stronghold of the "nesters," is almost an institution of the Midland country.

Notwithstanding the pity felt for them, the farming settlers had come to the Plains to stay. Their advance followed the railroads and decreed the passing of much of the cow country. Towns sprang up where cow camps once stood, and to the stories of the range came an additional lore, which I have called the contribution of the farming settler. The stories that, in part, go to make up this lore range from the typical buried treasure tales to stories of the supernatural. One of the last named will suffice.

Those familiar with the topography of the Plains country know that numerous canyons cut the surface along the eastern breaks. In one of these, about twelve miles south of Crosbyton, stands an old log house, once headquarters of the WIL S Ranch, located by Will Slaughter in the late seventies.[41] Legend relates that once, while the owners were freighting supplies from Fort Worth, some two hundred miles to the east, Indians ran in on the place and killed some women and children. To substantiate this statement, the story teller will point you to four graves in the front yard of the old place. The house was abandoned after the country was settled, and stood for years as a landmark of a past frontier, serene in its canyon setting, undisturbed in its traditions— only the rendezvous of pack rats and hoot owls.

---

[40] Ibid.
[41] N. Y. Bicknell to J. E. H., October 21, 1926.

Today, none but the venturous consider it a fit camping place, for there are few who care to disturb the spirits that are said to haunt the premises. It was a crisp October evening, with a half-full, waning moon giving that touch that makes night on the Plains so beautiful, when I turned my car out of Tahoka along the road that leads to Crosbyton. Beside me was Roy Howard, authority on legends of the supernatural in Crosby County. I was in search of some fragments of Plains history but a legend was not amiss, and as I splashed through the mudholes along the road, Roy recalled the origin of the story.

Upon the evening of January 12, 1923, Ed Wallace, a man named Davis, and two others went down into the canyon on a coon hunt. They camped for the night at the old ranch house. It consists of two rooms, in one of which is a fireplace. Beneath the room is a cellar, access to which is had by a stairway. While sitting around the fire that night, one of the men asked another for a chew of tobacco. The one of whom the request was made shuffled around and reached for his hip pocket. As he did, one of his feet went through a rotten place in the floor. Then, as if taking alarm at the disturbance, a baby was heard to cry in the cellar. The four men started for the stairs to investigate, but before reaching the cellar they met a woman with a child in her arms. Immediately a sound from without attracted their attention. They heard a man come riding at a run. They heard him draw rein at the edge of the porch, jump off, and quickly unsaddle. They heard him throw his saddle and bridle upon the porch, and slap his horse on the hip as the animal turned and trotted off. All four men left the woman standing on the stairs and went out to see who the rider might be. But no horse or rider was in sight. They decided that the creek would be a more comfortable place to spend the night and thereupon left the porch. As they passed through the front yard they saw a girl about 18 years of age, with long flowing hair, standing upon one of the graves. They rubbed their eyes and looked again, and saw that upon another of the graves stood an old woman, an old man, and a group of children. As the four watched the phantom group, it would disappear from one grave and in a moment reappear on another. Suddenly one of the men began suffering from a dry throat and started to the creek, some ten steps away, for a drink. Another ventured to address the girl, and asked her if their presence was interfering with the ghostly party. She replied: "Yes! God! Leave, leave, leave!" And all records for the mile run were unquestionably, though unofficially, shattered.

At that point in the story our old car hit an unusually boggy hole, and my friend jumped out and pushed it through to firmer ground. As he climbed back over the door and we moved along again, I advanced the idea that perhaps this story was more an index to the potency of West Texas "moonshine" than to the number of phantom spirits to be found in Crosby County. My idea was overruled, as Roy declared the four were men of temperate tastes, and would fight you in a minute if you attempted to offer that explanation to them. He went on to explain that the following day, January 13, 1923, witnessed no little excitement among the citizens of Crosbyton. Some five hundred of them are said to have set forth to investigate and discover the foundation of the story the four coon hunters told. They rode to the canyon and resolutely began the walk of a mile or two necessary to reach the log house. Out of the entire party of 500, some five or six reached the place,[42] nor is the failure of the others to do so to be attributed entirely to the West Texan's aversion to walking.

"Next January twelfth," concluded Roy, "I am going down there and spend the night. The haunts are supposed to appear then." That was only last fall, and I have not yet heard how fruitful his investigations proved.

These examples of the lore of the Llano Estacado will, perhaps, convey some conception as to the field that this geographical region offers to folk-lorists. Any one of the separate influences represented by the five social divisions— the Indian, the Mexican trader and hunter, the buffalo hide hunter, the Texas cowboy, and the farming settler—might be made the subject of interesting and fruitful investigation. Little has been written of the field. Therefore the study should be the more engaging. As were the trading opportunities of the first Mexicans, the grass to the first cowmen, the sod to the first farmers, the field is virgin. And, like all true folk-lore, that of the Staked Plains is to be furrowed from the soil.

---

[42]Roy Howard to J. E. H., October 20, 1926.

NAMES IN THE OLD CHEYENNE AND ARAPAHOE TERITORY AND THE TEXAS PANHANDLE

By DELLA I. YOUNG

Oil men call the divide between the North Fork of Red River and the South Canadian a turtle back. The spine of this turtle back is a mild depression along which the Washita River finds its crooked way. Numerous creeks and dry arroyos vein into the Washita; other water courses cut off toward the turtle's legs, entering the South Canadian on the north and the North Fork to the south.

Although the names of these various streams are derived from Indian, military, natural, and social sources, in almost every instance the name was originally applied by some cowboy, directed by a sense of humor or a sense of the fitness of things, for the sake of convenience, or on account of some whim. At the time of the opening of the Cheyenne and Arapahoe Territory (1892)—the name by which old timers still designate most of the turtle's back,—strange as it may seem, very few of the Indian geographical names were employed. Without exception, the Indian names that were employed were the names of chiefs or tribes; for example, Little Robe, White Shield, Kiowa.

One might easily follow Custer in his campaigns (1869) through Western Oklahoma by the trail of names he left, though the christening was done by the cowmen long after the passing of the great warrior. A creek in the quicksand of which were found embedded the running gears of a wagon was conveniently dubbed Wagon Creek. Custer's troops in their hurried flight from victory over Black Kettle on the Washita scattered canteens and pack saddles galore along the valley of a little stream that enters the Canadian from the north; and yet folk ask, "Why did they ever call this Pack Saddle Creek?" The town of Cheyenne is located on the east bank of the Sergeant Major, where the young Eliott bearing that military title so tragically lost his life as a result of his disobedience.

In locating a herd, a line camp, a roundup, or an especially fine motte of grass or watering place, the cowboys named the streams according to the adjacent fauna, flora, strata, or some property of the water itself; for example, Elk Creek, Buffalo, Red Deer, Wolf, Beaver Dam, Wild Horse, Turkey; Hackberry Creek, Hay, Timber, Cottonwood; Deep Creek, Sandstone, Sweetwater, and Croton, the last so named by Jim Fulton, a horse wrangler from the Laurel Leaf outfit, on account of the cathartic nature of its waters.

One stream is Wagon Sheet, because one of Tony Day's cowboys built part of his domicile on this stream with a wagon sheet. Another is Trunk Creek, from the fact that a certain opulent cowboy sporting a trunk and wishing to change his stamping ground, prevailed upon the driver of the chuck wagon to leave said trunk on the bank of a certain arroyo. The cowboy planned further that another chuck wagon crossing the trail of the first should pick up the trunk; but the best laid plans of even the riders of the range miscarry, for no wagon crossed the trail of the first. Thus the puncher lost his trunk, but the creek found its name.

Some three miles from the hundredth meridian a dry, sandy arroyo shambles off north to the South Canadian. Near a half century since, the cowmen farther up the river reported that a family had located on the banks of this sand bed. A house of logs with a roof of bark sheltered the family. There were a woman and a child. When one considers that about this time Pat Hennessey—after whom Hennessey, Oklahoma, is named—was burned alive at his wagon wheel and that Adobe Walls and Buffalo Wallow were made famous by Indian fights, he understands the surprise and anxiety of the Texas cowmen over the presence of a woman and a child near the Territory line. Even in that wild day strange rumors spread concerning this family. What was their mark and their brand? Whose outfit were they riding for? Were they hunters? No. They failed to visit other camps. They did not bid the lone cowman, "Ride in an' unsaddle."

Cow thieves! That explained.

Then one day, my narrator tells, a rider from the P O's, tired, hungry, and miles from home, dropped his reins before the bark-roofed house. It was empty, with cobwebs laced across the entrance. Whence these wayfarers came and whither they went, no one who talked knew, though to this day the arroyo shambles off to the river as Robber's Roost.

During '76, '77, and '78, the great herds of Goodnight, Creswell, and Pollard were moved from Colorado to the virgin pastures of the Texas Panhandle. Pollard located his headquarters on Elk Creek, a tributary of the South Canadian, about twenty miles west of the Territory line. On account of the Pollard brand, the outfit was known as the P O's. Soon afterwards the foreman of the Pollard Ranch moved his family down from Kansas to ranch headquarters. One day, the foreman's wife tells, a stranger rode into camp. After caring for his horse, he seated himself at the ever-ready table and said: "My name is Dietrich. I am from the East. I am hunting my brother. His name is Charles Dietrich."

The woman assured him that no such person was on the range. She was quite certain she knew every man from the Red to the North Canadian, and from the Territory line to Adobe Walls. "But," she said kindly, "we'll ask the men. They'll be in towards night."

On the arrival of the foreman, the stranger repeated his story, and added, "I've been told he rode on the P O range."

The boss listened and thought, but could say no more than, "No man by that name ever rode for the P O's."

The stranger described his brother, but made no headway until he added, " And he used to run wild horses."

"Wild horses!" mused the ranchman. "That is different. I think I know your man. He has worked on the P O range when we were short handed, but I never heard his name, Dietrich, before. He has a camp in the Territory. I'll send one of the boys with you tomorrow. I think we can find your man."

With the story of their over fifty-mile ride and wearying search, we are not particularly concerned, but by following a horse track that any man of the range could have told was made by a horse under the saddle, they found themselves late that evening at the door of a dugout in the red breaks of the Washita.

A red-faced, red-mustached, heavy-shouldered man, with the red of his habitation clinging to his hat and shirt, came blinking out of his doorway, wiping his doughy hand the while upon the legs of his California trousers.

Such was the long lost brother, no longer Charles Dietrich, but aptly Sour Dough Charley. And the glistening stream flowing past his door, from whose gypsy waters he mixed his famous bread, is to this day Sour Dough Creek.

About '78 the Texas Land and Cattle Company, a wealthy Scotch syndicate, established a camp on Home Ranch Creek, quite near the boundary between Texas and the Indian Territory. This company had immense tracts of grazing land leased in Texas, but the wild rye that grew along the widening valley of the Washita as it ambled along the turtle back possessed an irresistible lure for the cowman.

"By Jo," said B. Hopkins, foreman of the outfit, in relating the incident, "our saddle horses was pore in the fall, an' we jus' had to shove 'em down on that wild rye. Besides, Mr. Injun didn't need it, an' we give 'em more than enough beef to pay 'em. One fall, after the last beef herd had gone to market, and the mounts were all in, I sent some of the boys down the Washita to winter. Why, you haven't any idee how them ponies'd get rollin' hog fat on that wild rye. It's all killed out now. In a little while I started down. Never knowed what them blamed Injuns'd do. Packed a coupla ponies, and took old Dave Candill along.

"On the way down we kep' close to the Canadian all mornin'. As soon as we got to the Antelope Hills, old Dave begun watchin' for Injun sign. In the middle of the afternoon, we came to the head of a little crick. Dave was ridin' quite a ways ahead. He waved and I loped up. His eyes bugged out. You could a knocked 'em off with a little stick."

" 'Indians!' He could hardly talk.

" 'Naw,' I says. 'Whur?'

" 'Right here. Can't ya see? They been makin' bows an' arrers.'

"They'd been there all right cuttin' bows an' arrers from th' slender limbs of a clump of bois d'arc [osage orange] trees. I got down an' examined the whittlin's. I could tell they were dry and had been cut a month, but always after that when we talked about that crick, we called it the Bois d'Arc.

"We turned south there to get up on the divide. Old Dave was so scared he made me afraid. Jus' before night we struck a wide swale. I could tell it dreened towards th' Washita.

In a little bit we come to tall green grass an' water. I says, 'Here's a good place. Le's camp.' A coupla oak trees, the first I'd seen in that part, stood off a piece from the crick. I told Dave to unload the packs an' beds under them trees, an' I went ahead hobblin' the horses. I'll never forget how old Dave come tearin' back, sort of hissin'."

" 'Injuns!'

" 'Whur?' It made me mad fur a man to be always seein' Injuns.

" 'There! In that tree.'

"Sure enough, there was an Injun fastened to a coupla poles, with a tomahawk, fryin' pan, coffee pot, beads an' blankets, an' all tied up in the tree, but he was a dead Injun. An' that's how that crick an' all its branches got the name Dead Injun Crick."

During the days of Fort Elliott in the Texas Panhandle, communication with it was maintained by means of a mail service between Fort Elliott and Fort Reno. The mail route crossed the Canadian River at a point known as the Stage Stand. On the north side of the river, opposite from the Stage Stand, a cowman named Springer established himself in the day when Cattle was King.

Now Springer liked to play cards, and the stakes were for the highest amount any player would bet. Soldiers passing to and fro used to stop and give Springer an occasional bout. The story goes that two soldiers riding 'from Fort Elliott took shelter with Springer one night. Several days after, a cowman happening by and noticing Springer's gaunt saddle horse in the coral, stopped to investigate. Old Springer's body, with legs and arms stiffened in death, sat by his card-strewn table, while a bullet hole through his chest told the story of a gambler's quarrel. It was difficult for the kindly cowman, with help from the Stage Stand, to give the dead gambler decent burial.

The house soon fell to decay; the posts of his corral, standing in sub-irrigated land, grew to mighty trees; and honest men say that when a soldier or cowboy rides through that wood at night, old Springer leaps up behind the rider and, with stiffened knees thrust forward, rides out to the open. Thus the gambler-cowman's name and ghost still haunt that ranch. A creek so small it could scarcely be called a toe of the great turtle, just an artery that trickles toward the south and helps to form one of the appendages of the old Cheyenne and Arapahoe amphibian, goes by the creeping name of Starvation. Settlers seldom allude to it as Starvation Creek, but almost invariably employ the phrase, "Oveh on Starvation."

And why Starvation? Many are the answers.

A group of travellers, according to one story, cut off from food and water by the Indians, perished there. School children of the country tell how, "years ago," the bones of women and children were found along the dry arroyo.

Again, as another account runs, a detachment of soldiers camping on the "draw" had their horses and provisions stolen by the Indians. After hunger had drawn in their belts, two of the soldiers in desperation walked to Fort Elliott in the Texas Panhandle, fifty miles away. Old cowmen say that this tale could not be true as settlers were near at hand when Fort Elliott was established. One chronicler has it that horse thieves stole all the horses and chuck that a cow camp on the creek possessed and that the cowboys had to walk to Fort Elliott in order to keep from starving.

One old timer says that a band of horses perished here one desperately cold winter when the ground was so covered with ice and snow that stock all over the country starved and froze to death.

But ask of any farmer on a nearby creek, "Why do they call that Starvation?" and he readily answers, "Huh, if a feller tries to live oveh there he soon starves out."

Coming down the south bank of the Canadian River from the one hundredth meridian, one passes by Antelope Hills—piled up as if to go out of the way of the encroaching stream,—crosses in their turn three small creeks, and then comes upon what in early days was a beautiful flat, level, and velvety green with running mesquite. The soil is a black sandy loam as rich as the loess beds of China.

At the opening of the Cheyenne and Arapahoe Territory for settlement, an old lady named Nealy, with her numerous married sons and daughters, located claims upon this flat. When these settlers visited their neighbors, when they went to the distant market, when they made application for a school district, they proudly referred to their settlement as Nealy Flats. And Nealy Flats it should have been and would have been had the ever present wit and the ever healthy appetite of a certain cowboy not changed it.

Over the divide and a few miles south of what was Nealy Flats, heads Dead Indian Creek. While "Ma" Nealy and her tribe were taking up their claims, every quarter section along the clear waters of the creek named after the Indian in the tree was appropriated by some rider of the range. With these cowboys there was no mother, wife, sister, or daughter. Yet the cowboys were fond of feminine society, and the Nealys had no more than got settled before the horseback men had ridden them out as thoroughly as if they had been a strange herd of cattle.

The Nealy granddaughter, Jule, too tall, too long of limb, drooping, her long hands dangling behind; Adar, too wide, too dark, but gaily chattering; Idar, red of hair, white of throat, broad mouthed and heavy lipped; pale haired Deller, the youngest married daughter, tall, lean, and sunken at the belt— each in responding to the friendliness of the cowboys from Dead Indian Creek helped to change the proud name of their settlement. Among these "women folks" was the possibility of a clean shirt, and the cowboy must make one visit to take the shirt and another to claim it. Dellar and her loquacious Bob hoed nearest the cowboys. Dellar possessed a few hens; Bob, a little bunch of wide-horned cows that yielded a "right smart" of blue milk. A Sunday visit to Bob and Dellar promised custard pie.

Matt, a Dead Indian cowpuncher, laughed at the cold and laughed at the heat, laughed at the drouth and laughed at the flood. His eyes twinkled as he extolled the virtues of each of the neighboring girls; he chuckled softly as he talked of their awkward brothers, nicknaming one "Broad Axe" and another "Red Tom."

"Now you know, Windy, I cut your cows back the other day; so it's my turn to go after our shirts." Always it was Matt's turn.

But one Sunday he was feeling particularly jubilant over his turn. "Brig," he addressed his sod shanty companion, "it's Sunday. Sho' is. Pie day, Brig. Le's both go. Jes' think of that custard pie over on the flat. Why, Brig, there's so much pie there—why—why—it's Pie Flat."

Long since, Matt made his last ride, Bob his last corn furrow, and Dellar and Adar their last pie; Idar's pale face is deeply lined with the tears and smiles of motherhood; Brig with unspurred heel smokes his pipe on Dead Injun; Jule, Red Tom, and Broad Axe have drifted far from the flats of their youth. But a travelling stranger inquiring for a friend of his living in that part of the country will say, "He lives on Pie Flat."

NICKNAMES IN TEXAS OIL FIELDS

By Hartman Dignowity

Somewhere in Wyoming a "wild cat" driller had struck oil. The news of this discovery spread like wild fire. Overnight the country began to change. There was a bustle of busy men building derricks, laying pipe lines, and erecting storage tanks. The quiet of the countryside was changed into activity and feverish turmoil. Farmers who had lived in blissful isolation were forced into contact with the oil men.

In a field near one of the farm houses a woman and her 16-year-old daughter were working when a gang of drillers came in sight. "Look, Mama," the girl cried, "what kind of men are they?" The only men she knew were farmers and herders. "Hush, child!" warned the mother. "You had better go to the house. These are oil men and you are too young to know anything about them."

In that attitude the mother represents a large number of American citizens. Almost daily their imagination is inflamed by newspaper reports of the lawlessness and terrible people of the oil towns. Just at present (the spring of 1927) Texas papers are full of emergency measures for bringing law and order to Borger and other Texas oil towns. It seems as if nothing short of the Ranger force or the State militia can handle these men—these terrible oil men.

It has been my good fortune to have spent recently some weeks in close association with the oil men of Borger in the Texas Panhandle and then with others around McCamey in the Big Lake district. I did not find them at all as popular imagination pictures them. I found men too energetic and hard working to have time for the crimes attributed to them. To me the most interesting of the oil men are the pipe liners, laying pipe lines over mountains, through deserts, under rivers. Particularly did the nicknames of the pipe liners and other classes of oil men interest me.

Hard work and common inconveniences and dangers make friends of men. Similar interests and a common goal remove much formality among the men in the oil fields. They do not ask who you are but whether you can do the work. They care very little for your name, for the name may not fit you and even if they knew it the "men on the job" would very likely change it for you. Your name may be White, and yet your luck will be to be known throughout the fields as "Blacky." Nicknames are often spontaneous evaluations of co-workers. They may refer to the man's physique, to the way he does his work, to how he talks, or to his general behaviour. Often rivalry between men doing similar work, but using different machines, causes them to give each other descriptive names. For instance, the Standard, or cable tool, driller calls the man operating a rotary drill a "swivel neck," and the "swivel neck" retorts by calling the Standard man a "rope choker."

"Big Hole Ben" got his name from the fact that he will not work on casings less than ten inches in diameter. He is a "big hole" man and the larger the pipe the better he likes it. As soon as the well has progressed far enough to necessitate the setting of smaller casing, Ben leaves, for anybody can set small pipe, but the big casing takes a superior man.

Men who work long enough to make only one pay day are known as "pay day boys." "Pay Day Slim," "Pay Day Dan," "Pay Day Blacky," and such are common among the oil men.

"Tattoo Pete" was tattooed all over and must have been a sailor or a side show follower. Now he is working on a derrick floor.

"Big Boy," "Heavy," and similar terms indicating size and strength are often misleading in description, for the bearer of such names may be exceedingly light or small of stature. Often such names as "Little Bill," "Puny," and "Tiny" are given to men over six feet two inches in height. "Titanic Slim," though, was a large brawny man and very likely would not stand for any irony when the bunch gave him his name.

The woods are full of "Reds." It would alarm Judge Thayer to learn of "Fort Worth Red," "Denver Red," "Dallas Red," "Colorado Red," "Buttermilk Red," "Midnight Red," and "Three Day Red." "Society Red" got his name on account of his dislike for the fair sex. He would never attend any group activities at which ladies were present. "Poker Red" seems to be a fair indication of the man's ability or disability to play a game that is very much esteemed in the oil field.

Prohibition is one restriction from which the oil worker does not suffer very much, and we find such men as "Half Pint Joe," "Half Pint Mack," and "Half Pint Blacky." Some are called "Big Half Pints" or "Little Half Pints," according to the quantity of "hooch" they consume.

Many of the men are named for their native States; as, "Texas Tex," "Kentucky Colonel," "Alabama Joe," "Arkansas Red," and "Dakota Dan." One man's name is "Easy" because he talks with a peculiar slowness and a marked Georgian drawl.

"Spark Plug" is an active live wire who can run up and down a derrick with speed and endurance.

"Big Neck Jones" has the reputation of being able to bend a piece of pipe around his neck.

Men not endowed with physical strength are christened "Nubbin," "Squirrel," "Cricket," "Rabbit," and similar names, but one must remember that "Tiny" or "Puny" may be giants.

"Horse Power," a fellow with little of horse or power about him, got his name from his initials on the pay roll, where he appears as H. P. Brown.

"Mope Pole Slim" is a pipe liner who holds the mope pole, a long wooden pole which guides and keeps the pipe in line until the threads of one joint are well fitted into those of another.

"Bentover Slim" is a man who walks stooped and bent over; the chances are that he will carry this name to his grave.

Men who are either slow or lazy are given such names as "Molasses," "Mercury," "Hot Shot," "Sleepy," "Lighting," and "Speedy."

"Step and a Half" once suffered the misfortune of having his legs broken. In walking he takes one long step and then drags the other foot in such a manner that one foot always seems to move twice the distance of the other.

"Circus" got his name from the fact that he was once with a traveling show.

A driller was christened "Plush Bottom," because his "lazy bench"[1] had a pillow on which he would sit.

Some of the men are "overtime hogs." They try to work

---

[1]For explanation of the word see "Oil Field Diction," by A. R. McTee, **Publications** of the Texas Folk-Lore Society, No. IV, 1925, p. 65.—Editor.

all the time they can or are always willing and ready to go out on a job. One can find "Overtime Slims" and "Overtime Shortys" in nearly every oil field.

"Big Buckle" wore a belt with an oversized buckle on it when he first came on the job. He will never lose this name even though he should wear suspenders the rest of his life.

If you believe in intelligence tests or higher psychology you would come to the conclusion that the men in the oil field are better judges of human frailties and nature than many professors of psychology. Men who are mentally sluggish or exhibit signs of similar shortcomings are quickly dubbed with such names as "Arkansas" or "Arky"; men from that state seem to be considered defective or lacking in mental powers. Other "slow pokes" are called "Goofy," "Brightness," "Dizzy," "Sleeping Jesus," and "Unconscious."

Let me conclude by saying a few more words in defense of the oil men. It is a shame that oil boom towns are infested with parasites and pimps who suck the blood of the toilers. It was refreshing to meet the energetic and independent men —the real oil men—who, rich today and poor tomorrow, will share their last dollar with their "buddy." The oil man's game is one of uncertainty; he lives in the hope that either he or the company for which he is working will "strike it lucky." But, however luck may fall, the oil man works— and men who work are to be trusted.

THE DEVIL'S GROTTO

By Mody C. Boatright

For nearly two hundred miles as the crow flies—but not as the river runs—the Rio Grande flows southeast from Juarez and El Paso through a prison-like valley. Then between Ojinaga on the Mexican side and Presidio on the Texas side, the valley slightly widens to receive the Cibolo and Alamita creeks, which cut in from the north. For a hundred miles then the valley is pinched into the Grand Canyon of the Rio Grande. Twenty miles out from Presidio the Chinati Mountains in Texas rise to an apex of 7,000 feet above sea level; across in Mexico great palisades, pierced only by the Rio Conchos, tower thousands of feet and shut out the rain-bearing winds of the Pacific. The mountain slopes furnish the habitat of the creosote, the mesquite, the mimosa, and the various forms of cacti. The valley floor that supports the two little towns is the habitat of the *mestizo,* who fences his plat with stems of the barbed *ocotillo* and farms his cotton and corn very much as did his fathers in the days of the presidio system and the Chihuahua Trail.

In April the Great Spirit touches the heart of the desert, and the desert releases the beauty that for nine months has been dormant in the womb of the cactus. In an incredibly short time the yucca sends up its slender stalk; lateral buds appear, and then rich, waxy flowers, rivaled by those of the *sotol* and the *lechuguilla.* The dead, thorny stems of the *ocotillo* take on a leafy liveness and tip themselves with crimson, like spears stained with blood. The cacti light their flames of white, of lavender, of rose, and of saffron.

The Great Spirit speaks also to the heart of man, and the simple-minded *mestizo* is aware of some great power outside of him and beyond him—something at once kind and sinister, something that makes his cotton and his corn to grow, or withholds the divine rain—something to be feared, worshiped, appeased, propitiated.

Thus I found the valley on May 3, 1925. I cannot vouch for its appearance in the late sixteenth century when explorers from Spain traversed the region, setting up at intervals on the mountain peaks huge wooden crosses, symbols of their conquests for their king and their God.[1] The *mestizos* in the valley will tell you that there have been topographical changes within comparatively recent times, and that these changes resulted from a titanic struggle in which a great priest confounded the devil and shut him up in a cave.

About three miles from Presidio a rugged mountain arises abruptly from the Mexican side of the river to a height of some thousand or more feet. This is the Mountain of the Holy Cross. Near the summit, at the west end, is a notch visible for miles. In this notch is a sort of shrine surmounted by a cross. Nearby is the Devil's Grotto, the mention of which is likely to cause shuddering among the older inhabitants of the region, as I found when I broached the subject in a Presidio barber shop.

"Does the devil live there?" I asked one.

"*Quien sabe?*"

"Is he thought to live there?"

"It is strange," he said; "strange things have been seen. Once some children were playing on the hillside, and they saw a burro coming down from the cave, and the burro didn't have any tail. The children laughed because they thought it funny to see a burro without any tail, and they called their parents to look, but the burro was gone. . . . *Quien sabe?*"

Other natives told of strange happenings near the cave, seen, not indeed by themselves, but by their grandparents and their great grandparents. One grandmother, while gathering *mescal* on the hillside, saw a rabbit dancing on his hind feet, and then she saw that he didn't have any fore feet. She thought she could catch him, but when she reached for him, he was gone. She stuck a *lechuguilla* blade in her hand and suffered from an infection.

It was from Pedro that I secured the most complete version of the story. Pedro saw me and my companions wandering through the village, and with true hospitality he asked us to his house, where he entertained us with his antique harp of

---

[1]Rodriguez passed through what is now Presidio in the summer of 1581; Espejo arrived there on December 9, 1852. See Bolton, **Spanish Exploration in the Southwest,** pp. 137ff. and 163ff.

many strings. When we entered his *casita* of adobe we noticed two candles burning on an improvised altar in one end of the room. In the center of the altar, between the candles, was a chromo of the Son of Man on the cross. Above the Son was the Mother. Various saints had less conspicuous places. Paper and wax flowers in beer bottles were there in profusion, and by way of further decoration, two burnt-out electric light globes were suspended by strings from the low, beamed ceiling. This was Holy Cross day, and those who did not go over the river and take part in the processional would gather with their neighbors in their homes to render thanksgiving and prayer to the God and the good saint who, *muchos años pasados*, had wrought the deliverence of the valley.

This is substantially Pedro's version of the story:

Muchos años pasados—no living man knew how many— the valley had been prosperous and fertile. The rains came in the fall and in the spring; the Rio Grande flowed full and swift, and crude ditches were sufficient to lead its waters into the fields, where corn grew tall and cotton was never harmed by the pink boll-worm. Cattle were fat on the hillside, and goats yielded milk and mohair. All the inhabitants of the valley were happy.

Then came all manner of distress. Crops withered; the boll-worm came; cattle died of disease, and babies were born blind. At sunset when the people looked to the sky to implore a heavenly blessing, they would see a great rope stretched from Chinati Peak in Texas to the mountain in Mexico afterwards called Holy Cross. And upon this rope with many a weird grimace danced Satan, gloating over the mischief he had wrought and mocking those who tried to pray.

Now a saintly Spanish priest—Francisco, according to Pedro, but called Gomez by some—who was sojourning in the mountains, chanced one day to visit Presidio del Norte. Grieved to see the inhabitants thus prostrated by the evil one, the priest undertook their conversion. The cross, he said, was all-powerful, and to demonstrate the truth of his assertion, he asked that such an emblem be furnished him. When the devil made his customary appearance, this soldier of religion, armed with a crude wooden cross, advanced upon him. The devil's fiery breath might turn green hillsides into semi-deserts; it might cause the thorny cactus to spring up where the *alamo* had flourished; but behind the emblem of Christ, the priest was safe, and, thus protected, he advanced upon the enemy of man. The cable broke. The malignant one dropped into the valley. The priest pursued with renewed vigor. The devil resorted to his great physical strength, seizing great crags and hurling masses of rock and earth at the dauntless Francisco. But all in vain. The missiles were powerless. The devil was forced to retreat. He crossed the Rio Grande into what is now Mexico, fled up the mountainside, and finally took refuge in a cave, across the mouth of which Francisco placed the cross, effectively imprisoning his adversary. He then returned to the village and told the people of their redemption. He instructed them to make a shrine at the cave and to mount the cross near by. But once a year, he said, on the third of May, the anniversary of this victory, the cross might, with proper ceremony, be taken to the village that the people might be blessed with health, and to the farms that they might yield in abundance.

"Before the cross is removed," explained Pedro, "brush that has been blessed by the *padre* is placed around the cave and along the path to the river." This is lighted and kept burning while the cross is away. Pedro was not sure as to the exact purpose of the fire. He thought perhaps it was to keep the devil in confinement in the absence of the cross.

We left the home of Pedro, for we felt that to remain longer would be an intrusion. At dusk we looked toward the Mount of the Holy Cross. A tiny spark appeared at the notch; then sparks at intervals from the summit to the very river. Then flames shot up, and one imagined a great fiery serpent crawling out of the river and over the mountains. Then *mujeres* and *jovenes* began coming with bird-like step and entering the houses. From the street, we could catch a melody chanted in high nasal tones. A few words in the refrain came to us through the twilight; there were references to *"el diablo"* and *"la Santa Cruz."*

The cross itself is seldom brought across the river into Presidio these days; and since we did not visit Ojinaga, we did not see it. One respects the child-like faith of these simple people and does not intrude upon their worship.

The origin of the legend of the Devil's Grotto is fairly obvious. The early missionaries attempted to phrase the message of the church in terms which the Indians could comprehend. They did this to such an extent that one student of Mexican culture declares that in Mexico "the great mass of professing Catholics have retained in large part their primitive worship. . . . Mexico's patron saint, the Virgin of Guadalupe, owing its origin to an humble Indian who with difficulty persuaded the ecclesiastical authorities to accept the accounts of his 'vision,' is naught else but a slightly transformed Aztec deity, Tonantzin, patron of the local tribe of Totonaqui Indians, their goddess of earth and corn. Throughout, many native deities were similarly transmuted into Catholic saints."[2]

When we consider this further fact that the combat is supposed to have taken place on May 3, Holy Cross Day, it is not difficult to imagine some early missionary attempting to give content and significance to an occasion that without some such local legend would have meant little more than an empty ceremony.

Presidio now has an excellent highway. It hopes to have a railroad before a great while. It also has a high school in which United States history and the *Literary Digest* are studied. One wonders about the future of the custom. Already some of the youngsters doubt the truth of the legend; and one notices that the ceremonies are carried on largely by the old men and the women. To others the occasion is only a holiday. Will the Mexicans of the border forget the lore of their fathers, or will they learn a lesson from the Indians of the United States and perform their rites for the entertainment of the tourist and for the emolument of themselves?

---

[2]Gruening, Ernest, "The Mexican Renaissance," **The Century Magazine,** Vol. 107, pp. 522-523.

MYTHS OF THE TEJAS INDIANS

By Mattie Austin Hatcher

As a race they have withered from the land. Their arrows are broken and their springs are dried up; their cabins are in the dust. Their council fires have long since gone out on the shore, and their war cry is fast dying out in the untrodden west. Slowly and sadly they climb the mountains and read their doom in the setting sun. They are shrinking before the mighty tide which is pressing them away; they must soon hear the roar of the last wave that will settle over them forever. Ages hence, the inquisitive white man, as he stands by some growing city, will ponder on the structure of their disturbed remains and wonder to what manner of person they belonged. They will live only in the songs and chronicles of their exterminators. Let these be true to their rude virtues as men and pay tribute to their unhappy fate as a people.

Thus did Sam Houston plead for the preservation of the history, the myths, and the legends of the redmen of the Southwest, and especially of the Indians of Texas, whom he so earnestly defended. For did not he, like many a frontiersman, share in their beliefs, particularly in omens? Houston often related to his intimate friends three stories that show how the superstitions of the redmen were treasured in his heart. Once, on the eventful day of his marriage to the bride from whom he was soon to part forever, a raven, his "bird of destiny," fluttered before him in the dust of the road and uttered its direful note of warning. Again, while he paced the deck of the boat that was bearing him into exile, he was so tortured with thoughts of the bitter disappointment he had brought to General Jackson and the blight he had brought upon the life of this innocent bride, that he was on the point of ending his life, when an eagle swooped down near his head, soared aloft with loudest screams and was soon lost in rays of the setting sun—a sure sign to him that a glorious destiny awaited him in the West. Finally, he was induced to turn his face toward Texas and fame because a raven repeatedly rose into the air and then flew straight toward that fair land, where, on the eve of San Jacinto, "his ever watchful guardian angel, the American eagle," swooped down over his head and steeled his heart to victory.

Houston's prophecy of the disappearance of the Indians has proved all too true. But there is some consolation in the fact that within less than a century his pathetic plea has had its effect. Already has many "an inquisitive white man pondered over the structure of their disturbed remains" while writers are now eagerly seeking for the elusive myths of the vanquished and vanishing American aborigines.

Of the redmen of the Southwest none are more interesting than the Tejas Indians, who gave their name to a great empire along the northern banks of the Rio Grande. Tradition says that more than two hundred years before Columbus discovered America, a feud arose among the Aztecs and that, as a result, the *Nasonites* were driven forth and forbidden ever to return to the halls of the Montezumas. The exiles wandered far to the northward and finally reached the beautiful summits of the hills near San Marcos. They gazed with rapture upon the clear streams, the emerald valleys, the herds of buffalo and deer, and the droves of wild turkeys. Believing that they had reached the "Beautiful Hunting Ground," they cried out in delight, "Texas!" or, as the Anglo-American says, "Paradise." The untamed spirit of these children of the wilds, who finally located among the sighing pines of East Texas, lives still in a "War Song" translated by Schoolcraft in his *Indian Antiquities*:

> The eagles scream on high,
>   They whet their forked beaks;
> Raise, raise the battle-cry,
>   'Tis fame our leader seeks.
> The battle-birds sweep from the sky,
>   They thirst for the warrior's heart.
> They look from their circle on high,
>   And scorn every flesh but the brave.

To the missionaries who first led the way into the then unknown region across the Rio Grande and who lived for some time among the friendly tribes of East Texas we are indebted for the fullest records of the myths of the Tejas Indians. In the stories recorded by Fray Jesús María de Casañas in his *Informe*,[1] 1691, and by Fray Isidro Felix Espinosa in his *Chrónica Apostólica y Seráfica de Todos los Colegios de Propaganda Fide*,

---

[1] Ms. in University of Texas Archives.

about 1720, we read, in the present writer's translation, the following mythological accounts.

The Tejas Indians are not ignorant of God. Indeed, all of them know that there is only one God, whom in their language they call *Ayô-Caddi-Aymay*. In all their affairs they try by every possible means to keep him in a good humor. They never in any manner venture to speak of him in jest, because they believe that whenever he punishes them for anything it is a just punishment and that whatever he does is for the best.

Another thing which all of them believe implicitly is that an old man made heaven and that a woman who first sprang from an acorn gave them its outlines; they say that the old man and the acorn-woman formed heaven by placing timber in a circle. They further declare that this woman is in heaven and that she daily gives birth to the sun and moon, to the rain, the frost, the snow, the corn, the thunder, and the lighting.

They say that in the beginning of the world there was one woman only who had two daughters. One was a virgin while the other was not. One day the two sisters were alone, separated from their mother, when they were attacked in the following manner.

Suddenly there appeared a huge, misshapen creature of ferocious aspect, with horns so long that the ends could not be seen. The Indians call him *caddaja,* devil or demon. He attacked the pregnant sister, tore her with his claws, chewed her up, and swallowed her. The virgin escaped and climbed to the top of a very high tree. When the devil had finished eating her sister, he raised his eyes in search of the virgin in order that he might do the same thing with her. He tried to climb the tree; then, not being able to do so, he tried to cut the tree down with his horns and his claws. Seeing the danger in which she was placed, the maiden dropped down into a deep hole of water that was at the foot of the tree, and, diving down into it, came up at a distant point and escaped to her mother. The ugly giant began to suck up the water and drain it away so as to make a prisoner of the maiden. But she had fooled him and escaped. She told her mother everything that had happened, and together they went to the spot where the sister had been murdered. They searched among the bits that the demon had scattered while eating her and they found a drop of blood in an acorn shell. They covered this with another half shell. The mother put it in her bosom and carried it home. She put it in a jar, covered the mouth well, and put it in a corner. At night she heard a noise as if the jar were being scratched. Upon going to examine it, she found that the drop of blood had turned into a boy—the size of one's finger. She covered the jar again and the next night, hearing the same noise, found that the boy had grown to the stature of a man. She was very much pleased and at once made him a bow and arrow. He asked for his mother. They told him how the devil had eaten her, and he set out in search of the monster. When he found the devil he shot him so hard with the point of his arrow that the devil has never been seen since. The acorn-man returned to his grandmother and his aunt. They told him it was not good to stay on earth. He ascended with them to *Cachao-ayó*, as they call the heavens. And he has been there ever since, governing the world.

They say that when the soul leaves the body it travels toward the west and from thence rises into the air and goes close to the presence of the great captain whom they call *Ayó-Caddí*. Thence it goes to wait in a house located toward the south, called the House of Death. They believe that their enemies go to the dwelling place of *Texino*, the devil, and that he punishes them severely. They declare that if they do not pray when a friend dies the devil will take them to his house also. They also say that when a person dies his soul finally goes to still another house where a man guards souls until all the Indians are reunited. That man has some very large keys, "bigger than the oxen we have here." When all the souls are gathered together they will enter another world to live anew.

They believe that the Spaniards have *one* God, who gives them knives and clothing, but that the Indians have a different God, who gives them nothing but beans and such wild fruit as they can find. They say that through the place where the sun sets there runs a road that they must ascend into heaven. They say that their ancestors made the sky. To do so they built a high hill beyond the Cadodachos country. Standing on top of this hill, they were able to push up one half of the earth, thus forming the arch of the heavens above the other half upon which the hill rested. On this hill they plant corn and all kinds of plants as a votive offering.

They worship fire. For this worship, they have a house set apart wherein they always keep fire. They have appointed an old man whose duty it is to always keep it burning. They say that if it ever goes out everybody will die. The house is a large one, round and thatched, and within it is an altar made of reed mats. On the bed are three finer mats, two of them very small. On the benches to the sides of the doors are other reed mats in rolls. In front of the bed is a little square bench made of one piece of wood. It has four feet and is slightly raised from the ground. Upon this bench there is usually tobacco and a pipe with feathers, as well as earthenware vessels that are evidently incense burners. In these they burn buffalo fat and tobacco. A fire or a bonfire is always made of four very large logs, which point outward in the four cardinal directions. Here the old men gather for their councils and war dances or when they need rain for their crops.

They are very much afraid of angering the fire and they offer up to it the first tobacco and the first fruits of their corn, a portion of the game they kill, and a part of their other crops. They say that the fire created all these things for them. However, some of these people claim that men first came up from the sea and then spread over all the earth. They call the fire and water creatures *nicaddi*.

They say that in the beginning there were in the land many demons who murdered them and caused them great harm. They report that these demons were big and horrible. When their ancestors saw the suffering these demons inflicted, they transformed themselves into bears, dogs, otters, coyotes, and other animals. But at the same time they remained rational men and women.

About a gunshot's distance from the temple are two small houses. They call them the houses of the two *coninici*. These are the two children or small boys whom their "Great Captain" sent from *Cachao-ayó*, or the sky, to discuss their problems with them. The Indians explain that these two children were in these houses until about two years ago, when the Yojuanes, their enemies, burned these dwellings. This was when the friendly Indians saw the children ascend in smoke, and they have never come down again, although new houses have been built for them. In these houses are two little chests about three spans long with curious covers of painted reeds. They are upon an altar that rests upon four little forked poles. Within these little chests are four or five small platters or vessels of black wood, like circular shields. They are all curiously carved and have four feet. Some of them represent ducks and have heads and tails. Others have the heads and tails of alligators or lizards. Besides this, there are many feathers of various shapes and colors, handfuls of wild bird feathers, a white breast knot, some rolls of ornamental feathers, crowns made of skins and feathers, a bonnet of the same material, many carved crane bones—which serve them as flutes or fifes,—other flutes of carved reeds, and many other instruments used in their *mitotes* and other dances.

The grand *Xinesi* of the province has informed his vassals that whenever he wants to he talks to the two children, who came from the other side of heaven and whom he keeps in their houses. He says that these two children eat and drink and that whenever he wants to communicate with God, he does so through these two children. On certain occasions when he feels that his people do not bring enough corn and such other foods as they have, he lets it be known that the two children are angry and are unwilling to talk about matters of general welfare. On these occasions the two children make known to him that the people will not have good crops, that their enemies are sure to kill them, and that God is not going to bless them because they have not given their *Xinesi* a portion of their supplies. Their ruler then calls all of the people to his house and gives orders for all the old men and the *caddices* to come into the house where he keeps the two children. They all sit around the fire, which the *Xinesi* keeps burning day and night. The first thing he does is to take some live coals with a pair of tongs. He then mixes fat from the heart of a buffalo with tobacco and, having placed it upon a tall *tapestle* about two *varas* square, offers the incense to the two children, whom he has placed in their chests. At the sides of the *tapestle* are two small boxes of reeds into which he always puts a portion of the things the people bring him during the year. He announces to the assembled men that the boxes are now empty. As soon as he is through offering the incense, he puts out the fire and closes the door so that nothing can be seen distinctly. Thus all within is darkness. Those outside sing and dance, while those within are perfectly silent, listening to the voices—one that of a child, the other that of the *Xinesi*. He speaks to the children, asking them to tell God that the Tejas are now going to reform and to beg of him to give them in the future great quantities of corn, good health, fleetness in chasing the deer and buffalo, and great strength in fighting their enemies. He then takes in his hand a small calabash that is filled with small stones. He puts it down on the ground and when no sound issues therefrom, he explains that God is angry and does not wish to speak to them. They are all frightened when they are told that the calabash is on the floor making no sound. They cry out in a loud voice and promise the Great Captain, *Ayó-Caddi-Aymay,* to bring something of every kind of goods they have to present to the *Xinesi* and the two *coninici*. Satisfied with their promises, the *Xinesi* picks up the calabash and it instantly begins to rattle. One of the children now speaks, declaring that God is now speaking and wishes the people informed that if these promises are kept, he will give them everything they ask for through the agency of their *Xinesi*. The *Xinesi* then charges them to go out and hunt for game and promises that the two children will always keep God satisfied. The *Xinesi* is then left alone in the house, stirring the fire and grinding meal for the two children in a mortar that he keeps in the house.

In the month or "moon" of February, which they call *Sacabbi,* there is a mass meeting of all the people. Having previously hunted rabbits, wild cats, wild birds, and badgers, and having provided dry meats, which they have on hand the year round, and having secured ground meal and other edibles that are in season, they begin the celebration in the morning in the temple, where all the wise men and the medicine men are assembled. Two or three of them spend the morning in brewing tea from the laurel leaves. They then take the wing of an eagle, which they call *yugi,* and use it in their dances and songs. They salute the fire by throwing ground tobacco on it and by continually passing the pipe of tobacco from hand to hand. They then go through the motions to show that the eagle whose feathers they are using has risen on high to consult with the Captain who dwells there in regard to weather they are to have for the year. They feel sure that if they fan the fire in the winter with an eagle's wing, such a snow storm or heavy snow will come that everything will be killed. Often when they see us fanning the flames with a fan or a bird's wing, they try to take it out of our hands. They say we are either fools or crazy to do such a thing. They think we are not afraid because we are covered with clothing. They declare that our fire is different from theirs because it is made with a rock or iron, while theirs is made by rubbing two sticks together.

Before eating of their new corn crop, they summon a wise man from each house. He stands by one of the timbers in the house and says his prayers while the rest of the Indians cut a portion of the new crop. They roast a portion of it and grind part of it in mortars and make *atole* of it. When the wise men finish their prayers, those preparing the corn present some of it to each of the wise men, who throw part of it into the air and put the rest of it in their bosoms. It is very firmly fixed in the minds of the Indians that if they cut any part of the crop, large or small, ears or stalks, before these prayers are said, the guilty ones will surely be bitten by snakes.

Before they begin their planting they instruct all the women to provide food for a designated day. They all gather together, old women, girls, and young children. They make two or three mats of little strips of cane, which an old woman who acts as supervisor provides for them. These they turn over to a captain, who makes an offering of them to the fire in the great temple in order that they may have good crops that year. They end the ceremony by all eating together everything that has been provided. They then adjourn the meeting.

There is also another general meeting of the men and women held in the house of each captain, wherein a small fire is kept burning. Here they cut the wood to make their black-walnut hoes. They clean a spot of ground about a stone's throw in circumference and collect a lot of wood, which they stack up in big piles. They distribute dried deer meat, meal, and other foods that have been provided. One of their officials, a *tamma*, goes around and carefully collects the first fruits of the tobacco. These he delivers to his captain, whose duty it is to ward off the tempests by conjuring and to pray for rain and for blessings upon the crops.

They hold their most notable feast after the crops have been gathered. This is the festival that the greatest number of people attend. Six days prior to the appointed time, the men under each captain come together at his house, where there is a fire and where a spot has already been cleared off. The old men pray and distribute drinks of foamy laurel tea. When the day arrives, they all wear the very best things they have, fine deerskins ornamented with ruffles and white ornaments. Some wear very black deerskins decorated with the same ornaments. They all have necklaces and bracelets that they wear only on feast days. Quantities of food have been collected for the celebration.

It is night during the full moon in September. The first night the conjurers, medicine men, captains, and the necessary officials and servants spend within doors. The rest of the company lodge outside, by families. They build a bonfire for light as well as for warmth, as the cold is already beginning to be felt. After two old men pray, they stand for more than an hour and throw bits of meat and tobacco on the fire, which is in the middle of the room. They then sit down and all of the old men and captains are served with the rest of the meat. This they eat with their drink of wild herbs, which is served three or four times around from an earthenware vase. They then pass pipes of tobacco around to everybody. From time to time they draw and blow the smoke upwards, then toward the ground, and then toward the four winds. At midnight a crier begins to call all the people together. They come in by threes, one woman from each house, and each presents a pot or small vessel of fine meal and some rolls, which they call *bajan*, made of a thick paste of roasted corn and sunflower seed. The managers of the celebration deposit these in two big receptacles of their own. In this way all the families make their gifts. This ended, the gifts are divided among the old men, the captains, and the officials of the settlement. The celebration then ceases for a time. Some of the young men try to sleep while others sing to the accompaniment of music for the purpose of driving away sleep.

From midnight on one of the Indians is stationed as a watchman or sentinel. He watches to see when the Pleiades are in a certain position. They call these stars *Las Santas,* i.e., "The Women," because they believe that these stars are people. When "The Women" are in the right position, the watcher informs the chief conjurer, who, in company with another conjurer, goes to a circle made of green canes stuck up in the ground, where there is a big bonfire that several men continually feed. Two men seated on a raised platform serve as masters of ceremony. To their left the Indians are formed in the following manner: the old women in one file and the younger women, both married and unmarried, in a second row behind them. The little girls are in front of these two rows, while the young girls are at the end. To the right is an arbor with a bonfire under it. Three old men dressed in the very best they have go over to the fire, two of them following exactly in the footsteps of the leader, while the women and children begin singing. After a considerable time the three old men again approach the files, dancing as they come. When they reach the files, they stop and deliver a harangue in a hurried, high-pitched voice. As they pass in front of the files, each woman in turn presents them with a pot of meal and rolls made of various grains. At dawn all of them become more active, dancing to the music of a calabash, or gourd, filled with small stones. This is the accompaniment for their songs. They cease their singing at daybreak and five old men divide the offering that has been collected. After the song has been ended, they all await the rising of the sun. Certain young men and boys are sent out into the nearby woods as if calling or speaking to the sun for the purpose of hastening its coming. Just as it rises they run joyfully about as if giving thanks for their past crop and beseeching the sun to aid them in their future projects. All of a size and age are in one file. After the signal for starting is given, they all run as fast as they can to a tree about a gunshot's distance away and then return to the starting point. They do this two or three times until they give out.

All of the relatives of the men are intent upon seeing who gains the advantage, for the man who endures longest carries off all the laurels of the occasion. The wives and female relatives of the man who is left behind or who is worn out before finishing the race set up a terrible weeping, because when he goes to war, they say, he will on account of his lack of speed be left behind or killed as a captive. The ceremony lasts about an hour. They then take hollow logs, bury one end of them, and place green branches on the top of them. Next they select eight strong women, who, seated at the proper intervals, use each of the hollow logs as a drum, while the old men shake their gourds and about twenty men and women sing. This music is for the dance, in which all engage, old men and boys, women and girls. The dancers keep time but move only their feet. They continue until midday in this favorite frivolity, when, tired and sleepy, each goes home to rest after such strenuous exercise.

When the Indians gain a victory over their adversaries, they bring back the skulls of their enemies and keep them hanging in a tree until such time as they decide to bury them. They all gather together, men, women, and children, for this ceremony at the place the skulls have been kept. They build a number of bonfires; and, having provided their mournful instruments, they arrange their singers and bands of musicians, all painted black. They all seat themselves upon the ground and cover themselves from head to foot with buffalo robes. They all sing together with bowed heads. Then the women in one row and the men in another, sing. Then they dance, continuing nearly all night. Finally a decrepit old Indian, accompanied by a number of young men, approaches the tree where the skulls are hanging. Each has an arrow in his hand. They surround the tree, give a shout, turn in another direction, and repeat the gesture. From time to time they discharge a gun toward the skulls and all in unison raise a discordant shout. When the morning comes, they cover their faces with white dirt and carry away the skulls and bury them in a cemetery, which is near the fire temple. Here they spend the rest of the day in celebration.

At the beginning of May these Indians have a fête very much like that observed in certain villages of Europe, for the Zagales youth are accustomed on the first day of May to place an elm stripped of all leaves, save a bunch at the top, in the middle of the plaza. Here they hold a celebration with various games and contests, declaring that they are celebrating the May Day. In the same way the Tejas Indians celebrate by securing a very tall, straight pine. After cutting away all the leaves except those at the very top, they set it up on a level spot. They make two wide paths, cleaning off the surface of the ground so that they can run faster. These paths meet behind the tree and thus form a circle. Innumerable Indians gather together at the rising of the sun and begin to race along these paths, one after the other. The one who runs around the May tree the greatest number of times without pausing is the victor and receives the most applause. After they are tired out, they partake of the refreshments the Indian women have provided. This is their most celebrated feast day, for on it they test their ability to run swiftly when they are engaged in war. After this celebration, the Indians all go home rejoicing.

A NOTE ON FOUR NEGRO WORDS

By Robert Adger Law

In the course of an interesting article, "Reptiles of the South and Southwest in Folk-Lore," printed in the last number of the *Publications of the Texas Folk-Lore Society,* Mr. John K. Strecker writes:

> In the valleys of the Red River of Louisiana and the Sabine River of Louisiana and Texas, are to be found negroes who use many African words, the inheritance of their ancestors. A white man is a "buckra," which word is used on the Calabar coast of Africa to indicate a demon—a superior being. A ground-nut (peanut) is a "pinda," and "niam" (nēam) means "to eat." When a negro mother whips her child, she gives it an extra lick for "brawtus," and in a trade something is sometimes thrown in for "brawtus", the word evidently having the same meaning as the Creole "lagniappe" or the Mexican "pilón."

The most striking fact to my mind about this statement is that Mr. Strecker found all these words in Texas and Louisiana. I wonder if the same negroes speak of a terrapin as a "cooter." However that may be, all four words mentioned deserve a further brief note. Of the African origin of all except one, there seems to be no question.

"Buckra" is found in Webster and other dictionaries with about the same explanation as Mr. Strecker gives. But the *Century Dictionary* records also a derivative use, that of an adjective, meaning "white," as "buckra yam." Professor Reed Smith, writing recently of "Gullah" (*University of South Carolina Bulletin* No. 190, p. 134, November 1, 1926), notes both usages among the negroes of the Georgia and Carolina seacoast. My own impression, which may not be correct, is that the noun is commonly used with only one adjective, "po' buckra," and hence the term describes a particular class of whites. I find this interpretation apparently sustained by Joel Chandler Harris, who, in his Introduction to *Nights with Uncle Remus,* glosses "buckra" as "white man, overseer, boss."

"Pinder," as I have seen it spelled, was, during my youth in upper South Carolina, not regarded as a negro word, though African in origin. It was the common name among educated white people for peanuts, which the vulgar there called "goobers," and the low-country *élite,* living about Charleston, denominated "groun(d) nuts." Three well-reared Austin friends, all natives of upper South Carolina, bear out my memory on this point. Dr. L. W. Payne, Jr., writing for *Dialect Notes* in 1908, "A Brief Word-List from East Alabama," states that in that section of the South "groun(d) pea, peanut, goober, pinder" are "all four . . . used, but perhaps 'goober' is the favorite." "Goober" is also of African origin.

"Niam" I am personally not familiar with. Smith gives "nyam in the sense of eat," and quotes W. A. Craigie as sanctioning the African origin.

But the most interesting word cited by Mr. Strecker is the last one. I have frequently heard it from whites and negroes near Charleston, and, if recollection does not play me false, I once saw the word in the Charleston *News and Courier* spelled "broadus." The only dictionary mention of it I have ever seen is that of the *Century,* which in part follows:

> '*brotus* (brôtus), *n.* [*Cf.* E. dial. *brotts,* fragments, leavings. . .] Something added gratuitously; an additional number or quantity thrown in: same as *lagniappe*: used by negroes and others about Charleston, South Carolina."

Personally I am skeptical as to the etymology suggested and consider it much more likely that Mr. Strecker is correct in surmising that here we have another African word. Yet how can we explain its appearance in Texas and Louisiana, as well as in the conservative home of the Gullah dialect, when for many years it has been held to be a strict localism of Charleston and thereabouts? The ways of travel for dialect and folk-lore are past finding out.

BALLADS AND SONGS OF THE FRONTIER FOLK

By J. Frank Dobie

Considered objectively, the songs in the collection that follows are generally commonplace and devoid of literary merit. Yet because of their value to social history, their reflection of a people's experiences and attitudes towards life, they are worth preserving. Moreover, if considered in their proper setting, they do have a kind of literary merit. One time an old Scotch woman said of ballads that Sir Walter Scott was taking from her, "They were made for singing and no for reading." Much more than the Border Ballads were these frontier songs "made for singing and no for reading." Hearing them in camp or in a frontier home, one's imagination is stirred, one's elemental feelings are called to; in short, under proper conditions thousands of people have derived from just these songs the true *effect* of literature. Concerning one class of them, Charles A. Siringo, whose new book, *Riata and Spurs,* is most heartily recommended to all Texans, once said: "These old trail songs have caused the blood to stampede with joy through the veins of thousands of cowboys."

I am indebted to Mr. Carl A. Fehr, an Austin student in the University of Texas, for transcribing the music of the first group of songs.

I. Songs from Frontier Homes and Domestic Camps

The most interesting and fertile source for folk songs, as well as for other folk material, that I have ever found is the hospitable family of Mr. W. W. Burton in Austin, Texas —my friends. The Burtons are genuine old time *Texians,* thoroughly representative of frontier life. Mr. Burton was born in Brazos County, Texas, in 1844; Mrs. Burton has been in the state since 1866, having come from Illinois. The Burton men have ranched, rangered, freighted, farmed, prospected, hunted: in every motion of their beings they are men of the soil. The elder Burtons do not sing much now, but they know scores of old songs, and their daughter and their middle-aged sons are joyous singers.

SONG OF THE HAPPY HUNTERS

Three or four years back Wess Burton and I went on a deer hunt down in the Nueces River country. "The Happy Hunter" is one of the songs that he sang while, in the very opposite of a "dry camp," we were huddled under a wagon sheet protecting us from at least part of the cold rain. As he sang, we too were "happy hunters." He says that he learned the song from a man named Jerome J. Hill, of Dripping Springs, Texas.

1 Come, all who will, and listen.
    I'm going to sing a song,
  Of not so many verses;
    It won't detain you long.

2 'Tis of a band of hunters—
    You may all know them too;
  There's Pooney Plack and Fowler,
    Old Punch and Gov'nor Blue.

3 They live and hunt on Cow Creek,
    And on San José too.
  For brush they care but little,
    And always make it through.

4 The game they hunt is ven'son,
    Wild hogs and javelines;[1]
  Their food is beef and corn-dodgers,
    Along with pork and beans.

5 The captain of this little band
    Is Fowler, so they say;
  He beats his comrades hunting,
    And he hunts but half the day.

---

[1]In the Southwest, the English word **peccary** is never used for **javelina**, but, like **coyote**, the word is pronounced in more than one way. Here it is pronounced to rhyme with **bean**. In the seventh stanza it is pronounced in the Spanish manner, to fill out the meter.

6 He bids his men with courage,
    And he tells them on the spot,
  Like a true and faithful captain,
    "Boys, don't ever miss a shot."

7 Next comes Lieutenant Spooney,
    Though not so good for deer,
  But he chases javelinas
    And wild hogs on the fear.

8 There is a joke on Lieutenant Spooney,
    'Tis funny to relate;
  He catches pigs and makes them squeal
    And the mammies' lives he takes.

OLD GREY

"Old Grey," made up of a conversation between a man and his horse, is to me a singular song; I have been unable to find any other song like it. Miss Burton says that she learned it from a young man named Fount Backus, in Marble Falls, 1904.

1 It was on last Monday morning, all troubled in mind,
  I traveled far over some pleasures to find;
  Me being all alone excepting my horse,
  I traveled far over some raging discourse.

2 The very first word I ever heard Old Grey speak
  As over the head I hit him a lick,
  I'll tell you the truth though it sounds like a lie,
  He laid back his ears and made this reply:

3 "Oh, don't you abuse me, although you are a man;
  I endeavor to pack you as far as I can,

124   *Texas and Southwestern Lore*

    Over hills and rough ridges till I wear my feet out;
    By the honor of a master, I'll never give out.

4 "It was on last Monday morning you never gave me my dues,
   Rode me over rough country without any shoes,
   All over rough country and over rough ground,
   And all of my uses you never have found."

5 "You speak of your uses, you speak it with scorn.
   Don't I feed you a plenty of fodder and corn?
   And when I get down to jest warm my feet,
   Don't I feed you all the hay, Grey, you are able to eat?"

6 "Oh, when you are sober, I very well know
   You feed me a plenty and ride but slow,
   But when you get drunk, you pay for it all,
   You ride like the devil and feed none at all."

THE HONEST TRAMP

Miss Burton learned "The Honest Tramp" only a few years ago from a family who had recently moved to Austin from Liberty, Texas. I have no doubt that the song is old and of folk appropriation.

1 Let me sleep in your barn just tonight, sir;
    It's too cold to lie out on the ground,
  With the cold rain falling upon me
    And the north wind whistling around.

2 You may see that I use no tobacco,
    And I carry neither matches nor pipe;
  I am sure that I will do you no harm, sir.
    Let me sleep in your barn just tonight.

3 You ask me how long I've been tramping
    Or leading this kind of life.
  If you'll listen I'll tell you my story—
    Though it cuts through my heart like a knife.

4 It was three years ago last summer—
   I shall never forget that sad day—
When a stranger had come from the city,
   So tall, so handsome, and gay.

5 He was tall, fine dressed, and looked sporty;
   He looked like a man who had wealth,
And he said he had come to the country
   To stay just a while for his health.

6 My wife said she would like to be earning,
   With something to add to our home;
So she coaxed me until I consented
   That the stranger would stop in and board.

7 And one night when I came home from my work, sir,
   I was whistling and singing with joy,
Expecting a warm-hearted welcome
   To receive from my wife and my boy.

8 Nothing did I find but a letter
   That someone had placed on the stand,
And the moment my eyes fell upon it
   I picked it up in my hand.

9 And the words that were wrote there upon it
   Seemed to burn through my brain and drive me wild,
For they told me the stranger and Nellie
   Had run off and had taken my child.

10 Then I stopped at a farm house last summer;
    There they told me my baby had died;
It was there for the first time in my life, sir,
    I knelt to my knees and I cried.

11 Then they took me down to the church-yard;
    There they showed me a newly made mound,
And they told me that Nellie, my darling,
    Lay asleep in that cold, solid ground.

12 Now I'm sure there is a God up in heaven,
    Or, at least I've been taught to believe;
I am sure He will keep on the record
    The doom that he ought to receive.

THE DRUNKARD'S DREAM

"The Drunkard's Dream" is one of a numerous class of prohibition songs. Cox (*Folk-Songs of the South*, number 129) gives two versions of it of nine four-line stanzas each. He lists various occurrences of it and says that it is "common in English broadsides" under the title "The Husband's Dream." The music would indicate that the stanzas are each of eight lines. Miss Burton learned her version at the School for the Blind, Austin.

1 "Why, Durmont, you look healthy now,
    Your dress is neat and clean;
I never see you drunk about.
    Pray, tell me where you've been.
Your wife and family are all well;
    You once did use them strange;
You are kinder to them now.
    How came this happy change?"

2 "It was a dream, a warning voice,
    Sweet heaven sent to me,
To snatch me from a drunkard's curse—
    Great want and misery.
My wages were all spent in drinks.
    Oh, what a wretched view!
I almost broke my Mary's heart
    And starved my children too.

3 "What was my home or wife to me?
    I heeded not her sigh.
Her patient smile had welcomed me,
    Her tears bedimmed her eye.
My children too had oft awoke,
    'O father dear,' they said,

'Poor mother has been weeping so
   Because we have no bread.'

4 "My Mary's form did waste away,
   I saw her sunken eyes;
My babes on straw in sickness lay,
   I heard their wailing cry.
I laughed and sung in drunkard's joy,
   While Mary's tears did stream,
And like a beast I fell asleep
   And had this woeful dream.

5 "I thought once more I staggered home.
   There seemed a solemn gloom.
I missed my wife—where can she be?—
   And strangers in the room.
I heard them say: 'Poor thing, she's dead,
   She's led a wretched life.
Grief and want had broke her heart.
   Who would be a drunkard's wife?'

6 "I saw my children weeping 'round,
   I scarcely drew my breath.
They called and kissed her lifeless form
   Forever stilled in death.
'Oh, father, come and wake her up.
   The people say she's dead.
Make her smile and speak once more,
   We'll never cry for bread.'

7 " 'She is not dead,' I frantic cried,
   And rushed to where she lay
And madly kissed her once warm brow
   Forever cold as clay.
'Dear Mary, speak one word to me,
   No more I'll cause you pain,
No more I'll grieve your loving heart,
   Or ever drink again.

8 " 'Dear Mary, speak. 'Tis Durmont's call.'
   'Why so I do,' she cried.
I woke and there my Mary dear
   Was kneeling by my side.
I pressed her to my throbbing heart,
   While joyous tears did stream,
And ever since I've heaven blessed
   For sending me this dream."

NOT LONG SINCE A YOUNG GIRL AND I FELL IN LOVE

The next song was learned by Miss Burton from a young man who was "calling on her" some years ago. References in the song to Indian fighting show it to be at least a half century old. It might be classed as a cowboy song. The long title is as it was given to me.

1 Not long since, a young girl
   And I fell in love;
 I courted her as treasure
   As I would lay above.

2 She being like all other girls,
   I fear she would not do;
 Since I have come to study,
   My bargain I will rue.

3 She thought by her flattering tongue
   And by her silly voice
 That she would try to lead me
   To a fool's paradise.

4 Me being more wiser
   Than she taken me to be,
 I'll never prevent her marrying
   Since she's gone back on me.

5 So now at last we parted.
   She said, "My love, good-bye;
 If I never see you again,
   On the dreary plains you'll die.

6 "Remember what I've told you
   And keep it in your mind,
 For the girl that loves you the dearest
   Is the girl you left behind."

7 "I'll cross the Rocky Mountains,
       Where the savage Indians dwell;
   I'll cross the dreary plains,
       Where a many cowboy fell."

8 And now I am so lonely
       On the wild and dreary plain,
   For the girl I love so dearly
       I'll never see again.

9 Come, all you rambling cowboys,
       A warning take from me.
   Don't be so easy to fall in love
       With every girl you see.

10 Your head'll bend in trouble,
       Your heart will ache with pain.
    The girl you love so dearest
       You'll never see again.

THE HAUNTED WOOD

The ballad that follows, redolent of pioneer conditions rather romanticized, is supplied by Mr. Dan W. Gunn, a student in the University of Texas, 1925-1926. "When I was a child in Northeast Texas," says Mr. Gunn, "I heard my grandmother, who came to Texas from Alabama eighty years ago, sing 'The Haunted Wood' very often. I can still recall the powerful pictures to my mind and the delightful shivers to my body that her singing brought." The ballad has a distinct literary flavor, but I have been unable to find it in print.

1 In an olden time a river ran
       Between two mountain walls,
   And the place near where it started
       Was the place of the Haunted Falls.

2 On the bosom of that river
       Danced many a light canoe,
   While the waves were sweetly singing
       And the summer sky was blue.

3 On its banks there dwelt a white man
       With his wife and children three,
   And for many days the forest
       Echoed back their shouts of glee.

4 But to a little town the father
    One bright day for meal had gone,
  Left his wife and little children
    For a peaceful hour alone.

5 'Twas a solitary dwelling,
    For no one was living near,
  And the busy little mother
    Had no time for thought of fear.

6 Hark! the sound of traveling horses,
    And the mother turned in fright,
  Just in time to draw the door bolt
    When two Indians rode in sight.

7 Then she turned and kissed her children,
    Bade them neither speak nor cry,
  Cast them into a hidden closet,
    Then nerved herself to die.

8 With an angry push the chieftain
    Knocked the bolt from off the door.
  He saw the weeping woman
    Lying there upon the floor.

9 Then he shouted to his comrade,
    Who had seized a heavy stick,
  "Come and help. We'll drown this woman.
    Lose no time, I say. Be quick."

10 Then they seized that weeping woman
    Roughly there from off the floor,
  Caught her by her long dark tresses,
    Roughly dragged her to the shore.

11 Then they sang and danced about her,
    Heeding not her piteous cry,
  Dashed her on the rocks beneath her,
    And in agony she did die.

12 'Twas revenge that they had wanted,
    'Twas revenge that they had found,
  For they burned those sleeping babies
    And the cabin to the ground.

13 Now the old man wanders lonely
    Near the place where the cabin stood,
  And the people of the village
    Call the place Haunted Wood.

THE CALIFORNIAN'S LAMENT

Captain William F. Drannan, in his book, *Thirty-one Years on the Plains and in the Mountains, or The Last Voice from the Plains*,[2] tells how he heard the following song in 1853, when at the age of twenty-one, having won the soubriquet of "the boy scout," he came upon a band of emigrants near Bent's Fort, west of the Platte. The women among the emigrants were the first of his race that he had glimpsed in six years. "A little, fat, chubby young lady" from Missouri "sang a song entitled 'The Californian's Lament,'" and, continues Captain Drannan, "I thought it the prettiest song I had ever heard in my life. Environment so colors things."

In his long, honest, and interesting book Captain Drannan includes two other "poems": one an epitaph, the other a farewell at the end, entitled "The Old Scout's Lament." Both are frankly of his own composition. Yet "The Old Scout's Lament" has got itself printed word for word as a popular ballad,[3] and "The Californian's Lament," which must have been a genuine group ballad, has never, so far as I know, been included in a collection of frontier songs. The emigrants who sang it had camped all winter on the Platte. Very likely while they waited for spring to come they made up this and other songs for their own entertainment.

1 Now pay attention unto me,
  All you that remain at home,
  And think upon your friends
  Who have to California gone;
  And while in meditation
  It fills our hearts with pain,
  That many so near and dear to us
  We ne'er shall see again.

2 While in this sad condition,
  With sore and troubled minds,
  Thinking of our many friends
  And those we left behind,
  With our hearts sunk down in trouble,
  Our feelings we cannot tell;
  Although so far away from you,
  Again we say farewell.

---
[2]Chicago, 1900. See page 126.
[3]Lomax, **Cowboy Songs and Other Frontier Ballads**, p. 117.

3   With patience we submitted
    Our trials to endure,
    And on our weary journey
    The mountains to explore.
    But the fame of California
    Has begun to lose its hue—
    When the soul and body is parting
    What good can money do?

4   The fame of California
    Has passed away and gone;
    And many a poor miner
    Will never see his home.
    They are falling in the mountains high,
    And in the valleys too;
    They are sinking in the briny deep,
    No more to rise to view.

CUSTER'S LAST FIGHT

Somewhere in print must be more than one ballad on Custer's last fight. Few events of the old West have caused as much controversy and produced as much conversation as the fight without its messenger of defeat that the gallant Custer made on the Little Big Horn, June 25, 1876. Only last year the fiftieth anniversary of the battle was memorialized by a pageant of national importance. Yet the only song on Custer's fight that I have been able to find is one furnished by "Sandy" (his "real name" is Robert Alexander) Morris, just now of Lucille, New Mexico, and in this song Custer does not personally figure.

"Sandy" Morris is the most unflagging singer of cowboy songs that I have ever heard or heard of. Last year at the Cattlemen's Convention in Fort Worth he sang for three days and nights without stopping. He is known wherever cowmen in West Texas or New Mexico meet, his greatest concert being reserved for the "T-Anchor Roundup" of old time Panhandle cowboys held annually near Canyon. Most of his songs are those given by Mr. Lomax. At present he is herding sheep in New Mexico. I asked him if the sheep men did not have some songs. "No," he replied, "the sheepmen have no songs. I guess they are not smart enough to make them." He learned how to sing, he says, at camp meetings around Bonham. He used to ranch in New Mexico—"before the crash." I do not know what his sources are for the two songs he gave me, "Custer's Last Fight" and "The Orphant Girl." The latter is accessible in *Folk-Songs of the South*, by J. H. Cox, where full notes on it are provided; so it is not here included.

1 It was just before George Custer's last fight
    Two soldiers drew their reins,
With a clasping hand and a parting word,
    For they never might meet again.

2 One had blue eyes and curly hair,
    Nineteen but a month ago.
He had red on his cheeks and down on his chin;
    He was only a boy, you know.

3 The other was tall and dark and strong,
    But his faith in this world was dim.
He only trusted in those whom he loved,
    They were all the world to him.

4 "I have a picture in my breast.
    I will wear it in this fight,
A picture that is all in this world to me,
    And it shines like a morning light.

5 "Like a morning light was her love for me,
    And she cherished my lonely life.
It was little I cared for the frown on her face
    When she promised to be my wife.

6 "Write to her, Charlie, when I am gone;
    Send back this fond, fair face,
And tell her gently how I died,
    And where's my resting place."

7 Tears filled the eyes of the blue-eyed boy,
    And his heart was filled with pain,
Saying, "I'll do your bidding, comrade mine,
    If we never meet again.

8 "But if I get killed and you return,
    You must do as much for me.
I have a mother dear at home—
    Write to her tender-ly.

9 "She has lost us all one by one,
    Husband and son after son.

And I was the last of all of her boys
  To answer the country's call."

10 Just then the orders came to charge.
     For an instant hand touched hand.
   The last goodbye—then onward rode
     That brave, devoted band.

11 They rode together to the crest of the hill,
     Where the redskins shot like hail,
   Poured death among the ranks of the little band
     And scalped them as they fell.

12 They rode up the hill that they could gain,
     Against a dark and gathering gloom,
   And the few that were left of that gallant band
     Rode slowly back again.

13 And among the dead that were left behind
     Was the boy with the curly hair;
   And the tall dark form that rode by his side
     Lay dead beside him there.

14 So none was left to tell the girl
     The last words her lover had said,
   And the patient mother that was left at home
     Will learn that her last boy is dead.

OH, SUSAN, QUIT YOUR FOOLING

I want to include here a jocular song with which my father, who had one of the *soundest* voices for singing I have ever heard, used to make us children laugh. He was born on Buffalo Bayou, near Harrisburg, Texas, January 17, 1858, and probably learned the song early in boyhood before he left Harrisburg, a few years after the Civil War, to ranch in Live Oak County.

1 Oh, Susan, quit your fooling
    And give my heart to me,
  Oh, give me back my love again
    And I will let you be.

2 Her mouth was like an oven,
    Her foot was like a ham,
  Her eyes were like the owl's at night
    And her voice was never ca'm.

3 She looked so long and hollow,
  She looked just like a crane.
 Oh, I'm going away to leave you now,
  Goodbye, my Susan Jane.

4 Oh, Susan, I love you dearly;
  I ne'er can love again,
 But I'm going away to leave you now,
  Goodbye, my Susan Jane.

I MUST NOT WORK ON SUNDAY

I suppose that "I Must Not Work on Sunday" might be classed as a religious song, but I remember it chiefly as a "rockabye" song. I remember my father's singing it, too, as he rode along in a buggy or on horseback at the head of a quiet herd of cattle.

I must not work on Sunday, Sunday, Sunday,
I must not work on Sunday
Because it is a sin;
But I can work on Monday, Tuesday, Wednesday,
Thursday, Friday, Saturday
Till Sunday comes again.

II. BREAKFAST CALLS

And what cheer was there in the now silenced voice that called to us boys in the sleepy dawning:
  Wake up, Jacob!
   Day's a-breaking!
  Peas in the pot,
   And hoecakes a-baking!

I have heard of this call being used to rouse men in camp somewhere in the Rocky Mountains. Along in the eighties, I have been told, a camp cook on the Plains of the Texas Panhandle used to awaken the cowboys with a variant of it that went thus:

  Wake up, snakes! Day's a-breaking!

In *Allan's Lone Star Ballads*[4] there is an allusion to "Wake up Snakes and Bite a Biskit." I have never seen the song.

---
[4] By Francis D. Allan, Galveston, 1874, p. 72.

When the West lived out of doors and camp cooks were a distinct class of men, "breakfast calls" formed a gladsome and musical form of chant. Not all the camp singing by any means was around the shadow-beleaguered fire. In his wholesome little book, *The Bullwhacker*, William F. Hooker gives a sunlit picture of the breakfast summons that ox freighters heard in the Northwest sixty-five years ago.[5]

> At break of day the night-herder who has been out with the bulls all night . . . drives his herd into the corrals, usually singing some refrain of his own composition. . . . A half hour before the herder appears, the cook and his helper, both bullwhackers, doing their turn of a week, have been on the job with coffee and bacon, and as soon as the herder sounds his first note, the cook takes up the song, which is, perhaps:

> > Bacon in the pan,
> > Coffee in the pot;
> > Get up and get it—
> > Get it while it's hot.

W. B. Hester, of Rotan, Texas, who was ranching on the Canadian River in the early eighties, recalls a negro cook named Bob who was a "fine singer" and who on the long Beef Trail to Dodge City, "Cowboy Capital," used to sing out in the early morning a song he had composed. One line of it went thus:

> If you can't get up, there are men in Dodge that can.

Another old time trail driver[6] observes: "A camp cook could do more towards making life pleasant for those about him than any other man in the outfit, especially on those trail trips. A good-natured, hustling cook meant a lot to a trail boss. A cheery voice ringing out about daybreak, shouting, 'Roll out there, fellers, and hear the little birdies sing their praises to God!' or 'Arise and shine and give God the glory!' would make the most crusty waddie grin as he crawled out to partake of his morning meal—even when he was extremely short of sleep."

---

[5]Hooker, William F., **The Bullwhacker,** World Book Co., Yonkers-on-Hudson, 1924, p. 37.

[6]James H. Cook, **Fifty Years on the Old Frontier,** New Haven, 1923, p. 39.

III. TEXAS PATRIOTIC SONGS

The present is certainly not an age of sentiment. Recent appeals by the Legislature and Governor of Texas for a State song seem to have resulted in nothing suitable. One criticism made against the songs submitted is that they "lack sentiment." From this lack Texas songs of the last century do not suffer; frequently they have nothing but sentiment. The Texians—for a large portion of the citizens of the Lone Star State so called themselves until along in the seventies— liked to read patriotic verse and sing patriotic songs, as an examination of representative collections like Dixon's *Poetry and Poets of Texas* and Kyger's *Texas Gems* and of newspaper files will show.[7] Interest in such songs seems to have prevailed pretty widely until about the close of the century. Among people beyond the reach of commercial secretaries it yet exists. One of the best evidences of contemporary interest is to be found in the columns of Texas verse that until a few months ago were run under the editorship of Miss Katie Daffan in the Sunday edition of the *Houston Chronicle*.

TEXAS HEROES

One of the oldest of the patriotic songs adopted as their own by those Texas folk to whom Mier, San Jacinto, Austin, Houston, Wharton, Fannin, Travis, Scurry, and Green were household words, is "Texas Heroes." Like several other songs in this collection, it came to me from the Burton family of Austin. Mr. Burton, born in Texas in 1844, heard it in his childhood. He once knew the name of the composer, he says, but has forgotten it; however, he remembers having frequently heard that the song came into popularity soon after the battle of San Jacinto. Miss Burton, who is blind and who several years ago attended the Texas State School for the Blind in Austin, says that the song was there sung every San Jacinto Day for years. It is sung to the

---

[7]In a thesis, **Literary Trends as Indicated in Texas Newspapers, 1836-1846,** presented in partial fulfillment of the requirements for the degree of Master of Arts in the University of Texas, August, 1926, Mr. Paul Morgan has devoted a chapter to "Patriotic Verse" of the period of the republic.

tune of "Auld Lang Syne." A version of it printed in *Texas Gems,* compiled by J. C. F. Kyger (Denison, Texas, 1885), differs little from the Burton version. In an introductory note to the song Kyger says: "The author of this poem is not known. It was published in the *Texas Prairie Flower,* a monthly literary magazine." The *Texas Prairie Flower,* watered by Mrs. C. M. Winkler, bloomed at Corsicana only one year, 1883-1884.

Before the Civil War the celebration of San Jacinto Day was to many Texians as distinct a rite as the celebration of May Day in "merrie old England," and "Texas Heroes" must have been sung in many places on many a twenty-first of April. As a proper setting for the song and as a bit of folk history, a description of one of those San Jacinto celebrations is here in place.[8]

> The most conspicuous of the San Jacinto veterans [about Houston] was ... Tierwester, an old Frenchman. At the Battle of San Jacinto he had a powder horn slung to his neck. This powder horn was a cow's horn scraped very thin ... with a wooden plug at the large end and a small plug at the little end. During the battle a Mexican bullet struck this horn and entered through one side, but did not have enough force to go out of the other. Tierwester never removed the ball, but on San Jacinto Day he came to the reunion wearing [the] horn round his neck ... He would commence drinking early in the day ... The more he drank the louder he talked and the more viciously he would shake the horn and tell the story of the bullet it contained ... There was old man Jarmond, too, and a score or two of others ...
>
> One thing I have never seen mentioned in print and which seems forgotten by everybody, was the old "Liberty Pole" that was erected near the Houston House by the San Jacinto veterans and the people of Houston to commemorate Texas Independence ... I remember seeing only a part of it that was preserved by the veterans for many years. This liberty pole was a pine tree that had been trimmed and converted into a fine flag pole from which flew the Lone Star flag on festive occasions and always on San Jacinto Day. It did duty as long as Texas remained a republic, but by the time it was admitted as a state the old pole had grown so decayed and weak that it broke and fell to the ground. The veterans of San Jacinto, who had used

---

[8]Quoted from a delightful collection of anecdotes and reminiscenes, **True Stories of Old Houston and Houstonians,** by Dr. S. O. Young, Galveston, 1913, pp. 102-103; 106.

the pole as a rallying point for years, secured a piece of it, about twenty feet long, and on April 21, after an appropriate salute had been fired from the "Twin Sisters," the two brass cannon used by the Texans at the battle, the veterans shouldered the piece of liberty pole and headed for the nearest barroom. Placing the old pole on the counter was all that was necessary to "put the drinks on the house" and the veterans had whatever they called for without money and without price.

Then would begin a procession that would include every barroom in town. The veterans were welcomed everywhere, for it would have been considered as an unfriendly act by the proprietor had any saloon been overlooked.

About the fourth or fifth drink the war talk would commence and the Battle of San Jacinto would be fought over and over in a way that men of only one battle can [fight in talk]. . . .

I don't know what became of the piece of liberty pole, ... but it would be a priceless relic if it could be found. Now it must not be supposed . . . that the veterans were drinkers and roisterers. They were anything but that. They were the most honored and honorable citizens of the land.

(Sing to tune of "Auld Lang Syne.")

1 We lay the crown of memory
    Upon the place of rest
  Where noble heroes lie asleep
    Within earth's icy breast.

2 For those who fell at Alamo,
    And those who died at Mier,
  And those brave hearts still at Goliad,
    All claim the silent tear.

Chorus: Then strike the harp for those who fought
    For freedom long ago,
  At San Jacinto and the Mier
    And blood-stained Alamo.

3 On San Jacinto's crimson plain
    Brave Houston met the foe,
  And set his sturdy heel upon
    The chief of Mexico.

4 When Santa Anna's star went down,
    The Lone Star rose on high,
  And blazed aloft a brilliant light
    In freedom's cloudless sky.

5 Each veteran who stands today
    Beneath the scars of age

> Has made his name a shining mark
> On history's living page.
>
> 6 For those who wear upon the brow
> The crown of honored years
> And those who bravely died we offer
> A chaplet of our tears.

AWAY HERE IN TEXAS

There is little of the "Liberty Pole" spirit in the next song, wherein, after advertising the agricultural virtues of the State, the singer looks forward to being "ransomed from Texas." The song is really interesting as a blend of patriotism and religion. It has been supplied by Mrs. D. W. Walker, now living with Mrs. Joel E. Gunn, her daughter, in Austin. She came to Texas from Alabama in 1846, when she was three years old. Her family settled near Paris, and along in the early fifties she learned the song from her brother, James M. Biard, a circuit rider. She has sung the song to two generations of children.

> 1 Away here in Texas the bright sunny South
> The cold storms of winter defies;
> The dark lowering clouds which envelop the North
> Seldom darken our beautiful skies.
>
> 2 Away here in Texas the white cotton fields
> Look like plains covered over with snow,
> And corn in abundance at everywhere yields
> And oats most luxuriantly grow.
>
> 3 Away here in Texas a stranger I roam;
> I am unknown to all but a few;
> I travel in hopes of a far better home
> When I've taken my last sad adieu.
>
> 4 Away here is Texas my journey shall end,
> My body be laid in the tomb,
> And there it will rest till Christ shall descend
> When Gabriel his trumpet shall sound.
>
> 5 When, ransomed from Texas, my soul shall arise
> To meet my dear Lord in the air,
> The words of His promise shall bear me safe home
> Forever to dwell with Him there.

LEAVE IT! AH NO! THE LAND IS OUR OWN

Francis D. Allan in his *Lone Star Ballads* (Galveston, 1874, page 194), assigns the authorship of this song to Maud J. (also known as Maud Fuller) Young (1826-1882), in her day recognized in Texas as a leading patriotic poet. For years I have been trying to find her much eulogized *Legend of Sour Lake,* written in prose. Dr. S. O. Young, who died in Houston about a year ago and whose description of the "Liberty Pole" celebration has just been quoted, was her son. The poem was evidently composed shortly after the close of the Civil War, when the Confederate flag was "furled," when the land was "burdened with woes," and when various ex-Confederate Texans were leaving for Mexico and South America. To Texans of the old rock (May their tribe increase!) Texas comes first, the South second, and America third. America does not come at all in this song.

The verses printed below differ in nowise from those printed by Allan. Together with the music, they come from Mrs. John Creaton, of Austin, who secured them from Mrs. Fred Sterzing, Austin. She had a copy of the song with music taken down from the blackboard in Philip Bickler's school, which flourished in Austin in the early seventies before the city had public schools.

1 Leave it! Ah no! The land is our own,
    Though the flag that we loved is now furled.
  A Texian must roam o'er his own prairie plains
    Or find rest in the far spirit world.

Chorus: *Oh, the Lone Star State our home shall be*
  While its waters still roll to the Mexican sea. [*Repeat.*]

2 Where shall so blue a sky e'er be found
    As the heavens that bend o'er us here?
  Or where shall sweet flowers as fragrant and fair
    The wayfaring wanderer cheer?

3 Here do our Fannins and Travises rest,
    Our Scurry and Wharton and Green,
  And here may our heads repose on our breast
    When death's shadows fall on the scene.

4 Others may seek South American shores,
    Orizaba and fair Monterrey,
  But never! because she is burdened with woes,
    Shall our feet from our own loved state stray.

Oh, the Lone Star State our home shall be
While its blue rivers roll to the Mexican sea. [*Repeat.*]

5 Then there's our state, our own dear state,
    Right or wrong, enslaved or free;
  In poverty, wealth, enthroned, or disowned,
    Our mother, our queen she shall be.

Oh, the Lone Star State our home shall be
As long as her rivers run down to the sea. [*Repeat.*]

IV. CONFEDERATE SONGS

A large number of the Texas Confederates were frontiersmen and many of the "boys" who in the early sixties wore the gray and sang in army camps later wore spurs up the Chisholm Trail and sang in cow camps. From the early sixties on through the eighties the spirit of the Confederate States was strong over the West. Many a Texas trail driver could, upon reaching Kansas, the land of "jay hawkers" and of John Brown abolitionists, sing from the bottom of his heart:

  . . . And I don't want no pardon
    For what I was and am;
  I won't be reconstructed,
    And I don't care a damn.⁹

  When Boone Helm, noted desperado, was about to be hanged in Virginia City, Montana, in 1863, he yelled out, "Every man for his principles. Hurrah for Jeff Davis!" Then he kicked the box from under his own feet and a few minutes later was dead. Long after the Civil War had closed frontiersmen were singing army songs. Therefore Confederate songs have a legitimate place in any collection of balladry of the Southwest.

  Mr. W. W. Burton, of Austin, already spoken of, has given me a very definite picture of some of the army camp singing. "We had in our company during the Civil War," says he, "a fellow named Marshall Johnson from Waco, who was the greatest hand to make songs and speeches that I have ever known. Poor fellow, he got killed in a stampede one fall early in the seventies, up on the Bosque River, and the well known cowboy ditty, 'When Work Is Done This Fall,' was made on the occasion. Well, sometimes while we were in the army we would pile up a lot of pine logs and make a kind of platform, building a big fire out in front of it so that it would be in a good light. Marshall would mount up, r'aring to go. Then we could give him any subject on earth, and he would make a song or speech on it or preach a sermon. His favorite subjects were the general and the colonel. Any of us would have died for either of them, but we nearly all died laughing sometimes at the way Marshall took them off. Once in a while the general himself would come down to the fire and lie around and laugh with us boys while Marshall was making up his speeches or songs."

SHILOH: A CONFEDERATE SONG

  While just such a hearty detachment of Texas Confederates were floating down the Yazoo River one night in 1863, they "sang to the tune of Joe Bowers'"—though I fail to see how they made the meter fit the tune—some words very much more refined than those of the original song. The veteran recorder of these words says: "Our first night out some of

---

  9For a complete version of the song, "I'm a Good Old Rebel," see **Confederate Scrap Book**, by L. C. Daniel, Richmond, Va., 1893, pp. 104-108. Cf. Cox, p. 281.

the men relieved the monotony by playing cards, others by singing songs. I give one of the songs written by a member of our regiment, which has never appeared in print."[10]

Whether or not "Shiloh: A Confederate Song" appeared in print before Ralph J. Smith included it in his pamphlet, I can not say. I have not found it elsewhere, though Shiloh was a popular theme. Francis D. Allan in his *Lone Star Ballads* (Galveston, 1874), records three songs on the subject: "The Battle of Shiloh Hills," "Shiloh," and "The Drummer Boy of Shiloh," but they all differ distinctly from the Shiloh song recorded by Smith.

1 Draw near, my gallant comrades, and a story to you I'll sing,
   A sad and mournful song of war; tears to your eyes 'twill bring;
   One April morn on Shiloh's plains the rising sun displayed
   One hundred thousand soldiers in battle line arrayed.
   Soon drum and fife proclaimed the hour that we must march away,
   'Mid cannon's roar and musket's crack, to mingle in the fray.

Chorus: *On Shiloh's fields the bullets sped,*
   On Shiloh's hills full many bled,
   On Shiloh's plains lay thousands dead,
   While Shiloh's hills ran red with blood.

2 Time after time we charged the foe, who made a stubborn stand,
   And ere the sun had reached the west we fought them hand to hand.
   At last their solid ranks we broke and scattered them afar.
   And then the vale of night fell down and closed the scene of war.
   The memory of that bloody day the heart with anguish fills,
   For dead and dying everywhere lay thick on Shiloh's hills.

3 When morning's light once more appeared, drums beat to arms again,
   Unmindful of the dying and heedless of the slain;
   And soon the cannon's deadly mouth renewed its angry roar,
   Ten thousand fell and thousands sped to battle nevermore.
   Each place in ranks may be refilled, but not in heavy hearts
   That watch and pray for their return throughout our country's parts.

V. AMERICAN-MEXICAN SONGS

In the Southwest there has been—been pretty much forgotten, too—a considerable body of bi-lingual folk-songs.

[10]**Reminiscences of the Civil War and Other Sketches,** by Ralph J. Smith, San Marcos, Texas, pp. 9-10. The monograph is in the archives of the University of Texas.

Where so many men are as familiar with "Mexican" as with their own language and where hundreds of Mexican terms have passed into current speech, verse sandwiching Mexican into English is natural. I have forgotten two or three little songs of the kind that I used to know and can now produce but one stanza. That stanza comes from Judge O. W. Williams, of Fort Stockton, one of the best *lored* minds in all the Southwest. Concerning it he writes:

"In 1879 I was a 'prospector' in the neighborhood of Santa Fe, New Mexico, where I heard a kind of folk-song characteristic of the Americans then flocking into that land of *poco tiempo* and trying to accustom themselves to the lives and lingo of the natives. It struck me home, and I thought that I should never forget it. Nevertheless I have forgotten it and it may have been lost even in its home. Perhaps the few lines I am able to summon may serve to call up others from the hazy memory of some old-timer and thus save the song from oblivion. It relates to Johnnie Cox's troubles in the land of the double tongue and ran after this fashion":

> Johnnie Cox he live in Albuquer-ky,
> Johnnie Cox he was no fool, no fool.
> Sometime, sometime he eat the jerky,[11]
> All time he live on puro maiz azul.[12]

VI. SONGS OF THE BAD MAN

BUD BALLEW'S LAST DRAW

No collection of pioneer ballads would be complete without at least one bad-man jingle. "Bud Ballew's Last Draw" is thoroughly representative of the genre to which it belongs. For it I am indebted to Miss Elizabeth Settle Johnston, Lawton, Oklahoma, who in 1922 was teaching in Healdton, an oil town of that state.

"The poem," she says, "was recited in assembly by one of the junior high school boys, much to the horror of his teachers and to the delight of the other children. In 'Bud Ballew's Last Draw' you will find the real spirit of Healdton, which

---
[11]Jerky is dried beef, from Sp. **charqui** or **charque**.
[12]**Puro maiz azul**, bread made from blue grained corn. One of the popular Mexican songs of the border country is called "Puro Maiz."

is a 'Stay right in there, feller!' kind of town. It knew Bud well. Wildly drunk, Bud had driven through the streets, shooting up the town in true traditional fashion."

Born in Fannin County, Texas, in 1877, Bud Ballew twenty-three years later became a part of the congenial outlawry of the Indian Territory. In the latter years of his life he was associated with the notorious Sheriff Buck Garrett, of Ardmore, Oklahoma. The last time he reached for his pistol was on May 5, 1922, in Wichita Falls, Texas, where he had come to take part with cowboys in a roping contest. The chief of police in Wichita Falls, a former Texas Ranger, hearing that Bud was "cutting up," approached him—in a "soft drink parlor"—and demanded that he quiet down and hand over his gun. "Hell, you are out of luck," snorted the famous gunman, reaching for his hip. He never even got his six-shooter out of the holster; five shots from the ex-Texas Ranger bored into his vitals. Bud Ballew wore high-heeled boots and a wide-brimmed hat, and, though a rare horseman, drove habitually in an automobile. He loved Buck Garrett and he loved to "whoop 'em up." "Nothing but relief was felt when he was killed in Texas," says Miss Johnston. "Relief" in Healdton, I'll grant, but in the newspaper dispatches printed in the *Austin Statesman* for May 6, 1922, from which I have been extracting some heroical details, and in the ballad, recited "much to the delight of the other children," I find something much nearer regret than relief.

    1 Cynically smile the scoffers and say,
        "These wild West days are o'er,
    This movie stuff is merely guff"—
        But down in Ardmore,
    Bud Ballew was a fighting man,
        Sudden and sure on the draw.
    His dead hip shot would have cast his lot
        With the forces of the law.

    2 His deputy star, till he lost his job,
        Plus the name of Bud Ballew,
    Made a casual bluff most times enough;
        If not, he could see it through.
    So never a hand was raised
        When Bud mixed brawls with law and order,
    Till one day he strayed away
        Across the Texas border.

3 Down in a town called Wichita Falls
        Excitement charged the air.
    The worst and the best of the wooly West
        Were drawn by the rodeo there—
    Lids wide brimmed on every dome,
            Chaps, topping high-heeled boots,
    Jests on its lips, corn on its hips,
        The West on one of its toots.

4 Then down into a gay cafe
        Swaggered the bold Ballew.
    "I'm here," he said, "to scatter lead,
        And I yearn for a fight or two."
    Just a breath and the world went round
        And the crowd began to thin,
    But it checked its pace when it saw the face
        Of a man who'd just stepped in.

5 Calmly he walked across the room,
        His voice had quite a drawl,
    "Ballew, I thought you knew,
        This stuff won't go at all."
    Tiny he looked beside the Bud,
        Bulky and sinister there.
    Apart, apace, each face to face
        Studied his man with care.

6 Ballew knew the man he faced,
        The Chief of Police, but—"Hell!"
    Crash roared a gun, and roared again
        The voice of a forty-four.
    The throng amazed, eyes bulging, gazed
        As a man slipped to the floor.
    Calmly the victor knelt beside the one
        Who had defied the law.
    "Ballew," he said, but Bud was dead—
        Beaten at last to the draw.

BARNEY PAYNE

One of the songs the Burtons sing is about a young horse thief from Blanco County, Texas, who a number of years ago was sent to the penitentiary at Huntsville for stealing cattle. While he was in jail at Johnson City waiting to be "sent up," he is said to have composed the song about himself. He was a strong man, and his whine,

> Oh, to work I am not able,

was "all put on," says Mr. Burton. Nevertheless, Miss Burton, after she had sung the song to the accompaniment of an old time organ that she often plays, remarked that she had known people not to sleep all night after hearing the last stanza. The "pathetic line,"

> And to beg it is too low,

seemed especially to affect them.

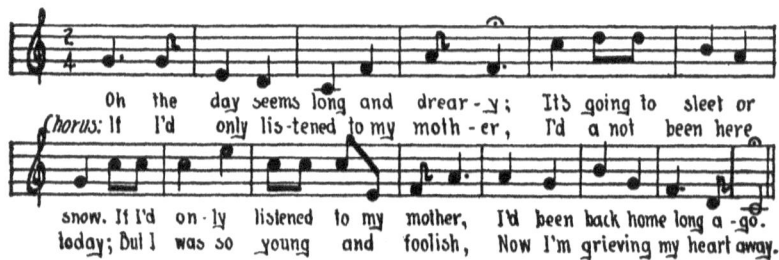

1 Oh, the day seems long and dreary;
   It's going to sleet or snow.
   If I'd only listened to my mother,
   I'd been back long ago.

   Chorus: If I'd only listened to my mother,
   I'd a not been here today,
   But I was so young and foolish;
   Now I'm grieving my life away.

2 Oh, listen to the mocking bird whistle
   And listen to the rain-crow sing,
   For the girl that I love so dearly
   She's wearing another man's ring.

3 Oh, where is my pocketbook of money,
   My forty-dollar watch and chain?
   All down at the gambling house, I reckon,
   Where the young man beat me at the game.

4 Oh, when I had a pocket of money,
   My friends came a-crowding around;
   But now when my pocketbook is empty
   Not a friend, not a friend, can be found.

5 Oh, to work I am not able,
    And to beg it is too low,
    And the track I'll take is stealing;
    Down to Huntsville jail I'll go.

BAD MAN YELLS

A certain class of chant-like yells emphasizing the badness of the man yelling them belongs to the lore of the bad man, I suppose, though oftener than not they originated in a spirit of mockery. The cowboy liked to "yip" them out when he was playing bad man—for the cowboy was truly "the playboy of the western world." Here is a yell that "hard customers" from the country around Harrisburg and Houston used to give fifty years ago. My father, who was a very quiet man, used to quote it to enforce his contempt for the "fly-up-the creeks" from whom he learned it.

    Raised in a canebrake,
    Fed in a hog trough,
    Suckled by a she bear,
    The click of a six-shooter is music to my ear!
        Wh-o-o-o-p-ee!

    The further up the creek you go
    The worse they get,
    And I come from the head of it!
        Wh-o-o-o-p-ee!

Another boast, adapted to a Texas river, was as follows:

    Born high up on the Guadalupe,
    Raised on thorny prickly pear,
    Quarrelled with alligators,
    And fought with grizzly bears!

A. J. Sowell, who knew Texas frontier life as few men who have written of it knew it, says in his *Rangers and Pioneers of Texas* (San Antonio, 1884, page 330): "Occasionally in some western village, you will hear a voice ring out on the night air in words something like these: 'Wild and woolly,' 'Hard to curry,' 'Raised a pet but gone wild,' 'Walked the Chisholm Trail backwards,' 'Fought Indians and killed buffalo,' 'Hide out, little ones,' and then you may expect a few shots from a revolver. It is a cowboy out on a little spree, but likely he will not hurt anyone, as some friend who is sober generally comes to him, relieves him of his pistol, and all is soon quiet again." Sowell adds that such yelling cowboys were exceptions.

VII. RANGER SONGS

As the bad man has been a theme for song and story over the great Western country to which he in a peculiar way belonged, so his pursuer, the Texas ranger, has also been. One of the undying ballads of the frontiers that stretched from the Rio Bravo to the Canadian Rockies, from the Brazos to the Pacific, is the song of "The Dying Ranger," printed in a hundred places. It represents a numerous class of range-made compositions. The ranger was a hero to all kinds of people; with intense and manly pride he was a hero to himself; the *esprit de corps* of the organization to which he belonged was more intense than that of any other armed body of men west of the British Isles. He liked to make songs depicting his own experiences; buoyant, vigorous, eager, he liked to sing any kind of song, make any kind of noise. "We had a fashion," remembers one of them, "common to cowboys, rangers, and all plainsmen, of yelling like wild Indians at times, for nothing at all except to give vent to our exuberant spirits, born of the free big life of the prairies."[13]

What a picture of the canorous nature of the Texas ranger does N. A. Jennings, just quoted, give! Early in 1875, with a Philadelphia accent still fresh on his young tongue and a lust for adventure rushing the blood through his young heart, he joined Captain L. H. McNelly's company of rangers at Laredo on the Texas border. A tired tenderfoot, he slept heavily the first night. And then:

> The first faint glimmering of dawn was lighting the sky in the east when I awoke. . . . The awakening was peculiar. It began with a confused dream, in which I thought myself in a church where all the congregation were singing the hymn, 'There's one wide river and that wide river is Jordan.' I remember that I looked about me and recognized many persons whom I had often seen in the church which I attended in Philadelphia, only, instead of being in that church, I was in a little backwoods Sunday-school in the mountains of East Tennessee.

---
[13]Jennings, N. A., **A Texas Ranger**, N. Y. 1899 p. 269. For references to the book that follow, see pp. 101-103; 123.

The singing grew louder, and at last I awoke with a start. Even then it did not cease, but assailed my waking senses with renewed vigor. I sat up and found myself surrounded by fifteen or twenty rangers, all of them looking at me and singing about that 'one wide river' as loud as they could howl.

It surprised me not a little to see those wild and reckless border riders beginning the day so devoutly, and I looked at them in blank amazement. This seemed to stimulate them to greater exertions, for they not only continued to sing, but presently began to dance with a slow, measured step, as though they were performing some strange religious rite. They joined hands as they danced and circled around me. Gradually, they increased their speed until, in the end, they were all whirling about me in a bewildering, dizzy ring, like so many madmen.

Of a sudden they stopped and gave a series of wild, blood-curdling yells, such as are never heard save in the far West. There the men on the great silent plains feel sometimes that they must let out their voices with all their power, just to break the monotony of that stillness which is one of the most impressive features of a seemingly limitless prairie. Having thus given vent to their feelings in the early morning, the rangers started off in various directions to attend to their horses and prepare breakfast.

Among McNelly's company, it turned out, was one ranger named McKay who "had a fine tenor voice and sang old Scotch songs in a way to make homesickness epidemic at night about the campfires." Two other rangers were improvisers: one made verse "of no mean order"; the other, verse "of the cowboy variety."

A. J. Sowell, an experienced ranger of the same period and subsequently a firm-handed writer, gives a significant episode.[14] In the summer of 1871 a band of rangers had scouted all day in the Palo Pinto country without water. When they finally reached the Brazos, their pack mule dashed ahead, lost his footing on the steep bank, and rolled over and over until he landed in the refreshing water below. "Then when rangers and mounts had drunken," says Sowell, "one of our men became very poetical and made a song on our unfortunate little mule, who was now standing very contentedly up to his middle in the water, and [who] seemed to be trying to take in enough to last him the balance of the scout. I

---

[14]A. J. Sowell, **Rangers and Pioneers of Texas**, San Antonio, 1884, p. 355. A rare and entertaining book.

will give you a few lines of the song as a sample of the poetical genius of a Texas ranger:

> Our pack mule Balaam took a tare,
> And down the hill he run,
> But struck his foot against a rock,
> And down poor Balaam come."

TEXAS RANGERS AFTER THE MOB

I cannot say how "popular" the ballad of "Texas Rangers after the Mob" ever became. I am afraid, however, that it does show the "poetical genius" of the ranger. It is extracted from a considerable group of songs and ballads appended by Sergeant W. J. L. Sullivan to his book, *Twelve Years in the Saddle for Law and Order on the Frontiers of Texas* (Austin, 1909). Sullivan assigns the authorship to himself and another ranger named Allen Maddox. The ballad celebrates the part rangers took in putting a stop to cow thieving, murdering, and mob law around San Saba in 1890.

1 Governor Culberson, from among the rest,
  Chose four Rangers, whom he thought best.
  He ordered us to San Saba to put down crime—
  We met in Goldthwaite, all on time,
  Two from the Panhandle, two from the Rio Grande,
  Which made a jolly little Ranger band.

2 We stopped at a hotel to stay all night;
  From what the people said, we expected a fight.
  They puffed and blowed, and said we were in danger,
  For a bushwhacker didn't like a Ranger.
  We laughed at such talk and considered it fun,
  But wherever we went, we carried our gun.

3 We had a six-shooter, a Winchester too
  That would shoot a buffalo through and through.
  Next morning at early dawn,
  We were off to San Saba as sure as you're born,
  In a wagon, with sheet and bows;
  How we stood it, the good Lord knows.

4 The roads were rough as rough could be—
  Why it did not kill us, I cannot see.
  Over mountains and hills through the dust,

Over rocks till I thought die I must.
We stopped in San Saba all that night,
Still expecting a hard little fight.

5 We rose next morning, gathered up our tricks,
Our camping outfit we began to fix.
We got a pair of mules and a wagon too,
Cooking utensils, and something to chew.
We wanted a cook, for we expected to be slain,
So the job was given to Buck Chamberlain.

6 We stopped in a town a day or two,
Met some of the girls, as pretty as ever we knew.
Then to the Colorado River we soon did go,
When to return we did not know.
The sheriff went along to pilot us through;
He knew the country—Buck did too.

7 We stopped at noon; got something to eat.
For economy, Buck was hard to beat.
He got on the wagon, taking a chew,
And said, "Come on, boys; better go through."
He drove into the creek, his lines all slack,
Stalled his mules, and then looked back.

8 Sullivan, Barker and Edgar Neal,
All jumped off and grabbed a wheel.
Maddox jumped off and grabbed one too.
Buck hit old Jack and yelled, "Get up, Sue!"
We made it to the river and pitched our tent;
To have a mess of fish we were all bent.

9 Still we were hearing a lot of the mob,
But we felt as though we were on to our job.
We rode over the country, went where we pleased,
But kept our eyes on all the big trees.
So we sent to Sheriff Bell for a good watchdog—
It would tickle you to death to see him catch a hog.

10 He caught by the tail, dropped down behind—
They went over that hill simply flying.
Here are the Texas Rangers, I know it is a hard life;
You had better find a girl and ask her to be your wife.
Now, if you trust in God, He will carry you through.
So goodbye, Ranger boys, I'll bid you adieu.

VIII. Cowboy Songs

Since Mr. John A. Lomax seventeen years ago brought out his *Cowboy Songs and Other Frontier Ballads* (1910)—a book that has deservedly gone through edition after edition—we have all chimed in on the subject, adding, however, very few significant songs. I have chimed,[15] and now I am chiming again. The subject is so interesting and important that scraps pertaining to it are worth recording.

One observation I should like to make. Nearly everybody has stressed the utilitarian purpose of cowboy songs—to keep cattle quiet. Such a purpose did occasion in the aggregate miles of verses. But while he sang to "make the little dogies lay down," the cowboy, like country people in their isolated homes, like the emigrant, the outlaw, and the ranger, sang also because he liked to sing, because meter and melody afforded an outlet to the natural feeling welling up in his wholesome nature. "I once punched cattle on the T-Bar Ranch," wrote R. L. Smith, of Killeen, Texas, to me a year or so ago, "and as we followed a long string of white-faces across the bed of an old alkali lake reflecting the moon's light, while the wind swept across the plains and the coyotes howled from the head of Laguna Rica, I wanted to answer the forces of nature, and did answer them, in wild half-maniac-like compositions of my own. In such times as this ballads are born."

What I wish to say is that in cowboy songs human nature as well as cowboy nature is expressing itself. Billie Fox, an old-time buffalo hunter and then range rider of the Cherokee Strip, now living near Marshall, Oklahoma, expressed himself to me in this manner: "There was one peeler in my outfit who used to sing just a line or two of 'Oh, Listen to the Crickets,' and how beautiful his soothing voice and the words sounded away across the herd in the still night! Singing was company to us just as much as it was to the cattle. One time when I was line-riding I met a peeler from another range. We stopped down under some shade trees next to a spring and exchanged songs. Each taught the other the tunes, and then each wrote down the words for the other to

---

[15]In an article entitled "Cowboy Songs," **The Country Gentleman, January 10, 1925.**

learn. Of course we learned a verse or two of each song while we were learning the tune. Lots of the boys couldn't sing but just sorter hummed, putting in words now and then."

Whenever cowboys had worked together long enough on a ranch to build up an *espirit de corps* they were likely to have something of song pride. Roy S. Scott,[16] who was familiar with the big cow outfits on the Little Missouri River twenty-five or thirty years ago, recalls how "just singing" played an important part in the social life of the cowboys. "Nearly every well established ranch," he says, "had for its own individual song a set of verses of its own making. Some 'smart' cowboy would lead off composing these verses, which the outfit would take up, chorusing in whenever the song was sung. When a puncher from another outfit drifted into camp he was expected to sing any new songs he might know or new stanzas to an old song, and to teach them to the camp he was visiting. In exchange he took the novelties possessed by his hosts. Thus songs like 'The Old Chisholm Trail' became of interminable length."

A good deal has been said on the sly about the unprintable nature of *genuine* cowboy songs. I have more than once heard it asserted that the songs printed do not represent the cowboy. It is time to deal with the subject frankly. It must be admitted that a good many of the cowboy songs were too raw for gentle ears; that many of them were as wild as the cattle they were sung to. In a society vigorously and exclusively masculine a great deal of the song and talk naturally turns on sex, and frequently it is downright obscene. John Rigby, cattle inspector at Beeville and old-time trail driver, tells a story that will illustrate.

Along in the eighties his outfit was camped on Wolf Creek in the Indian Territory—a place noted for stampedes and the number of men that had been killed there by lightning. It was a stormy night with the lightning playing ball on the tips of the long horns and dancing on the manes of the horses. Some distance down the creek from Rigby's camp another

---

[16]Mr. Scott will be remembered as the author of an interesting article on "The Cowboy Dance of the Northwest," **Publications** of the Texas Folk-Lore Society, 1925.

herd was being held, and that evening word had come up that a woman was with the outfit. As the lightning raced and played and the cattle milled about, the cowboys sang. One of them had a voice like the thunder itself and he pitched it to the racket of the elements. The song he sang was vile, and the men in Rigby's camp could hear him plainly. Presently the boss said to one of his men:

"Jim, go out there and tell that damn fool to quiet down a little. There's a woman in camp about four miles down the creek, and we shore don't want her to hear them songs Alec's a-singing."

Jim rode out to the herd, but the song continued. The storm got worse, and soon all hands were called to help hold the herd.

The boss rode around to where the high singer was holding forth and said to him, "Alec, for God's sake quiet down."

"What for?" Alec replied. "Don't you know we've got to sing to these cattle to keep 'em from running?"

"Yes," replied the boss, "but there's a woman in camp about four miles down the creek, and we shore don't want her hearing them songs you are howling over."

Roy S. Scott has added this comment: "In the singing about camp a cowboy would often cut loose with a song too vile to repeat; great cheers and a hurray would usually follow and there would be calls for more. After the climax in this class of songs had been reached, some puncher would strike up an old-time religious hymn, and that also would be cheered to the echo."

The cowboy was a healthy being. In him natural animal spirits ran high. On the trail or on remote ranches he was separated by hundreds of miles from the good women he invariably revered. The last woman he had seen, perhaps, was a dance hall trull; the next woman he met would be a dance hall trull. His song was often a dance hall memory, though it might be innocent enough. J. E. Folts, trail driver and for years chief deputy sheriff of Harris County, talked to me on the subject a few months before his death, early in 1925.

With his outfit one trip up the trail there was a cowboy who had but one tune and but one stanza to that tune. But this he sang over and over. The first two lines of the song were supposed to be addressed to a dance hall "lady." In the second two lines she made reply. After each couplet the cowboy would let out the long wail of the "Texas Lullaby," and he always ended each couplet with a rising whine. His song ran thus:

"I'll buy fer you fine ribbins
Fer to tie in yer hai-r-r."
Who, who, whoo- wh-o-o, wh-o-o, wh-o-o, oo-oo-o-o-o-o-o-o-o.

"I don't want none uv yer fine ribbins
Fer to tie in my hai-r-r."
Who, who, whoo- wh-o-o, wh-o-o, wh-o-o, oo-oo-o-o-o-o-o-o-o.

DON'T GROW WEARY, BOYS

The cowboys parodied many of the popular songs. Some of the parodies are unprintable; others are not. "The Burial of Sir John Moore" and "Over the Wall" were transmuted into obscene imitations. Dr. J. W. Hargus, of Asherton, Texas, who drove cattle to Kansas from Texas in 1866 and then remained in the north to study medicine, remembers a peculiar little song called "Don't Grow Weary, Boys," which was sung to the tune of the then popular "If Ever I Cease to Love." It bears a strong resemblance to "Rye Whiskey." Three stanzas of it ran thus:

1 Ducks in the mill-pond eating up moss,
  Devil on the hillside kicking like a hoss.

  Chorus: *Don't grow weary, boys,*
  Don't grow weary, boys,
  For we're going to the ball.

2 Meat on the goose-foot, marrow in the bone,
  Devil on the hillside—don't you hear him groan?

3 Beefsteak when I'm hungry, liquor when I'm dry,
  Greenbacks when I'm hard up, and religion when I die.

If many of the cowboy songs were so broad as to be unprintable, more of them, and the most representative ones, are altogether printable. I have the testimony of two old punchers of the Cherokee Strip, Frank Orner, of Stillwater, Oklahoma, and Billie Fox, of Marshall, Oklahoma, that "Bonnie Black Bess," that fine old English song about Dick Turpin's beautiful mare, was the favorite song of the cowboys in the Indian Territory. The songs that all the cowboys

158   *Texas and Southwestern Lore*

knew and sang, whatever others some of them might know and sing, were "Sam Bass," "Little Joe the Wrangler," "Oh, Bury Me Not on the Lone Prairie," and other such songs now familiar to the whole country.

ON RED RIVER SHORE

Of course cowboy songs of a kind are still being invented and in some places a few of the old ones are still being sung. But most of the modern cowboy songs lack the narrative element that is characteristic of the older songs. The narrative element or the absence of it in a cowboy song will go a long way towards determining whether it was composed before or after about 1890. The circumstances made use of in the song "On Red River Shore" make me confident that it is at least thirty-five years old. So far as I know it has never before appeared in print. It was given to me in the spring of 1925 by J. E. Wilburn and Joe Parks, two Oklahoma boys living in the Lawton country, just north of Red River. They said that it was a familiar song among old-timers of that country.

1 At the foot of yon mountain,
       Where the fountain doth flow,
   The greatest creation,
       Where the soft wind doth blow,

There lived a fair maiden;
    She's the one I adore,
She's the one I would marry
    On Red River shore.

2 I spoke to her kindly,
    Saying, "Will you marry me?
My fortune's not great"—
    "No matter," said she.
"Your beauty's a plenty,
    You're the one I adore,
You're the one I would marry
    On Red River shore."

3 I asked her old father
    Would he give her to me.
"No, sir, she shan't marry
    No cowboy," said he.
So I jumped on my bronco,
    And away I did ride
And left my true love
    On Red River side.

4 She wrote me a letter
    And she wrote it so kind,
And in this letter
    These words you could find:
"Come back to me, darling,
    You're the one I adore,
You're the one I would marry
    On Red River shore."

5 So I jumped on my bronco,
    And away I did ride
To marry my true love
    On the Red River side.
But her father the secret had learned
    And gathered an army of twenty and four
To fight this young cowboy
    On the Red River shore.

6 I drew my six-shooter,
    Shooting round after round,
Till six men were wounded
    And seven were down.
No use of an army
    Of twenty and four.
I'm bound for my true love
    On Red River shore.

THE 3 L BUCEROS[17]

"The 3 L Buceros" was, according to T. M. Turner, an old-time trail driver, "composed on the Chisholm Trail in 1870 in front of a herd of cattle grazing their way to Abilene, Kansas," at that time the wildest cow town in the West. The cattle were owned by W. G. and P. B. (the "Captain Ples" of the song) Butler, widely known cowmen of Karnes County, Texas. Their brand was 3 L. *Bucero* is one of the various corruptions of *vaquero,* a much more familiar word in Southwest Texas at that time than its now widely misused equivalent, *cowboy.*

1 Come, all you 3 L buceros,
To you I'll sing a little song.
The words are few—it won't take long—
It's about this crowd I compose this song.

2 It was on the eleventh day of March
We crossed the flooding San Antone;
Our hearts were sad, but bear in mind
The ones we love we leave behind.

3 We drive our beeves from sun to sun,
We keep them slowly moving on,
And when night comes we circle 'round
And bed our scalawags[18] on the ground.

4 Sometimes it rains, sometimes it sleets,
Sometimes the wind blows from the east;
The lightnings flash, the thunders roar,
But there's no rest for a bucero.

5 There's Captain Ples, he is our boss;
Sometimes he quirts and spurs his horse;
Sometimes he yells and stamps the ground
Just to see his buceros gin around.

6 There is our cook, Lorenzo Dowe,
He's nearly dead to get a frau.
At Abilene, our journey's end,
He'll rope the girls with the Grecian bend.

---

[17]Taken from **The Pioneer Magazine of Texas,** San Antonio, October 1923, page 7.
[18]Rough, wild steers.

7 Now when we get to Abilene,
   We'll wash up, boys, and dress up clean,
   And when we travel back this road,
   We'll be dressed up in our store-bought jeans.

8 If Captain Ples wants me again
   To drive his beeves to Abilene,
   I'll say, "Dear friend, I'm pretty darn green,
   But I'll drive your beeves to Abilene."

I'D LIKE TO BE IN TEXAS WHEN THEY ROUNDUP IN THE SPRING

Going on two years ago I came across two lines of a new cowboy song in an unpublished play by Mr. Andy Adams—unquestionably the most faithful and effective writer that has ever written of cowboy life. I wrote to him requesting a full version of the song. He sent me two stanzas and the chorus, saying that he had been familiar with it for about fifteen years, having obtained it from W. E. Hawks, an old-time ranchman now living in Burlington, Vermont. However, he added that he himself was responsible for most of the second stanza. A few months after this correspondence I was in Fort Worth attending a meeting of the Texas and Southwestern Cattlemen's Association. There I met Lon Fishback, a young man living in Fort Worth, who, dressed up in a well-creased pair of grey leggins that had never seen sweat or saddle, was singing the song in the lobby of a hotel and selling copies of it with the music. His version comprised two stanzas and chorus, the first stanza being almost identical with the first stanza sent by Mr. Adams. I am printing them and then printing as the third stanza the addition by Mr. Adams. The music is as given by Lon Fishback. Mr. W. W. Burton, already referred to, told me that he heard this song forty or fifty years ago at a celebration in the then young town of Colorado City, Texas.

1 In the lobby of a big hotel, in New York town one day,
  Sat a bunch of fellows telling yarns to pass the time away.
  They told of places where they'd been and different sights they'd seen;
  Some of them praised Chicago town and others New Orleans.
  In a corner in an old armchair sat a man whose hair was grey;
  He listened to them eagerly, to what they had to say.

They asked him where he'd like to be; his clear old voice did ring:
"I'd like to be in Texas when they roundup in the spring.

Chorus: *"I can see the cattle grazing o'er the hills at early morn;*
I can see the camp-fires smoking at the breaking of the dawn;
I can hear the broncos neighing! I can hear the cowboys sing!
I'd like to be in Texas when they roundup in the spring."

2 They all sat still and listened to each word he had to say;
They knew the old man sitting there had once been young and gay.
They asked him for a story of his life upon the plains.
He slowly then removed his hat and quietly thus began:
"I've seen them stampede o'er the hills until you'd think they'd never stop;
I've seen them run for miles and miles until their leader dropped.
I was foreman on a cow ranch—the calling of a king.
I'd like to be in Texas when they roundup in the spring.

3 "There's a grave in sunny Texas where Mollie Deming sleeps,
'Mid a grove of mossy liveoaks that constant vigil keeps.
In my heart's a recollection of a long, long by-gone day
When we rode the range together like truant kids astray.
Her gentle spirit calls me in the watches of the night,
And I hear her laughter freshening the dew of early light.
Yes, I was foreman of that cow ranch—the calling of a king,
And I'd like to be in Texas when they roundup in the spring."

BOW-LEGGED IKE

"Bow-Legged Ike," which follows, is extracted from a book entitled *Cattle Ranch to College* by Russell Doubleday.[19] John Worth, of whom the book is a biography, heard it from a horse wrangler named Curran, in Montana, about 1875. The description of the wrangler belongs with the song.

> Curran was of medium height, stoop-shouldered, and rather bow-legged from long contact with a horse's round body. He was awkward and stiff when afoot, an appearance accentuated by the suit of canvas and leather that he wore. In the saddle he was another being, graceful, supple, strong—seemingly a part of the beast he rode. His skin was tanned and seamed by long years of exposure to the sun. He might be the very hero himself of the song.

---

[19]N. Y., 1899, pp. 227-228.

1   Bowlegged Ike on horseback was sent
    From some place, straight down on this broad continent.

2   His father could ride and his mother could too,
    They straddled the whole way from Kalamazoo.

3   Born on the plains, when he first sniffed the air,
    He cried for to mount on the spavined gray mare.

4   And when he got big and could hang to the horn,
    'Twas the happiest day since the time he was born.

5   He'd stop his horse loping with one good, strong yank,
    He'd rake him on shoulder and rake him on flank.

6   He was only sixteen when he broke "Outlaw Nell,"
    The horse that had sent nigh a score of men to Hell.

7   He climbed to the saddle and there sat still,
    While she bucked him all day with no sign of a spill.

8   Five years later on, a cayuse struck the trail
    Whose record made even old punchers turn pale.

9   He was really a terror, could dance on his ear,
    And sling a man farther than that stump to here.

10 A man heard of Ike, grinned, and bet his whole pile
    His sorrel could shake him before one could smile.

11 So the crowd they came round and they staked all they had,
    While Ike, sorter innocent, said, "Is he **bad**?"

12 And during their laugh—for the sorrel, you see,
    Had eat up two ropes and was trying for me—

13 Ike patted his neck. "Nice pony," says he,
    And was into the saddle as quick as a flea.

14 That sorrel he jumped and he twisted and bucked,
    And the men laughed, expecting that Ike would be chucked.

15 But soon the cayuse was fair swimming in sweat
    While Ike, looking bored, rolled a neat cigarette.

16 And then from range to range he hunted a cayuse
    That could even **in-ter-est** him, but it wasn't any use.

17 So he got quite melancholic, wondering why such an earth,
    Where the horses "had no sperrits," should have given himself birth.

HOME, SWEET HOME

Frequently a cowboy ballad centers around some ranch or brand—pretty good evidence of its local composition. One of the best and most honorably known names in the cattle country is that of Slaughter. On the old New Orleans Trail in East Texas, out in Palo Pinto County, then on the South Plains and elsewhere, the Slaughters have been cattle people in Texas since the days of colonization. I am glad to have "found" a cowboy song that seems to have grown up in a Slaughter outfit. Two versions of it from widely separated sources, neither of which I am now able to name, have come to me. I have amalgamated the two.

1 We were lying on a prairie
    On Slaughter's ranch one night,
With our heads upon our saddles
    While the fire was burning bright.

2 Some were telling stories
    And some were singing songs,
While others were idly smoking
    As the long hours rolled along.

3 At last we fell to talking
    Of distant friends so dear,
When a boy raised up in his saddle
    And brushed away a tear.

4 "Now though it's only a Kansas dugout
    I left behind to roam,
I'd give my saddle and my pony
    To be at home, sweet home."

5 We all asked why he had left his home,
    If it was so dear to him.
He looked the rough crowd over
    And spoke in a voice that was dim.

6 "I fell in love with a neighbor girl,
    Her cheeks were soft and white.
Another feller loved her too;
    It ended in a fight.

7 "This feller his name was Thomas Jones—
    We'd known each other from boys;

> We had rode each other's horses,
> We had shared each other's joys.

8 "Tom was tall and slender,
> His face was young and fair;
> His eyes were the color of heaven,
> He had dark curly hair.

9 "Oh now it makes me· shudder
> To think of that awful night;
> When Tom and I began fighting
> I stuck him with my knife.

10 "I fell right down on my knees
> And tried to stop the blood
> That from his side came spurting
> All in a crimson flood.

11 "And now whenever I sleep,
> I dream I hear him say:
> 'Bob, old boy, you'll be sorry—
> I'll be gone before it's day.'

12 "Now, boys, you can see the reason
> Why I am compelled to roam;
> But I'd give my pony and saddle
> To be at home, sweet home."

THE COWBOY'S HYMN

All the anthologies include "The Cowboy's Hymn," or, as it is sometimes called, "The Cowboy's Dream." N. Howard Thorp, in his *Songs of the Cowboys,* ascribes the authorship to the father of Captain Dan W. Roberts of Texas Ranger fame, and W. J. L. Sullivan, in *Twelve Years in the Saddle,* makes the same ascription. Captain Roberts, who lives in Austin and who will be 86 years old next October (1927), says that he has no knowledge of his father's having written the "hymn," though his father was inclined to be religious and sometimes made up jingles "of a humorous turn." His father was in Texas before the battle of San Jacinto; he died about thirty years ago in Gillespie County.

Whoever the author may have been—and it is a pity that the authorship cannot be established—the version given by

Ballads and Songs of the Frontier Folk   167

W. J. L. Sullivan differs so much from the anthological versions that it is worth including here. The figures of speech in this song have always struck me as highly picturesque and native to the range. That is one reason why the song has been one of the three or four most popular songs peculiar to range people. Thirty-five years ago an old time Tarrant County cowboy, named W. S. James, who had turned preacher, wrote a book to be sold by butcher boys on the trains.[20] At the conclusion of this book he gives one of his sermons preached to cattle people, and the climax of the sermon is "The Cowboy's Hymn." The version that James quotes is almost identical with that quoted by Sullivan.

1 When I think of the last great roundup
    On the eve of eternity's dawn,
I think of the host of cowboys
    That have been with us here and have gone;

2 I think of those big-hearted fellows,
    Who'll divide with you blanket and bread,
With a piece of stray beef well roasted,
    And charge for it never a red.

3 I wonder if any will greet me
    On the sands of that evergreen shore
With a hearty "God bless you, old fellow,"
    That you've met with so often before.

4 And I often look upward and wonder
    If the green fields will seem half so fair,
If any the wrong trail have taken
    And will fail to be over there.

5 The trail that leads down to perdition
    Is paved all the way with good deeds,
But in the great roundup of ages,
    Dear boys, this won't answer your needs.

6 The trail to green pastures, though narrow,
    Leads straight to the home in the sky,
And Jesus will give you your passport
    To the land in the sweet by and by.

---

[20]James, W. S., **Cowboy Life in Texas,** or **Twenty-Seven Years a Maverick,** Chicago, 1893.
    Under the title of "The Stampede on the Turkey Track Range," included in his **Tales from the X-Bar Horse Camp,** Chicago, 1920,

7 Jesus has taken the contract
    To deliver all those who believe,
   At the headquarters ranch of the Father,
    In the great range where none can deceive.

8 The Inspector will stand at the gateway
    Where the herd, one and all, must go by,
   And the roundup by the angels in judgment
    Must pass 'neath His all-searching eye.

9 No maverick or slick[21] will be tallied
    In that great book of life in His home,
   For He knows all the brands and the ear-marks
    That down through all ages have come.

10 But along with the strays and sleepers[22]
    The tailings[23] must turn from the gate;
   No road brand to give them admission,
    But that awful sad cry, "Too late!"

11 But I trust in that last great roundup,
    When the Rider shall cut the big herd,
   That the cowboy will be represented
    In the ear-mark and brand of the Lord,

12 To be shipped to that bright, mystic region,
    Over there in green pastures to lie,
   And be led by the crystal still waters
    To the home in the sweet by and by.

WITH THREE THOUSAND TEXAS STEERS

A representative maker of "popular" cowboy songs is Mr. Ben Thorne, of Hennessey, Oklahoma. More than a half

---

Will C. Barnes has written a very realistic story around the song. He gives the music to the song and includes a stanza about "the cows from the Jimpsons" that I have not seen elsewhere.

[21]**Slick,** another name for maverick; the term is also applied to unbranded horses, whereas **maverick** is generally applied only to unbranded cattle.

[22]A **sleeper** is an animal that has been marked but not branded. Cow thieves used to ride over the range ear-marking various calves. At the spring branding, when the hair is still long, the owners or their legitimate representatives would see the marks and consider the calves branded. Later, when the calves were weaned, the cow thieves would slip in and run their brands on the **sleepers,** changing the ear-mark.

[23]Cut-backs, rejected animals.

century ago he was trailing cattle from Texas to Nebraska; then he "choused dogies" all over the old Cherokee Strip. When I went to see him two years ago he told me a hundred interesting incidents of the old range days and then sang to me some of his songs. "I just kinder make the songs up as I go around," he explained. "I make the tune up at the same time. I've been doing this kind of thing all my life, and now that I can't sing my songs any more to the cattle, I sing them about the days when I worked cattle."

In the fall of 1925 he sang "Three Thousand Texas Steers," which he had recently composed, to the annual "Roundup" of the Cow Punchers' Association of the Cherokee Strip, held at the 101 Ranch.

1 It was down in lower Texas,
    Along the southern line,
  That we bunched three thousand longhorns
    In the spring of '79—

2 Three thousand wild old coast steers
    Road-branded "Lazy L."
  All the way up that trail, boys,
    We shorely did smell hell.

3 Old Spike Jenkins was our ramrod,
    A grand old scout was he.
  When we crossed the River Concho
    The boy he saved was me.

4 Two of us in the whirlpool,
    And one must there go down—
  Never to reach his destination,
    The Ogallala town.

5 We all searched for his body
    The hours twenty-four;
  We found his horse and saddle,
    But we never saw him more.

6 Little Jackie, as we called him,
    Was dear to every one.
  Old Spike he did mourn for him
    As though he were a son.

7 But now those rollicky old beef-steers
    Forced our attention and time,

And they took us on a dirty race
   Before we crossed the line.

8 It was three nights out from the Brazos
   That they made a nasty run—
Every puncher in the saddle
   From dusk till morning's sun.

9 "How many are there missing?"
   We took them through the count.
When we got our final tally
   We were ninety big steers out.

10 So we rode that country over
   For many miles around,
And that night forty big beef-steers
   Walked in on the bed ground.

11 So, "It's throw 'em on the trail, boys!
   Yonder rolls the mighty Red!
Tonight we sleep in the Indian country
   With these three thousand head."

12 Now there is an old-time maxim
   That says: "Jest look before you leap."
It was easier said than done—
   Old Red flowed wide and deep.

13 "I'll bust her on the point," said Spike.
   "Boys, you feed 'em in the swing,
And we'll cross that raging torrent
   As if we were all on wing."

14 With the Concho Twin on the east side point
   And old Spike out on the left,
We brought 'em down to the entering point—
   A hundred steers abreast.

15 They took the water with a rush;
   The current they seemed to ride;
Soon the cattle and the punchers
   Were swimming side by side.

16 Those muddy waters beat around us
   Like boats in a stormy sea,
But we all landed safely
   In the big I. T.[24]

---

[24]Indian Territory.

OLD-TIME COWBOY

It is fitting to round out this collection of frontier songs with the reminiscent "Old-Time Cowboy," which is still sung in some cow camps of West Texas. While it is comparatively recent in composition, it must "be getting up in years." It bears no resemblance to "Old-Time Cowboy" given by Mr. Lomax (page 365). In the manner of hitting off characters it suggests "The Days of Forty-Nine" (Lomax, pp. 9-11). The song was sent to me by Miss Flora Eckert, of Fredericksburg, Texas, who secured it from some cowboys in the Junction country. The meter and the closing lines suggest Tennyson's "May Queen," and it might be better to arrange the verses in long couplets as Tennyson does:

> To lie within the light of God, as I lie upon your breast—
> And the wicked cease from troubling and the weary are at rest.

1 Ofttimes I get to thinking
    Of the changes time has wrought
  Since upon these western ranges
    Long ago I cast my lot.

2 I was young and full of ginger
    In the days of long ago;
  Now my limbs are all rheumatic,
    And my hair is touched with snow.

3 In them days the Sioux Indians
    Were roaming everywhere,
  And it made us feel somewhat uneasy
    For the safety of our hair.

4 Ofttimes I get to comparing
    The cowboys of today
  With those weather-tanned old riders,
    Now respectable and gray.

5 We had no dandy riders,
    With their fancy brown shirts,
  And we had no love-knot ribbons
    Tied by girls upon our quirts.

6 We had no shindigs at the ranch-houses
    As they have them nowadays,

With a lot of purty cowgirls
  To join in our hurrays.

7 We lived in tents and dugouts,
    With our blankets for a bed,
  And our saddles for a pillow
    On which to lay our head.

8 Our rifles and revolvers
    Beside us we would lay,
  To get them *poco pronto*
    If the Indians made a play.

9 Oh, you bet you never saw us,
    And it's true as preachin', boss,
  With a hundred dollar saddle
    And a twenty dollar hoss.

10 Ofttimes I get to thinking
    Of old Bean Stew Maxine,
  And a lot of my old companions
    Now away up in the line.

11 Texas Jack, the holy terror,
    Reckless, brave, and bold,
  Is a high-toned legislator
    Up in Denver, I am told.

12 Lightning Jack, who was always
    A-spoiling for a fight,
  In the church of Kansas City
    Is a bright and shining light.

13 Andy Dozen, who used to maverick,[25]
    I'm surprised to hear,
  Has a government position
    And a fortune every year.

14 Hungry Tom, a fiend for eating,
    Got quite rich, I understand;
  He is now up in Congress,
    Playing style to beat the band.

15 But the news that surprises me
    Is of little Tommie Dell,

---

[25]That is to say, was not always careful as to whose animal he branded.

Who used to swear at heaven
And could crack a joke on hell,

16 The toughest boy on all the ranches,
With our outfit of tough old boys;
He's preaching of the gospel
Up in southern Illinois.

17 Jim's the only old survivor
Of the cowboys of the past
Who has stayed to cowboy custom
And will hold it to the last.

18 Oh, I wonder if they would know me,
Recognize old Shaw,
Who was with them punching cattle
On the Little Arkansas.

19 Oh, I wonder if they will own me,
Though I'm not so stylish dressed,
When the wicked rise from heaven
And the weary are at rest.

THE SOURCE OF "OH, BURY ME NOT ON THE LONE PRAIRIE"

Finally, I wish to say something concerning the best known, perhaps, of all cowboy songs, "Oh, Bury Me Not on the Lone Prairie," called also "The Dying Cowboy." Various editors and compilers have noted its source as being "The Ocean Burial," first printed in 1850. Professor J. H. Cox, in *Folk-Songs of the South* (pages 247-251) has printed a forty-line oral version of it together with fragmentary forms of "The Dying Cowboy," which he calls "The Lone Prairie." A version of the music of "Oh, Bury Me Not on the Lone Prairie," together with 32 lines of verse, was contributed from Uvalde, Texas, to the *Journal of American Folk-Lore,* Vol. 14 (1901), page 186, by Mrs. Annie Laurie Ellis. Then in Volume 25 of the *Journal,* page 278 and following, Phillips Barry, in "Some Aspects of Folk-Song," gave, with six eight-line stanzas, two tunes to "The Ocean Burial," adding an adaptation of it to trapper life. The first of the three stanzas of this adaptation runs thus:

Oh, a trapper lay at the point of death,
And short his bank account, short his breath,
And as he lay this prayer breathed he,
"Oh, bury me not on the lone prairie."

The words of "The Ocean Burial" as given by Mr. Barry, transcribed from *Folk-Songs of the North Atlantic States,* differ only slightly from those here reproduced, but both of the tunes are entirely different from the tune below.

So far as I know, however, the original song has never been printed in full alongside a complete text of the cowboy derivative. Through the courtesy of Mr. William A. Anderson, of Houston, a very helpful member of the Society, the original song is here reproduced, and it is followed immediately by a full version of "Oh, Bury Me Not on the Lone Prairie," contributed by Mr. John R. Craddock.

The song as loaned to the Society by Mr. Anderson is in a miscellaneous collection of privately bound music sheets. The title page of the original of the cowboy song reads as follows (with Spencerian flourishes not possible to print):

NEW AND IMPROVED EDITION
THE
OCEAN BURIAL
A
FAVORITE AND TOUCHING BALLAD

The Music Composed & Affectionately Inscribed to his
SISTER

by

George N. Allen

25 cts nett

BOSTON Published by OLIVER DITSON 115 Washington St.
Entered according to act of Congress AD 1850 by O. Ditson
in Clerks Office of the Dist' Court of Mass.

The "new and improved edition" seems, from the date printed at the bottom of each page of music, to have been issued in 1891. According to Dr. Louise Pound (*American Ballads and Songs*), W. H. Saunders wrote the words of the song and Allen, whose name alone appears on the title page of the edition in hand, the music.

N. Howard Thorp, in his *Songs of the Cowboys*, credits the authorship of the cowboy version to H. Clemons, Deadwood, Dakota, 1872. In my opinion, however, very little credence should be placed in such a statement. Somebody, sometime, began the song, but who or when will probably never be known. Doubtless the song as it has come down was added to by many a lone hand circling a Texas herd under the stars. Fifty years ago and more it was being sung "up the trail," on roundups, around camp fires.

One interesting little story has come to me regarding the origin of the song. I give it as an interesting story—and there is no better reason in the world for giving it—but as nothing else. A former student of mine named Hewitt was a few years ago teaching at Lohn in McCulloch County. While there he heard that out on the prairie about twenty miles from Brady is a solitary grave, unmarked by stone, that folk of the country say is the grave of the cowboy who composed "Oh, Bury Me Not on the Lone Prairie." Hewitt tried to find out the name of the cowboy, but no one could tell him, though he found many people in the country who could sing the song and more who associated it with that grave

> on the lone prairie
> Where the coyote howls and the owl sports free.

The Craddock version of "Oh, Bury Me Not on the Lone Prairie" has two more stanzas than the version given by Mr. Lomax. John Craddock says that it is a composite of all the stanzas he has ever heard. It was sung wherever cowboys drifted or Texas longhorns ranged, and no doubt there are somewhere other stanzas, some of them curiously corrupted. For instance, in a booklet that prints half a dozen stanzas of the song,[26] the following strange phenomenon is recorded:

> Where the dewdrops fall, and the butterfly rests,
> And the wild rose blooms on the sparrow's crest.

---

[26]Sloan, W. W., **Poems and Selections**, San Antonio, Texas, 1911, p. 43.

As I compare the verses of the original song with those of the cowboy imitation, the latter seem to me as much superior to the former as some of the songs retouched by Burns are to their originals. The dying cowboy tells his story straight and his words are picturesque and realistic with actual details of the range over which he had made his last ride. I must confess that hearing this song sung affects me in the same way that the clink of spurs on gravel in the dead of night or the stamping of horses' hoofs and the flop of saddles on horses' backs in the silent, dewy morning before first dawn, have always affected me. If other people are not so affected by it, it is because their imaginations have not been prepared for the suggestions it makes—or because they have not been told often enough by "authorities" that they ought to respond to it in a certain way.

1 "Oh bury me not in the deep, deep sea."
  The words came low and mournfully,
  From the pallid lips of a youth who lay,
  On his cabin couch at the close of day.
  He had wasted and pined 'till o'er his brow,
  The death-shade had slowly passed, and now,
  When the land and his fond loved home were nigh,
  They had gathered around him to see him die.

2 "O bury me not in the deep, deep sea,
  Where the billowy shroud will roll over me,
  Where no light will break through the dark, cold wave,
  And no sun-beam rest upon my grave.
  It matters not, I have oft been told,
  Where the body shall lie when the heart is cold,
  Yet grant ye, O! grant ye, this boon to me,
  O! bury me not in the deep, deep sea.

3 "For in fancy I've listened to the well known words,
  The free, wild winds, and the songs of the birds;
  I have thought of home, of cot and bower,
  And of scenes that I loved in childhood's hour.
  I had ever hoped to be laid when I died,
  In the church-yard there, on the green hillside;
  By the bones of my father's my grave should be.
  O! bury me not in the deep, deep sea.

4 "Let my death slumbers be where a mother's prayer,
  And a sister's tear shall be mingled there;
  O! 'twill be sweet, ere the heart's throb is o'er,
  To know when its fountains shall gush no more,
  That those it so fondly hath yearned for will come
  To plant the first wild flower of spring on my tomb;
  Let me lie where those loved ones will weep over me,
  O! bury me not in the deep, deep sea.

5 "And there is another; her tears would be shed,
  For him who lay far in an ocean bed;
  In hours that it pains me to think of now,
  She hath twined these locks, and hath kissed this brow.
  In the hair she hath wreathed, shall the sea snake hiss?

And the brow she hath pressed, shall the cold wave kiss?
For the sake of that bright one that waiteth for me,
O! bury me not in the deep, deep sea.

6 "She hath been in my dreams"—his voice failed there;
They gave no heed to his dying prayer;
They have lowered him slow o'er the vessel's side,
Above him has closed the dark, cold tide;
Where to dip their light wings the sea-fowls rest,
Where the blue waves dance o'er the ocean's crest;
Where the billows bound, and the winds sport free;
They have buried him there, in the deep, deep sea.

OH, BURY ME NOT ON THE LONE PRAIRIE

"Oh, bury me not on the lone prairie"—
These words came slow and mournfully
From the pallid lips of a youth who lay
On his cold damp bed at the close of day.

He had wasted and pined till on his brow
Death's shades were slowly gathering now;
He thought of his home and his loved ones nigh,
As the cowboys gathered to see him die.

Chorus:[27] *"Oh bury me not on the lone prairie,*
Where the wild coyotes will howl o'er me,
Where the west wind sweeps and the grasses wave,
And sunbeams rest on the prairie grave.

Again he listened to the well-known words,
To the wind's soft sigh and the song of birds;
And he thought of his home and his native bowers,
Where he loved to roam in his childhood hours.

"It matters not, I've oft been told,
Where the body lies when the heart grows cold.
Yet grant, oh, grant, this wish to me,
Oh, bury me not on the lone prairie.

"Then bury me not on the lone prairie
In a narrow grave six foot by three,
Where the buffalo paws on the prairie sea.
Oh, bury me not on the lone prairie.

---
[27] Only those stanzas not ending with the line
        Oh, bury me not on the lone prairie,
are, as a general rule, followed by the chorus.—John R. Craddock.

"I've always wished that when I died
My grave might be on the old hillside.
There let the place of my last rest be.
Oh, bury me not on the lone prairie.

"O'er me then a mother's prayer
And a sister's tears might mingle there,
Where my friends can come and weep o'er me.
Oh, bury me not on the lone prairie.

"Oh, bury me not on the lone prairie.
In a narrow grave just six by three,
Where the buzzard awaits and the wind blows free.
Oh, bury me not on the lone prairie.

"There is another whose tears may shed
For one who lies on a prairie bed.
It pained me then and it pains me now—
She has curled these locks, she has kissed this brow.

"Oh, why did I roam o'er the wild prairie?
She's waiting there at home for me,
But her lovely face ne'er more I'll see.
Oh, bury me not on the lone prairie.

"These locks she has curled, shall the rattlesnake kiss?
This brow she has kissed, shall the cold grave press?
For the sake of her who will weep for me,
Oh, bury me not on the lone prairie.

"Oh, bury me not on the lone prairie,
Where the wild coyotes will howl o'er me,
Where the buzzard beats and the wind goes free.
Oh, bury me not on the lone prairie.

"Oh, bury me not"—and his voice failed there,
But we took no heed of the dying prayer;
In a narrow grave six foot by three,
We buried him there on the lone prairie.

Where the dewdrops glow and the butterflies rest,
And the flowers bloom o'er the prairie's crest;
Where the wild coyote and winds sport free
On a wet saddle blanket lay a cowboy-ee.

"Oh, bury me not on the lone prairie,
Where the wild coyotes will howl o'er me,

Where the rattlesnakes hiss and the crow flies free,
Oh, bury me not on the lone prairie."

Oh, we buried him there on the lone prairie,
Where the wild rose blooms and the wind blows free;
Oh, his young face ne'er more to see,
For we buried him there on the wild prairie.

Yes, we buried him there on the lone prairie,
Where the owl all night hoots mournfully,
And the buzzard beats and the wind blows free
O'er his lonely grave on the lone prairie.

May the light-winged butterfly pause to rest
O'er him who sleeps on the prairie's crest;
May the Texas rose in the breezes wave
O'er him who sleeps in the prairie grave.

And the cowboys now as they roam the plain—
For they marked the spot where his bones are lain—
Fling a handful of roses o'er his grave,
With a prayer to God his soul to save.

"Oh, bury me not on the lone prairie,
Where the wolves can howl and growl o'er me.
Fling a handful of roses o'er my grave
With a prayer to Him who my soul will save."

SONGS THE COWBOYS SING

By John R. Craddock

These songs were for the most part obtained at the foot of the Plains, in Dickens County, Texas, where I was reared. They are songs that furnished entertainment to the people of that country before the phonograph and the radio came in; in those days the people used to meet for "singings," at which they would both sing and dance. They are the songs also that cowboys of the Swenson, Matador, and other ranches of the region used to sing—and sometimes yet sing—to pass the time along in camp or on the range or in entertaining each other. Like the old darkey songs, they are often hard to set to music. The cowboys and cow people in general sang them with a nasal twang that easily lengthened out short beats and as easily shortened down extra syllables. Nearly all regular cowboys still sing more or less, and wherever a few of them gather together one or two can be found that are noted for their memory and their ability to carry tunes. These troubadours of the range often improvise songs. The most popular songs, like "Utah Carl," "The Z Bar Dun," "Little Joe the Wrangler," etc., have been so often printed, in Lomax's *Cowboy Songs* and in other places, that they are not here reproduced.

THREE GAY PUNCHERS

The first song is still popular among punchers throughout Dickens, Kent, and Stonewall counties. From the brands used, I judge that the originators of the ballad worked from New Mexico back to the Three A's of Stonewall County; however, I have not been able to trail down the improviser of the lines.

> We are three gay punchers from Yellowstone Flat;
> We wear the high heels, also the white hat.
> We are noted in Texas and on the Staked Plains,
> And also in Montana, on the Yellowstone Range.

We ride the Frazier saddles,[1] our chaps are the best,
Our boots, spurs, and bits can't be beat in the West.
We ride to the wagon, we ride in pursuit,
We hear the cook holler, "Chuck-away, grab-a-root."

We make a bed down on the ground frozen hard,
For, boys, we'll soon be called to our guard.
We ride up the cow trail, take down the rawhide;
There is never a bronco but what we will ride.

We rope 'em, ride, brand 'em, as in the days of old,
And on the left shoulder we stamp the Shoe Sole.[2]
We work the J Q, also the Bar S,
But as for the Three A's [A A A] we like 'em the best.

We steal out their horses, to the dances we go,
And if we get boozy, we pull off a show.
It's now for cowpunching I have no more use,
I'll hang up my saddle and coil up my noose.

I am tired of cowpunching, the work is so rough;
I'll do like my pardner, go east and play tough.
For saddle and bridle I have no more use;
I'll ride back to Three A's and turn Grey Walt a-loose.

So hang saddle and bridle where they will keep dry,
For, boys, we will need 'em in the sweet by and by.

THE WILD BOY

"The Wild Boy,"[3] like "Three Gay Punchers," is common to New Mexico and West Texas. It seems to have originated in the vicinity of the Rocky Mountains. All singers of the ballad stick closely to the words as given.

> My parents reared me ten-der-lee,
> They had no child but me,
> But I was bent on rambling—
> With them I couldn't agree.

---

[1] A brand of saddles manufactured at Pueblo, Colorado, still well-known all over the cattle world.

[2] A ranch brand made in the form of a half-sole.

[3] The first stanza of this song is almost identical with the first two lines of "My Parents Reared Me Tenderly" (Cox, No. 85, p. 300) and with the first two lines of the second stanza of "Lackey Bill" (Lomax, p. 83), but the narrative is entirely different.—Editor.

I started up the cow trail
    To see some Western land.
I met up with a wild bunch,
    And likewise killed a man.

I stole a many a fat horse,
    Stole him from the poor,
And over the Rocky Mountains
    I made his iron hoofs roar.

One morning, one morning,
    I think it was in May,
The sheriff rode up to me,
    Says, "I'm a-looking for you today."

He took me down to the new jail,
    And there I walked in.
My parents all deserted me,
    As likewise did my kin.

Except one old rich uncle,
    Far out in the West;
A-hearing of my trouble,
    They say he could not rest.

He went my bail at the Ute jail,
    He paid my debts by scores.
It's once I've been a wild boy,
    I won't be any more.

There's Agnes and there's Mabel,
    There's Mary likewise;
My deeds and desperation
    Brought tears into their eyes.

I've stolen many a fat horse,
    Stolen him from the poor.
It's once I've been a wild boy,
    I won't be any more.

THE YOUNG COMPANIONS

For "the Young Companions"[4] I am indebted to "Buddie" Grubbs, of the Red Mud community; however, the ballad is common both east and west of the New Mexico line. The

---

[4] An interesting variant to Lomax's "Young Companions," page 81, and to me preferable.—Editor.

doleful tune to which it is sung is well fitted to the downfall of the hero.

Come, all my young companions, wherever you may be,
And I'll tell you all a story,—to shun bad compan-ee.
My home's in Arizona, among those desert hills;
My childhood and my fireside are in my memory still.

I had a darling old mother, she always prayed for me;
The very last words she uttered were a prayer to God for me.
Says, "Oh, keep my boy from evil. May God direct his ways;
My blessings are upon you throughout your manhood days."

Well, I bid adieu to loved ones, to kind friends bid farewell,
I landed in Chicago—the very depths of hell.
It was there I took to drinking, I sinned both night and day,
And ever in my bosom those feeble words would say:

"God, keep my boy from evil. May God direct his ways;
My blessings are upon you throughout your manhood days."
Well, I courted a fair young damsel; her name I will not tell,
For why should I disgrace her since I am doomed for hell?

It was on a moonlit evening, the stars were shining bright,
When I drew my ugly dagger and bade her spirit take flight.
The justice overtook me, and, as well you now may see,
My soul is doomed forever, throughout eter-ni-tee.

And ever in my bosom, those dying words do say,
"God, keep my boy from evil throughout his manhood's day."
I am standing on the scaffold, my moments are not long;
You may forget this singer, but don't forget this song.

TONIGHT MY HEART'S IN TEXAS

A favorite song with a girl in our country used to be "Tonight My Heart's in Texas," but I secured my version from a fiddler at a cowboy dance on Red Mud three or four years ago.

In the Lone Star State of Texas
 By the silvery Rio Grande,
A couple strolled one evening,
 Lingering hand in hand.

'Twas a ranchman's pretty daughter
 And the lad she loved so dear;

On the morrow they must part
    For many and many a year.

To Europe she was going
    To become a lady grand,
And she went away next morning
    From the silvery Rio Grande.

Her father hoped some earl
    Or else a count she'd wed,
But her heart was true to Jack.
    One day a letter came and thus it read:

Chorus: Tonight my heart's in Texas
             Though I'm far across the sea,
         For the band is playing Dixie
             And in Dixie I long to be.
         Dad says some earl I'll marry,
             But you have my heart and hand.
         Tonight my heart's in Texas
             By the silvery Rio Grande.

At a stately hall in England
    Stood a Texas lass one night.
The scene was one of splendor
    And the lamps were dazzling bright.

An earl knelt there before her,
    Begging her to take his hand;
But her thoughts were far away
    By the silvery Rio Grande.

"I can't say, 'Yes,'" she answered.
    "Your title I cannot take.
There's a lad away in Texas—
    They call him Texas Jack.

"Long ago I promised
    That Texas lad to wed.
'Twas only yesterday I wrote,
    And this the letter said:— *Chorus.*

Old Tom Harkey, "a stove-up cowpuncher," used to play the fiddle and sing in the wagon yard at Spur. One evening I heard him sing this snatch[5] of song:

---

[5]See Lomax, "The Jolly Cowboy," 284; Thorp, 86. Charles A. Siringo, **Riata and Spurs,** Boston, 1927, pp. 242-243, has a very interesting comment on the song.—Editor.

My lover is a cowboy;
    He's honest, kind, and true.
He rides a Spanish pony,
    And he totes tobacco to-o.

And when he comes to see me,
    He rides a many a mile
Over the lonely prairie
    To greet me with a smile.

I do not know when or where I learned the remaining songs. I've heard them all my life. The first is a kind of chant well punctuated with yells. To understand it you will have to understand the cowboy's innocent way of dramatizing himself. It is not at all expressive of the bad man. Probably it originated as a satire on the would-be bad man.

O I'm wild and wooly
    And full of fleas.
Ain't never been curried
    Below the knees.

I'm a wild she wolf
    From Bitter Creek,
And it's my night
    to ho-o-o-wl.

The next song[6] sounds like a garbled version of "Sing Polly Wolly Doodle All Day."

Oh, I came to the river
    And I couldn't get across;
I paid five dollars
    For an old grey horse.

I put him in the river
    And he couldn't swim;
So I gave him hell
    With a hick'ry limb.

I spurred him in the shoulder,
    I spurred him in the flank,

---

[6]Compare with "The Old Gray Horse," Perrow, "Songs and Rhymes from the South," JAFL, 26, 124.—Editor.

> And you oughter seen the sucker fish,
>   A-swimming for the bank.

The next two stanzas might be a part of the three preceding, for all the sense they make, but I've always heard them separately.

> O I just kept a-running
>   Till I got tired,
> And then I went
>   To the wagon yard.
>
> I stuck my head
>   In a woodpecker hole,
> And I couldn't get it out
>   To save my soul.

The last snatch is on the theme that all cowboys—all "boys," let us say—like to dwell on: the theme of love and a girl.

> I got a little girl,
> A purty little girl.
> She won't go back on me.
>
> She can dance and sing
> And cut the pigeon wing,
> But she won't go back on me.

One spring a few years ago, while we were working cattle on our ranch, I made up a song that I called "The Wandering Cowboy" and imparted it to the cow crowd. Six months later in a camp on the S M S Ranch, I heard a cowboy named Floyd Cain singing it; I am told that it is still sung in the S M S country.

THE WANDERING COWBOY

> I am a wandering cowboy,
>   From ranch to ranch I roam;
> At every ranch when welcome,
>   I make myself at home.
>
> Two years I worked for the Double L,
>   And one for the O Bar O;

Then drifted west from Texas,
   To the plains of Mexico.

There I met up with a rancher
   Who was looking for a hand;
So when springtime greened the valleys,
   I was burning the Bar S brand.

I worked on through the summer;
   Then early in the fall,
Over the distant ranges,
   There came the old, old call.

So I drifted to Arizona,
   To work for Uncle Bob,
A-tailing up the weak ones
   On a winter feeding job.

But the ranch camp grew too lonely,
   With never rest or change;
So I saddled up one morning
   And struck for a distant range.

One night in wild Wyoming,
   When the stars hung bright and low,
I lay in my tarp a dreaming
   Of the far off home ranch-o,

Where the cottonwood leaves are whispering,
   In the evening soft and low;
'Tis there my heart's a-turning,
   And homeward I must go.

It is now I'm tired of rambling.
   No longer will I roam
When my pony I've unsaddled
   In the old corral at home.

SONGS OF THE OPEN RANGE

By INA SIRES

(EDITOR'S NOTE.—It was not until preparations for this issue of the Publications had been almost completed that I learned of the work being done by Miss Sires. Realizing the interest that a large number of the Society's membership would have in her new book of cowboy songs, I wrote to Miss Sires asking for a brief statement of her work and a sample of her material. She very accomodatingly responded as follows. For further information concerning her, see "Contributors," toward the end of the volume.)

The accurate knowledge of any primitive people is found in their songs, for these express what is nearest the heart of the people. In accordance with this universal principle, the American cowboy lives in ballads that speak the heart of the Old West—the West of yesterday, boisterous, reckless, romantic, and somehow tragic; a land of promise and adventure, of freedom and open skies, but sometimes a land of loneliness and failure.

For the last five years I have been making a collection of cowboy songs—both words and melodies—thinking that these songs would be of value in furnishing future generations with a truer conception than the prevailing one of what the cowboy really was. Making this collection has been a slow process, for the songs are scattered all over those states west of the Mississippi where here and there remains an isolated relic of a past institution.

My work has been lightened by the collections of Mr. N. Howard Thorp and Mr. John A. Lomax. The collection of the latter contains a few melodies, but these deserve a wider recognition apart from the words of the songs, for they belong distinctly to the cowboys. In them is the greyness of the prairies, the mournful minor note of a Texas norther, and a rhythm that fits into the gait of the cowboy's pony. The songs and their tunes were born of the saddle. Although the origin of some of the cowboy songs may be traced back to ballads of other nations, and the tunes are borrowed ones, there are songs, both words and melodies, that even the most discriminating critic must admit are indigenous to American soil.

I have several ballads that so far as I know have not appeared in print, but my chief work has been to preserve the melodies. I have secured these directly from the cowboys, by visiting ranches, attending dances, and riding on roundups in the western states where people still dance all night to the tune of the fiddle. One summer I taught on a ranch in Montana, out twenty-five miles from Malta. The school children and their mothers were especially helpful in securing melodies. The first year after I graduated from Baylor University I taught in Arizona. I spent week-ends on ranches and after school closed stayed and rode on the spring roundup. I spent two years in Kansas City teaching in the city schools, getting my material in shape for publication. Friends at the stock yards helped me get songs from any one who chanced in that knew melodies I did not have. I now have seventy-three distinct melodies, and there are any number of variations. Some twenty-five or thirty of what, in my judgment, are the best and most characteristic songs both as to words and melodies will appear in my book, *Songs of the Open Range*.

The folk songs of other nations are more varied and polished than are these of the cowboys. In other countries the ballads and folk songs are the result of centuries of growth; in America the cowboy came and went in less than a century. Nevertheless, despite imperfect meter and other crudities, many of the songs are beautiful and ring with the sincerity of the cowboy's country.

THE GRASS OF UNCLE SAM

One of the most characteristic ballads that I have is "The Grass of Uncle Sam."[1] Here, true to form, the stranger gets the bucking horse.

---

[1] "The Grass of Uncle Sam," with music and five stanzas of eight lines each, is to be found in **Cattle Ranch to College**, by Russell Doubleday (Grosset and Dunlap, New York, 1899, pp. 269-271). The opening stanza runs thus:

> Now, people of the Eastern towns,
>   It's little that you know
> About the Western prairies
>   Where the beef you eat does grow;
> Where the horses they run wild
>   With the mountain sheep and ram;
> And the cowboy sleeps contented
>   On the grass of Uncle Sam.—Editor.

We are out to the roundup to brand the sucking calves;
The stranger gets the bucking horse and how we all laugh.
He throws his arms into the sky, his legs get in a jam,
And he turns a flying somersault on the grass of Uncle Sam.

The angry bull takes after him with blood in both his eyes.
We run, but when his back is turned, he gets a big surprise;
Our ropes jerk out his feet behind and down he goes *kerslam*,
And we drag the fighting out of him, on the grass of Uncle Sam.

Sometimes the horse thief comes around to steal our horses true;
We are always looking out for him and sometimes get him too.
We ask him if he is ready, and when he says, "I am,"
The bottom of his feet they itch, for the grass of Uncle Sam.

And, when pay day comes around, to town we go for fun;
The dollars we have hoarded up are blowed in every one.
Then broke we hit the trail for camp, but we don't care a damn,
For wages are good when the grass is good, the grass of Uncle Sam.

PRETTY LITTLE MAIDEN

I have found a few cowboy love songs that, I think, have not appeared in print. "Pretty Little Maiden,"[2] found in Arizona, expresses the cowboy's idea of what he admires in a sweetheart.

> Pretty little maiden out in the garden,
>   Cowboy up by her side did ride,
> Saying, "Pretty little maid, won't you marry me?
>   Oh, come, little one, and be my bride."
>
> Oh, no, oh, no," this maiden answered.
>   "How can you impose on a girl like me?

---

[2]This song has had a wide vogue in America as well as in England, where it originated as "The Sailor's Return." The details changed to make the cowboy fit into the sailor's part are hardly so vital as those wrought on "The Ocean Burial," for a consideration of which see **ante,** p. 194 ff. Cox, **Folk-Songs of the South,** give a full discussion of "Pretty Little Maiden" and two versions, under the title of "A Pretty Fair Maiden," p. 316ff.—Editor.

For I have a sweetheart among the cowboys,
  Though he's been gone for many a day."

"Perhaps your sweetheart has been drowned,
  Or perhaps by some Indian killed,
Or perhaps he's found and married another girl,
  And never will return to you again."

"Well, if my sweetheart has been drowned,
  Or if by an Indian slain,
Or if he has found and married another girl,
  I'll love the girl that married him."

He pulled his hands from out his pocket;
  His fingers they were soft and white,
And on one finger shone a ring,
  And at his feet this maid did fall.

He picked her up, held her to his bosom,
  He gave her kisses one, two, three.
He picked her up, held her to his bosom,
  Saying, "Pretty little girl, will you marry me?"

"Oh, yes, oh, yes," this maiden answered,
  "Though you have been gone for many a day;
If you had been gone for a thousand ages,
  No other man could have married me."

THE TEXAS COWBOY[1]

Contributed by ARBIE MOORE

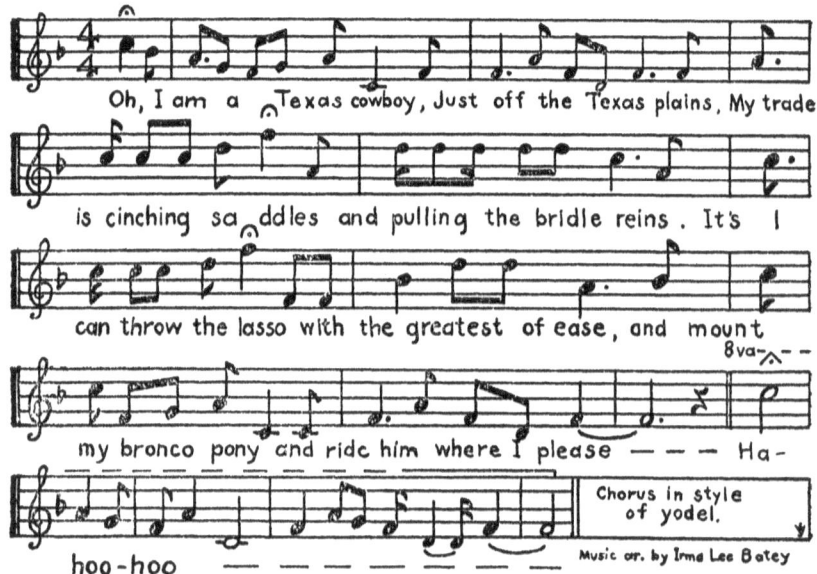

O, I am a Texas cowboy,
　Just off the Texas Plains;
My trade is cinching saddles,
　And pulling bridle reins.
It's I can throw the lasso
　With the greatest of ease,
And mount my bronco pony,
　And ride him when I please.
　　Ho-hoo-hoo-hoo-hoo.

---

[1]Reprinted by permission of Mr. Victor J. Smith, Curator of the West Texas Historical and Scientific Society, from **Publications,** No. I, December, 1926, of the West Texas Historical and Scientific Society, page 36. Two or three lines of the song seem to be borrowed from "The Lone Star Trail" (Lomax, 310). In the **Journal of American Folk-Lore** for 1913 Vol. 26, p. 188, G. F. Will, "Four Cowboy Songs," reports, without music, a full version of "The Texas Cowboy" as coming from Bismarck, North Dakota.—Editor.

The Texas Cowboy

O, it's on the rolling prairie,
  Free from toil and strife,
Behind a bunch of longhorns,
  I'll journey all my life.
It's if I had a little stake, boys,
  It's married I would be,
For the dearest girl in all the world
  Has fell in love with me.
    Ho-hoo-hoo-hoo-hoo.

O, it's on the rolling prairies,
  Where the dusty billows rise,
Fifty miles from water
  And the grass a-scorching dry,
The boss is mad and ringy,
  Just as plain as you can see.
I am bound to quit the trail, boys,
  And an honest farmer be.
    Ho-hoo-hoo-hoo-hoo.

O, it's when there comes a rain, boys,
  One of the general kind,
The lake all full of water,
  And the grass a-waving fine,
The boss'll shed his frown, boys,
  And fall in smiles, you see.
I am bound to quit the homestead,
  And a roving cowboy be.
    Ho-hoo-hoo-hoo-hoo.

O, it's when we get them bedded,
  You'll think it's for the night,
Some horse'll shake a saddle
  And give the herd a fright;
They'll rise to their feet,
  And then they'll dash away,
And in less than half a moment's time
  You'll hear some cowboy say,
    Ho-hoo-hoo-hoo-hoo.

O, it's when you get them bedded,
  You'll feel most forlorn,
A cloud in the west a-risin',
  Fire playin' on their horns.
The boss'll say, "Stay with 'em boys,
  Your pay you'll get in gold."
I am bound to follow the F A steers
  Until I am too old.
    Ho-hoo-hoo-hoo-hoo.

COWBOY SONGS AGAIN

By J. Evetts Haley

For a long time I had hoped to meet an authority on folklore who had never read a book upon the subject. In the Midland country a few years ago, when I was eating sourdough biscuits from Tom Grammar's skillets at the back end of a chuck wagon and sleeping six hours a night on the grama grass, my vaulting ambition other than being able to "flank" more calves than any cowpuncher in the outfit was to become well-versed in cowboy ballads. That desire was all the more remarkable when I recall that Professor Lackey's attempts to make me carry a tune always ended in dismal failure. But the desire persisted. Hence it was that I forgot to eat when I met that human anthology of western ballads—James W. Mullens. All his knowledge of the field had been gained from oral sources. Although I traveled more than five thousand miles across the plains and over the hills of West Texas and New Mexico before I found him, the experience was worth the travel.

Curiosity to know more of the history of the Southwest took me to Roswell, N. M. There upon the banks of the Rio Hondo I listened to the songs of the old frontier, sung by a man who had learned them in the cow camps of the Southwest and on night herd along the Goodnight-Loving Trail. Any man who has never found occasion to memorize a song from a printed collection, but can sing a hundred or more from memory will always be a wonder to me. "Honey Jim" Mullens will long have my gratitude for the songs he sang to me upon that crisp January night.

Even though his tunes were limited, his repertoire of ballads was marvelous. How the blood quickened as he sang in the night time "The Buffalo Hunters' Song," "Quantrell's Call," "Adieu to Old El-lum," and "The Lone Star Trail"! For variety he sang in Spanish "Como Los Rayos del Sol," and tried his voice upon a few sailor songs. He knew the history of many of these ballads for the last fifty years.

Not often can a ballad be traced to its source. When it can be, the interest attached to its origin is increased many fold through the light it may throw on the origin of ballads generally.

THE JUICE OF THE FORBIDDEN FRUIT

According to Mullens, at least one ballad was in the making in the Davis Mountains in 1883. There were but a few ranches in the region at that time. Sergeant Percival, head tailor in the Tenth Cavalry, had broken over the measured limitations of his calling and was in the cattle business near the mouth of Limpia Canyon. The cowboys he employed to run the "Circle An'" ranch were paid $30 a month to ride the range—not to compose ballads. Towns were widely scattered, and civilizing influences were at a premium; but by rare good fortune some of the cowboys of the region had the cultural advantage of hearing a vaudeville ditty in the fall. All but the "swing" and theme of it were forgotten, however, before winter drove the boys into the closer seclusion of their camps.

The long winter evenings passed slowly, and cowboys from a neighboring outfit would sometimes spend the night at the "Circle An'" camp. Among those who gathered there one night was Billie Pascal, who recalled the popular ditty and prepared to write it down. There had been but four or five lines in the original, but since no two cowpunchers agreed as to what they were, each wrote his version; the results revealed so much variation that five of the stanzas were selected, emended, and combined into a song. Tom Morgan, Jim Jones, Charlie Hill, Tom Storey, Beulah Davenport, "Honey Jim" Mullens, and "Hard Tack," a Texas Ranger, collaborated to produce the ballad.

The different versions are not so much an indictment of the memory of the cowboy as they are an index of his productive imagination and the potency of the "juice of the forbidden fruit."

> Along about the time old Eve she did climb
>   That apple tree, first she ever saw,
> It made her heart sore when she threw down the core
>   For poor old Adam to chaw.

Then Eve, without Adam or evil intention,
　　Got up an invention so cute;
From an old-fashioned mill, soon managed to distill
　　The juice of the forbidden fruit.

And, ever since then, all manner of men,
　　The crippled, the blind, and the mute,
The lawyers and clerks, politicians and Turks,
　　Drink the juice of the forbidden fruit.
There's Heny Ward Beecher and our Sunday School teacher,
　　Drink what they call "sassafras root,"
But you bet all the same, if it had its right name,
　　It's the juice of the forbidden fruit.

There's Oscar Wilde, takes his with a smile,
　　As he admits, while he smokes his cheroot;
Mrs. Langtry, they say, was carried astray
　　By drinking the juice of the fruit.
There's Cleveland and Blaine, their glasses will drain,
　　When engaged in a political dispute;
Ben Butler, they say, when elected so gay,
　　Drank the juice of the forbidden fruit.

And there is Frank James, who's now out on bail,
　　Governor Crittenden's orders to suit;
There's Charles and Bob Ford, drank out of a gourd
　　The juice of the forbidden fruit.
There's my girl, Sarah Ann, she will down the can,
　　Whenever we have a dispute;
Right then we make up and together we sup
　　The juice of the forbidden fruit.

The clerks and the mayor they all have their shares;
　　The police up a dark alley will scoot,
And whistle a short tune at the door of some saloon
　　For the juice of the forbidden fruit.
There's the cowboy so gay, you often hear say,
　　Totes a "cutter" and Winchester to boot;
He'll raise hell all around and take in a small town,
　　When he's full of the juice of this fruit.

　　This is an unusual ballad to have originated in a cow camp. It deals with men and events foreign to cowboy life that become all the more interesting for being balladized in a remote cow camp.
　　Of course many songs sprang up around the trail life of the cowboy. "The Lone Star Trail" was one of the favorites,

but perhaps none equalled in popularity "The Old Chisholm Trail." One reason for its wide appeal was the ease with which parodies might be made upon it and additional verses added to suit the fancy of the singer, so that by the time the herd reached Kansas or the northern ranges the cowboy might be singing of his own experiences rather than those of the original author.[1]

THE HILLS OF MEXICO

Among the songs which found life along the Goodnight-Loving Trail worthy of perpetuation is one called "The Hills of Mexico." No mention of the name of the trail is made in the song but there are two geographical references which make the route certain. The driver started his herd from Fort Griffin, and the cowboy tells of his troubles upon Boggy Creek, more generally known as the Delaware, which flows into the Pecos in southern New Mexico. And it was while driving over this Goodnight-Loving Trail with a cowman from Mason County, in the early eighties, that James Mullens learned the ballad. It must be patterned after the song of "The Buffalo Skinners" (Lomax, 158-161), which begins by telling what "happened in Jacksboro in the spring of seventy-three." Various lines in one ballad are identical with lines in the other, and in each the unjust employer comes to a just end. A fragmentary form of "The Hills of Mexico" appears under the title of "Boggus Creek" in "Miscellany of Texas Folk-Lore," by W. P. Webb, *Publications* Number II of the Texas Folk-Lore Society, 1923.

> I found myself in Griffin in the spring of '83,
> When a noted cow driver one morning came to me.
> Says: "How do you do, young fellow? Say, how'd you like to go
> And spend one summer pleasantly out in New Mexico?"
>
> I being out of employment, to the driver thus did say:
> "A-going out in New Mexico, depends upon the pay.
> If you pay to me good wages, transportation to and fro,
> I believe I'll go along with you out in New Mexico."
>
> "Of course I'll pay good wages, and transportation, too,
> Provided that you stay with me the summer season through.

---

[1] See Lomax, J. A., **Cowboy Songs and other Frontier Ballads**, 58, 310.

> But if you do get homesick, and want to Griffin go,
> I will even loan you a horse to ride from the hills of Mexico."
>
> With all this flattering talk he enlisted quite a train,
> Some ten or twelve in number, strong, able-bodied men.
> Our trip was quite a pleasant one, over the road we had to go,
> Until we reached old Boggy Creek out in New Mexico.
>
> Right there our pleasures ended—our troubles then begun;
> The first hailstorm that came on us, Christ, how those cattle run!
> In running through thorns and stickers we had but little show,
> And the Indians watched to pick us off the hills of Mexico.
>
> The summer season ended, the driver could not pay.
> The outfit was so extravagant he was in debt today.
> That's bankrupt law among the cowboys. Christ, this will never do.
> That's why we left his bones to bleach out in New Mexico.
>
> So, now, we'll cross old Boggy Creek and homeward we are bound;
> No more in this cursed country will ever we be found.
> Go home to our wives and sweethearts—tell others not to go
> To that God-forsaken country they call New Mexico.

The most popular ballads were and are sung with many variations. These have come about, one may safely assume, from three principal causes: the changes incident to their oral transmission, additions made to supply the gaps left by forgotten portions, and those changes designedly made to suit the fancy or taste of the singer. However they may have come about, the variations of "The Buffalo Hunters' Song" are worthy of notice.

THE BUFFALO HUNTERS' SONG

This ballad was current upon the buffalo range to the west of Fort Griffin in 1875. It is the more interesting because the tune to which it was sung was adapted to the ballad of "Sam Bass."[2] It was sung not only by hunters and cowboys, but by freighters from Fort Worth to the little frontier town of Griffin (near the site of Albany) long before Bass made Round Rock famous. While most of the details of the version here given are the same as those given by Mr. Lomax,[3] the divergencies seem sufficient for printing it.

---

[2]James W. Mullens to J. E. H., Jan. 14, 1927.
[3]Lomax, **Cowboy Songs,** 185.

Come, all you girls of fashion, to you these lines I'll write,
 I'm going out on the buffalo range, on which I take delight,
I'm going out on the buffalo range, as we poor hunters do—
 Those old, sore-footed fellows can stay at home with you.

Our game is the antelope, the buffalo, and deer,
 That roam these wide prairies without the least of fear,
And when we come upon them our guns have effects—
 They raise their tails, punch the breeze, and almost break their necks.

Our fires are made of buffalo chips, our beds are on the ground,
 Our houses are of buffalo robes, we build 'em tall and round;
Our furniture's the camp kettle, the coffee pot, and pan,
 Our chuck is bread and buffalo meat, well mingled with the sand.

The buffalo bull's a noble beast, most noble of his band,
 And sometimes he refuses to throw us up his hand;
His shaggy mane pitched forward, his head he raises high,
 As if to say, "Old Hunter, look out for your eye."

Around him with Sharps rifles and the needle gun so true,
 Which causes him to bite the dust, we send our bullets through.
We rob him of his robe and think it is no harm—
 They buy us chuck and clothing, to keep our bodies warm.

Our neighbors are the Comanches, likewise the Kickapoo,[4]
 Their mode of emigration is riding ponies, too,
And if they were to emigrate I'm sure I wouldn't care—
 'Cause I dont' like the way they've got of raising hunters' hair.

BACKWARD, TURN BACKWARD

Many frontier ballads are merely parodies upon familiar songs or poems. A ballad that I happened upon in the summer of 1920 will illustrate. Flint Cosby and I were working together on the old Long S Ranch north of Big Spring. We were on the trail with a herd of cattle, and Flint and I were bringing up the "drags." Flint was a good cowhand and, characteristically, a proportionately poor singer; but no minstrel of the ranges ever had a more appreciative audience than Flint had that day.

---

[4]"The northern hunters substituted Cheyenne and Arapahoe."—Mullens.

Three years ago I read the ballad at the annual banquet of the Panhandle-Plains Historical Society at Canyon. It was printed in a newspaper and its authorship erroneously accredited to me.[5] I do not know who the author is, but I have found the song a favorite wherever it has been heard, especially among the old time cowboys of the Plains country. Its reminiscent spirit appeals to those who have lived in the cow country and who are nearing "the end of the trail." It is a parody on "Rock Me to Sleep," by Elizabeth Akers Allen.

>Backward, turn backward, oh time on your wheels,
>Airplanes, wagons, and automobiles.
>Dress me once more in a sombrero that flaps,
>Spurs, a flannel shirt, boots, slicker, and chaps.
>Give me a six-shooter or two in my hand,
>And show me a steer to rope and brand.
>Out where the sage brush is dusty and gray,
>Make me a cowboy again for a day.
>
>Give me a bronc that knows how to dance,
>Buckskin of color and wicked of glance,
>New to the feeling of bridle and bits;
>Give me a quirt that will sting where it hits,
>Strap on poncho behind in roll,
>And pass me the lariat, so dear to my soul;
>Then over the trail let me lope far away. .
>Make me a cowboy again for a day.
>
>Thunder of hoofs over range as we ride,
>Hissing of iron and smoking of hide,
>Bellow of cattle and snort of cayuse,
>Longhorns from Texas as wild as the deuce;
>Midnight stampedes and milling of herds,
>Yells from the cowmen, too angry for words;
>Right in the midst of it all I would stay.
>Make me a cowboy again for a day.
>
>Under the star-studded canopy vast,
>Camp-fire, coffee, and comfort at last;
>Tales of the ranchmen and rustlers retold
>Over the pipes as the embers grow cold;
>These are the tunes that old memories play.
>Make me a cowboy again for a day.

---

[5]It was printed in **The Prairie,** Canyon, Texas, and has since been copied by many papers of the Southwest.

THE BALLAD OF "DAVY CROCKETT"

Contributed by Julia Beazley

(NOTE.—"Davy Crockett" is an interesting example of a folk-lorized negro minstrel song. "Pompey Smash" was a popular song on the minstrel stage before the middle of the nineteenth century. It is included in *The Negro Singer's Own Book* (Philadelphia, n. d.) and in *Lloyd's Ethiopian Song Book* (London, 1847). It has been twice before reported as a transformed folk song: in H. M. Belden's *A Partial List of Song Ballads and other Popular Poetry Known in Missouri,* No. 59; and in J. H. Cox's *Folk-Songs of the South,* No. 177. But neither of these versions is as complete as the one reported here by Miss Beazley, nor has any folk tune, so far as I know, been heretofore recorded.—L. W. Payne, Jr.)

Nearly a generation ago, before the advent of motor cars and motor boats, I heard some sailors on the Texas coast singing "Davy Crockett." They were old time sailor men, and the ruggedness of the meter of the song in nowise hampered their gusto in singing it. For the music of the song I am indebted to Mrs. Tom C. Rowe, of Houston, who transcribed it, and to Mrs. Melton, who sang it. The words as sung by Mrs. Melton are slightly different from those originally learned by me, but the meter is the same.

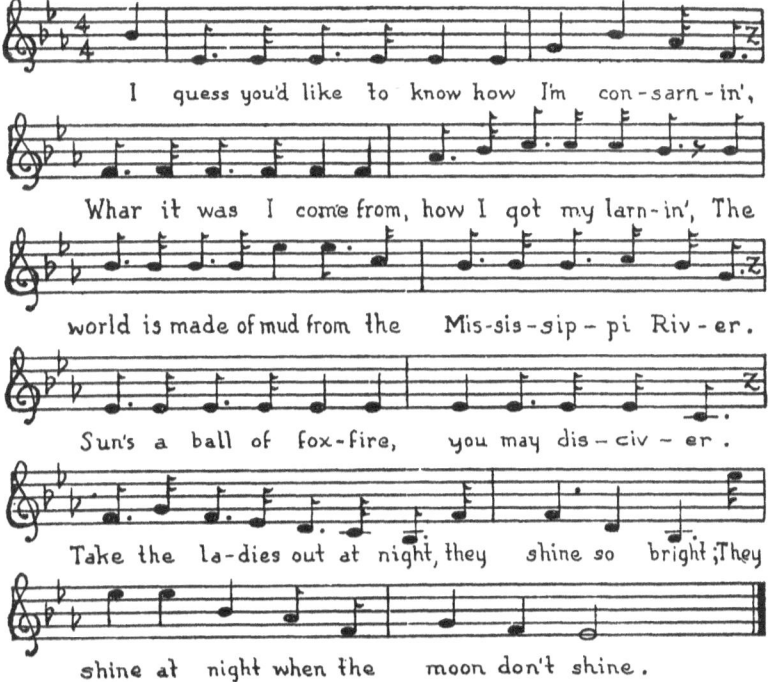

Now, don't you want to know something concernin'
Where it was I come from and where I got my learnin'?
Oh, the world is made of mud out o' the Mississippi River!
The sun's a ball of foxfire, as well you may disciver.

Take the ladies out at night. They shine so bright
They make the world light when the moon is out of sight.
And so one day as I was goin' a-spoonin'
I met Colonel Davy, and he was goin' a-coonin'.

Says I, "Where's your gun?" "I ain't got none."
"How you goin' to kill a coon when you haven't got a gun?"
Says he, "Pompcalf, just follow after Davy,
And he'll soon show you how to grin a coon crazy."

I followed on a piece and thar sot a squirrel,
A-settin' on a log and a-eatin' sheep sorrel.
When Davy that did see, he looked around at me,
Saying, "All I want now is a brace agin your knee."

And thar I braced a great big sinner.
He grinned six times hard enough to git his dinner!
The critter on the log didn't seem to mind him—
Jest kep a-settin' thar and wouldn't look behind him.

Then it was he said, "The critter must be dead.
See the bark a-flyin' all around the critter's head?"
I walked right up the truth to disciver.
Drot! It was a pine knot so hard it made me shiver.

Says he, "Pompcalf, don't you begin to laugh—
I'll pin back my ears, and I'll bite you half in half!"
I flung down my gun and all my ammunition.
Says I, "Davy Crockett, I can cool your ambition!"

He throwed back his head and he blowed like a steamer.
Says he, "Pompcalf, I'm a Tennessee screamer!"
Then we locked horns and we wallered in the thorns.
I never had such a fight since the hour I was born.

We fought a day and a night and then agreed to drop it.
I was purty badly whipped—and so was Davy Crockett.
I looked all around and found my head a-missin'—
He'd bit off my head and I had swallered his'n.!

A variant of the ending was:

Then we did agree to let each other be—
I was too much for him and he was too much for me.

"ANNIE BREEN FROM OLD KAINTUCK"

Contributed by GEORGE E. HASTINGS

Some time ago Mr. Charles J. Finger, the Arkansas writer, while on the public square in Fayetteville, came upon a crowd gathered about a wandering blind boy, who was playing a guitar and singing old songs. In the minstrel's repertoire was one song of his own composition, which he said he had "got, words and music in five puncheons to noon." The meaning of this quaint expression seems to be that he had finished the song at noon, and that the time spent in composition was that required by a sunbeam shining through the roof of his cabin to move across five puncheons on the floor. Mr. Finger secured the words and music and sent them to the contributor. Later he published the words in his magazine, *All's Well*.

The last line of the stanza was spoken, not sung.

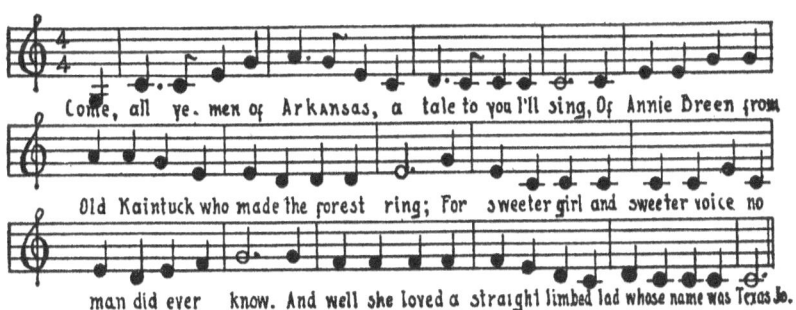

Come, all ye men of Arkansas, a tale to you I'll sing
Of Annie Breen from Old Kaintuck, who made the forest ring;
For sweeter girl and sweeter voice no man did ever know,
And well she loved a straight-limbed lad whose name was Texas Jo.

To meetin' she and Jo they went, and oh, her eyes did shine
To see him full of manly strength, so clear and tall and fine;
To be his wife and helping hand she wanted as her fate,
But sad the story that befell, as now I will relate.

One morn when birds were singin' and the lilacs were a-bloom,
There came unto the little town—and here he took a room—
A evil-hearted city man who said he'd made his stake;
And then it was the serpent in the Paradise did wake.

At meetin' after prayers were said, sweet Ann sang clear and fine,
The stranger said upon his knees, "That girl she must be mine";
So arm in arm they both walked home and wandered up and down,
Which caused the neighbors who loved Ann to shake their heads and frown.

He entered in and brought a stain on Annie Breen's fair life,
He told her that he loved her well, would take her for his wife.
When Jo got wind how matters stood his heart was like a stone;
With ne'er a word of parting he went off to Texas alone.

Before a year in a shallow grave lay Annie and her child,
And when the news reached brave Jo's ears, that lad went almost wild.
He saddled up and cantered hard and rode both long and fast,
And in Fort Smith he found the man who had ruined Ann, at last.

Then words were spoke and shots rang out and Jo fell on the floor;
He said, "In spite of all what's been I love sweet Ann the more."
His face was white as driven snow, his breath came gasping low;
He said, "My soul is clean and to my Maker it must go."

Before he closed his dimming eye he said, "My work's not done,"
And turning to his aching side he drew his faithful gun.
"You done your mischief, stranger, but from life you now must part.
His finger pressed the trigger and he shot him through the heart.

SONGS AND BALLADS—GRAVE AND GAY

By L. W. Payne, Jr.

From time to time I have picked up various old songs and ballads from students, teachers, and others who have heard me talk on balladry and folk-lore. I had in mind the gathering of a rather extensive collection of these old songs as sung in various parts of Texas, and eventually making a book of them; but, as usual with the folk-lorist, other things have intervened, and the accumulation of new material has distinctly slowed down. Since the larger project is likely to be put off indefinitely, I thought it might be well to gather together a few of the songs, particularly those which have not been widely published heretofore, and make them accessible through the *Publications of the Texas Folk-Lore Society*. I wish here to thank the many correspondents who have furnished me with songs and tunes, and to make especial acknowledgment to Miss Anne Garrison, of the University Conservatory of Music, for her very efficient help in transcribing and editing the tunes throughout the article.

RATTLESNAKE

The first song that I collected in Texas was a version of "Springfield Mountain," known as "Rattlesnake." In 1910, Mr. John E. Rylee, one of my freshman law students from Hood County, told me that he had spent the preceding summer on a ranch in Hood County, and that there he had learned from the cowboys "one of the darndest songs you ever heard." Side by side we walked around the campus while he taught me the words and music to this "darndest song." I gave the verses to Mr. Lomax just in time for him to include them as the last selection in his book, *Cowboy Songs and Ballads*, under the title "Rattlesnake" with the erroneous subtitle, "A Ranch Haying Song." I later discovered what I had previously suspected, namely, that this is no indigenous cowboy song at all, but merely an adaptation of "Springfield Mountain," a ballad that has had an extensive history in this country.

The ballad had its origin in a real incident and a real poem in commemoration of a young man from Western Massachusetts, Timothy Mirrick (or Merrick), who died from a snake bite on August 7, 1761. The author of the verses, said to be Nathan Torrey, of Springfield, Massachusetts, though there is a tradition, as Dr. J. G. Holland states in his *History of Western Massachusetts,* wherein the poem was first printed (1855), that the reputed author was a young lady to whom Timothy Mirrick was engaged to be married. The origin of the ballad is, then, more or less definitely fixed. The method of its transformation, like all real folk processes, is veiled in obscurity. All we know is that the people became interested in the story, made a song of it, and started it on its career as a traditional ballad. Beginning in Massachusetts, it has, like the Star of Empire, traveled westward. Outside of New England, it has been reported from Wisconsin, Kentucky, Missouri, Ohio, and now from West Texas, the original historical and tragic poem being finally transmuted into a semihumorous cowboy song with a peculiar stuttering or repetitional rime. I cannot here enter into a discussion of the twenty-odd versions of the ballad that have already been printed in the *Journal of American Folk-Lore and elsewhere.*[1a] Suffice it to say that of the nine or ten different tunes which have been recorded from different parts of the country, all are entirely different from the tune I learned from Mr. Rylee. I find evidences of the repetition of a syllable such as *well-i-ell-i-ell-i-ell* in some of the versions. And I also find several nonsense refrains, but no one of them is exactly like the refrain in the Texas version. I give, first, the original poem as it is printed in the *Journal of American Folk-Lore,* Vol. 13 (1900), p. 107, from J. G. Holland's *History of Western Massachusetts.* The title of the song is "Springfield Mountain."

    1 On Springfield mountains there did dwell
      A likeley youth was known full well
      Lieutenant Merrick onley son
      A likeley youth near twenty-one.

    2 One friday morning he did go
      in to the medow and did mow

[1a]See JAFL, Vols. 13, p. 107; 18, p. 295; 22, p. 366; 28, p. 169; 35, p. 415, etc.; Pound, **American Songs and Ballads,** No. 42.

Songs and Ballads—Grave and Gay

A round or two then he did feal
A pisen serpent at his heal.

3 When he received his deadly wond
He dropt his sythe a pon the ground
And strate for home wase his intent
Calling aloude still as he went.

4 Tho all around his voys wase hered
but none of his friends to him apiere
they thought it was some workmen calld
and there poor Timothy alone must fall.

5 So soon his Carfull father went
to seak his son with discontent
And there hes fond onley son he found
ded as a stone a pon the ground.

6 And there he lay down sopose to rest
withe both his hands Acrost his brest
his mouth and eyes Closed fast
And there poor man he slept his last.

7 his father vieude his track with greate concern
Where he had ran across the corn
unevin tracks where he did go
did appear to stagger two and frow.

8 The seventh of August sixty one
this fatull axadint was done
Let this a warning be to all
to be prepared when god does call.

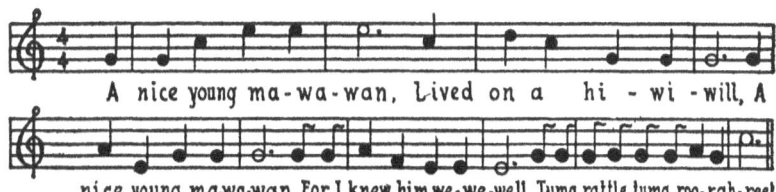

A nice young ma-wa-wan, Lived on a hi-wi-will, A nice young ma-wa-wan, For I knew him we-we-well. Tuma rattle, tuma roo-rah-ree!

1 A nice young ma-wa-wan
Lived on a hi-wi-will,
A nice young ma-wa-wan,
For I know him we-we-well.
Tuma rattle, tuma roo-rah-ree!

2 This nice young ma-wa-wan
  Went out to mo-wo-wow,
  To see if he-we-wee
  Could make a sho-wo-wow.
    Tuma rattle, etc.

3 He scarcely mo-wo-wowed
  Half round the fie-wie-wield,
  Till up jumped, come a rattle, come a sna-wa-wake
  And bit him on the he-we-weel.

4 He laid right dow-wow-wown
  Upon the grou-wou-wound
  And shut his ey-wy-wyes
  And looked all a-row-wow-wound.

5 "O pappy da-wa-wad,
  Go tell my ga-wa-wal
  That I'm a-goin' t' di-wi-wie,
  For I know I sha-wa-wall.

6 "O pappy da-wa-wad,
  Go spread the new-wu-wus,
  An' here come Sa-wa-wall
  Without her sho-wu-wus."

7 "O John, O Jo-wa-wahn,
  Why did you go-wo-wo
  Way down in the mea-we-we
  Dow, so far to mo-wo-wow?"

8 "O Sall, O Sa-wa-wall,
  Why don't you know-wo-wow,
  When the grass gits ri-wi-wipe
  It must be mo-wow-wowed?"

9 Come, all young gir-wi-wirls,
  And shed a tear-wear-wear
  For this young ma-wa-wan
  That died right here-were-were.

10 Come, all young me-we-wen,
   And warning ta-wa-wake
   And don't git bi-wi-wit
   By a rattle-sna-wa-wake.
     Tuma rattle, tuma roo-rah-ree!

THE OLD MILL

"The Old Mill" was contributed in 1925 by Mrs. Jeane L. Maxwell, 811 East Lamar Street, Sherman, Texas. Mrs. Maxwell's father, Mr. F. H. Lair, is a descendant of a Kentucky family connected with the Goodes and Hatfields, who were involved in one of the desperate Kentucky feuds. The following ballad, sung by Mr. Lair to his daughter about 1890, was brought to Texas from the Kentucky mountains. Five or six stanzas have been lost, but the story is fairly complete. I find a slight similarity between this ballad and two versions of five stanzas each (A and B of No. 45 in Miss Pound's *American Ballads and Songs*) of a ballad called "The Old Shawnee" and "On the Banks of the Old Pedee" respectively. In these versions the murder is based on the rejected lover motif, though no such motif appears in the version given here. The lines which suggest comparison are: "I ask my love to take a walk," "O Willie dear, don't murder me, For I am not fit to die," and "He took her by her long black hair." In the A version, the lover leaves the dead girl's body by the river, and in the B version he throws it into the water. In both versions a knife is the instrument with which the girl is killed. In the present version the more brutal fence rail is used. Under the title of "The Wexford Girl (The Cruel Miller)," Professor Cox, in *Folk-Songs of the South*, No. 90, traces the ballad back into the eighteenth century. In both versions of the song recorded by Professor Cox the miller beats the young lady over the head with a "stake."

1 In a lonely spot by an old, old mill,
   I spied a pretty fair maid;
  The devil brought it in my mind
   To take her life away. . . .

2 I met her at her sister's house
    At eight o'clock one night;
  And little did the poor girl think
    At her I had a spite.

3 I asked if she'd take a walk;
    She answered, "With a will."
  We walked along, then, side by side,
    Until we reached the old mill.

4 How I recall the lonely spot,
    That still, secluded place!
  I snatched a rail from off the fence
    And struck her in the face.

5 She fell upon her bended knees,
    And "Mercy!" she did cry,
  "Oh! please, sir, do not murder me,
    For I'm not prepared to die!"

6 But little attention I paid to her,
    While mercy she did implore;
  I raised the heavy rail aloft,
    And struck her yet once more . . .

7 I saw her cold and innocent blood
    Had stained her bosom o'er;
  I knew that, try howe'er I would,
    I'd cover it nevermore!

8 Amongst her long and coal-black hair
    My fingers I did entwine;
  I dragged her to the river-brink
    And plunged her body in . . .

9 And as I was returning home,
    I met my servant John;
  He asked me why I trembled so,
    And why so pale and wan . . .

10 I lit my candle and went to bed,
    Expecting to take my rest;
   Alas! I found that all of hell
    Was burning in my breast!

11 Come, all ye young and handsome men,
    And hear my warning true:
   Don't let the devil take your heart,
    And make a fiend of you!

SISTER MARY

"Sister Mary" is a lovely old dirge, evidently composed by an imaginative mind. There may be a few omissions, and perhaps there are a few changes and additions due to oral transmission. It was sent in by Miss Emily M. Richie, formerly a student in the University of Texas, now a teacher in California. She comes from Scotch ancestors who were reared in North Ireland and who settled in Ohio and Wisconsin when they came to America. Several members of the family could sing, and Miss Richie has taken down from them a number of ballads, among them good versions of "Fair Charlotte," "Polly Vaughn," and "James Bird," the manuscripts of which I have now in my collection.

1 'Twas a stormy night in winter,
    And the winds blew cold and wet.
I heard some strains of music
    That I never shall forget.

2 I was sitting in my cabin
    With my Mary fair and young,
When a light shone in the window
    And a band of singers sung:

Chorus: "*We're coming, Sister Mary,
    We're coming by and by;
Be ready, Sister Mary,
    For the time is drawing nigh.*" [1]

3 When the next night came I heard them
    And the third night, too, they sang [sung]

---

[1] The chorus is sung only after stanzas in which the sense demands it. It would not be sung after the first stanza, for example.

As I watched beside the pillow
      Of my Mary fair and young.—*Chorus.*

4 As I watched I heard a rustling
      As the rustling of a wing,
   And close beside her pillow
      I heard the bright ones sing.—*Chorus.*

5 I tried to wake my Mary,
      But my tongue would not obey
   Till the song so strange had ended
      And the singers flown away.

6 Then I woke her from her slumbers,
      And I told her everything;
   But we could not guess the meaning
      Of the song I heard them sing.—*Chorus.*

7 Then I tried to wake my Mary,
      But my sorrow was complete
   When I found her heart of kindness
      Had forever ceased to beat.

8 And now I'm sad and lonely
      From summer's morn till spring,
   And often in the twilight
      I think I hear them sing.—*Chorus.*

BROWN-EYED LEE

The following ballad, *Brown-Eyed Lee,* is certainly a local production based on a real incident that happened in 1899 in Bell County, Texas, and was perhaps composed by the unlucky hero himself. The song was obtained for me in February, 1923, by a sophomore student, Mr. J. B. Coltharp, of Coryell County, who induced a boyhood friend of his to copy off the song. Dee Riddle (or as he facetiously signed himself, "Ree Diddle, the Thrasher Baggar"), of Turnerville, Texas, lives near Cave Creek in Coryell County. Dee says the ballad is based on the real experience of a cousin of his, though he does not clearly identify this cousin as the author of the song.

Songs and Ballads—Grave and Gay

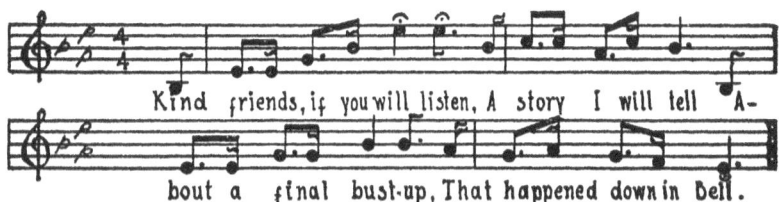

Kind friends, if you will listen, A story I will tell About a final bust-up, That happened down in Bell.

1 Kind friends, if you will listen,
    A story I will tell
About a final bust-up
    That happened down in Bell.

2 I courted a brown-eyed angel
    That goes by the name of Lee,
And when I popped the question,
    She said she would marry me.

3 She told me that she loved me,
    And loved no one but me,
And I pressed a kiss upon the lips
    Of my darling angel Lee.

4 My rapture at that moment
    No human could explain,
To know that I had loved her
    And had not loved in vain.

5 I went and bought my license,
    March, eighteen ninety-nine,
Expecting in a few more days
    That darling would be mine.

6 Her mother grew quite angry,
    And said it could not be;
She said she had picked another man out
    For brown-eyed Lee.

7 She talked to friends and neighbors,
    And said that she would fight;
She said she'd get her old six-shooter
    And put old Red to flight.

8 But lovers laughed at shooters
    And the old she-devil, too;
I said I would have my darling
    If she didn't prove untrue.

9 I borrowed Dad's old buggy
       And got Jim's forty-one;
   I started down to Kerns's,
       Thinking I would have some fun.

10 And passing Mr. O'Dell's,
       Out came Frankie's son,
   To bring a letter from the old folks,
       Saying, "Harry, don't you come."

11 I thought the matter over,
       Not knowing what to do,
   When something seemed to whisper,
       "Are you going to prove untrue?"

12 I am not one to craw-fish
       When I am in a tight;
   I said, "I will have my angel
       And not be put to flight."

13 I went on down to Kerns's
       With the devil in my head;
   I said I'd have my darling
       Or leave the old folks dead.

14 Good fortune fell upon me;
       My darling proved untrue;
   I gave her back her letters
       And bid her kind adieu.

15 I pressed her to my aching heart
       And kissed her last farewell,
   And prayed a permanent prayer to God
       To send her Ma to hell.

16 She stood and gazed upon us,
       As if she thought it were fun;
   I caught myself a time or two
       A-reaching for my gun.

17 I went back home all broken-hearted
       And almost wished I was dead,
   Till something seemed to whisper,
       "It was best for you, Old Red."

18 I sold my cows to J. M. G.,
       My corn to K. M. P.,

And cursed the day that I first met
   That darling angel Lee.

19 I sold my horse and saddle
       And caught a north-bound train,
    Leaving the darling girl behind
       That I had loved in vain.

20 I landed in Paul's Valley,
       All right-side-up-with-care,
    And dreamed of the girl I loved that night
       With dark brown eyes and hair.

21 When I got up next morning
       To see what I could see,
    And every sound that I could hear
       Would speak the name of Lee.

22 I stepped into a billiard hall,
       Thinks, "I'll have a game,"
    And every ball that I would knock
       Would speak the same dear name.

23 I drank two glasses of whiskey
       And emptied a bottle of wine,
    And cursed the very day that I first met
       That darling girl of mine.

24 I hopped a freighter's wagon,
       Went to Midland town,
    And hired to a man by the name of Smith
       And quietly settled down.

25 Although I am broken-hearted,
       There is one thing I know well,
    That the one that caused this bust-up
       Will some day scorch in Hell.

26 She will cast her eyes to heaven,
       To Jesus on His throne,
    And ask for a drop of water
       To cool her scorching tongue.

27 But Jesus will answer her:
       "Go to the old Scratch;
    You are the very hypocrite
       That busted up this match.

28 "Depart from me, you cursed;
    You are the devil's own,
Old Red shall find a resting place
    On the right hand of my throne."

29 Now, kind friends, remember
    The H. M. P.
I could not help but love the girl
    That wore the name of Lee.

30 I loved her, oh, I loved her,
    Yes, more than tongue can tell;
I know that there is no other
    That I could love so well.

31 And in my dreams at night
    My darling's face I see,
And it seems to whisper,
    "Dear one, remember me."

32 And every night I go to bed,
    I pray a permanent prayer
For the girl I loved so well
    With dark brown eyes and hair.

BRING ME OUT MY BOTTLE

Dee Riddle very kindly added another song, called "**Bring Me Out My Bottle.**" This is doubtless by the same author, being apparently a sort of aftermath of the experience related in the previous ballad. I imagine it is sung to the same tune.

1 Bring me out my bottle
    And good old corkscrew too,
And when I get the stopper out,
    I'll set 'em up to you.

2 I went to see my girl the other night;
    She met me at the door;
She threw her arms around my neck,
    Saying, "You cannot come any more."

3 I don't know what I've said to her,
    And I don't know what I have done,
But the boys all say I fight a little booze,
    But I fight just for fun.

4 Laying around the depot,
        Waiting for an express train,
    Four good old quarts of Hill and Hill,
        And I am going to get drunk again.

5 I stepped up to the express man
        And said, "Is there anything doing for me?"
    "Well, I don't know, my lad,
        But I will just step back and see."

6 He handed me out a package
        Addressed in my own name;
    Four good old quarts of Hill and Hill,
        And I am going to get drunk again.

7 Now my train is leaving;
        I will bid you all adieu,
    But when I stop, get off, and get drunk,
        I seldom think of you.

8 Now my song is over;
        I will sing to you no more;
    But don't you wish you'd been in my place
        When she met me at the door?

A PACKAGE OF OLD LETTERS

"A Package of Old Letters" was contributed by Professor Jay B. Hubbell of Southern Methodist University. He says that the song came to him in 1924 from a student from East Texas. Another and fuller version of this ballad is recorded by E. C. Perrow in *Journal of American Folk-Lore*, Vol. 28, p. 172 (1915).

1 In a little rosewood casket
        That is sitting on the stand
    Lies a package of old letters
        Written by a loved one's hand.

2 You may bring them now, dear sister,
        Read them o'er to me tonight;
    I have often tried but could not
        For the tears would blind my sight.

3 You have brought them; thank you, darling,
        Come and sit here by my bed,
    And press gently to your bosom
        This poor, aching, throbbing head.

4 When I'm dead and in my coffin
        And the shroud is round me wound
    And the narrow bed is ready
        In the solemn churchyard ground,

5 Place these letters and this picture
        Both together o'er my heart,
    And the little ring he gave me
        From my finger never part.

6 You may read them now, dear sister,
        While I gently fall asleep,
    Fall asleep to wake in Jesus,
        Darling sister, do not weep.

THE DEATH OF LITTLE JOE

"The Death of Little Joe" and "Johnny Sands" were transcribed for me by Mrs. Grace Du Pré Ridings of Sherman, Texas, in August, 1925. She writes: "They were sung to me by my sister, Mrs. Preston Stimpson (then Arabella Dupree), who now lives in Chattanooga, Oklahoma. She learned them from my mother, Amelia Wofford Dupree, and our aunt, Mrs. Josephine Slagle, who now lives in Monkstown, Texas. I remember hearing them as early as 1887, but they have been sung in our family for generations."

1 What will the birds do, Mother, next spring,
        The little brown birds at my door?
    Will they hop upon my step and chirp at my window,
        Asking why Joe wanders there no more?

What will the kitten do, Mother, all alone?
  Will he stop in his frolic for a day?
Will he lie on the rug by the side of my bed
  As he did when I first went away?

2 Love Tige, mother, love Tige, I say,
  For I know he will mourn for me true;
Keep him from cold as he useless grows,
  Sleeping all the long winter through.
Show him my coat, Mother, so he'll not forget;
  Little Master, oh, then, will be dead.
Speak to him kindly and often of Joe,
  And pat him on his black shaggy head.

3 What will Thomas, the gardener, say
  When you ask him for flowers for me?
Will he give you a rose that he's tended with care,
  The first fairest bloom of the tree?
I saw the tears come in his honest old eyes,
  Though he said it was the wind that brought them there,
As he looked at my cheeks growing paler each day,
  And his hands trembled over my hair.

4 Poor Uncle Jack in the far away West,
  Will be sad o'er the letter that you write;
Only tell him, dearest Mother, I've gone to the front,
  Marching nearer and nearer the fight!
And you, darling Mother, will miss me awhile,
  Yet in Heaven no larger will I grow,
And then a kind angel will know at the gate
  When you ask for your darling little Joe.

JOHNNY SANDS

"Johnny Sands" is a comic song-ballad widely known in the eighteen forties and still surviving among the people. The text was accurately summarized by H. M. Belden in his *A Partial List of Song-Ballads and Other Popular Poetry Known in Missouri* (No. 46, in the second edition, 1910.) A. H. Tolman gives this summary in the *Journal of American Folk-Lore,* Vol. 29, pp. 178-179 and notes that E. C. Perrow had previously published a version of it in the same journal, Vol. 28, p. 174. In the article referred to above Professor Tolman also gives another song called "The Old Woman of Slapsadam," which treats the same subject but is quite different from "Johnny Sands" in matter and form. In Vol. 35, p.

385, of the *Journal of American Folk-Lore,* Tolman reverts to his previous note on "Johnny Sands" and reports a text sent in by Miss Mary O. Eddy, of Perrysville, Ohio. Professor Kittredge adds to the entry a note giving the history of the song. The music was composed by John Sinclair and published by Oliver Ditson at Boston under copyright of 1842. The song became widely known through traveling "troupes" and was included in many popular song books from 1859 on down to the end of the century. Miss Pound includes, in her *American Ballads and Songs,* two versions very similar to the one given below. (See No. 48, pp. 114-116.) The only excuse I have for reprinting the song is to record the tune as sent in by Mrs. Ridings. I am giving the text as reported by Mrs. L. A. Scott, of McKinney, Texas, since it is better adapted to the tune and is almost identical with Mrs. Ridings' version. (See the foregoing note on "The Death of Little Joe.")

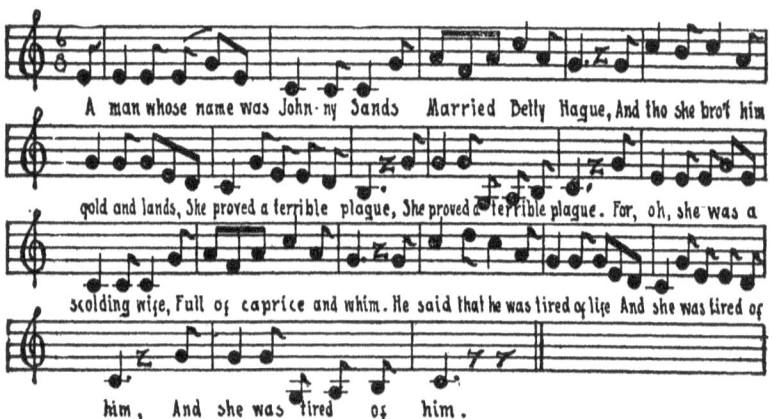

1   A man whose name was Johnny Sands
        Married Betty Hague,
    And though she brought him gold and lands,
        She proved a terrible plague,
        She proved a terrible plague.
    For, oh, she was a scolding wife,
        Full of caprice and whim.
    He said that he was tired of life,
        And she was tired of him,
        And she was tired of him.

2 Says he, "I'll go and drown myself
    In the river that runs below."
 Says she, "Pray do, you silly elf,
    I've wished it long ago,
    I've wished it long ago."
 Says he, "Upon the brink I'll stand,
    While you run down the hill
 And push me in with all your might."
    Says she, "My love, I will,"
    Says she, "My love, I will."

3 "For fear that I should courage lack
    And try to save my life,
 Pray tie my hands behind my back."
    "I will," replied his wife,
    "I will," replied his wife.
 She tied his hands behind his back,
    And when securely done,
 He took his stand upon the brink,
    And she prepared to run,
    And she prepared to run.

4 Now as he stands upon the brink,
    She comes with all her force,
 But as she came he stepped aside,
    And she fell in of course,
    And she fell in of course.
 Splashing, dashing like a fish,
    "Oh, save me, Johnny Sands!"
 "I can't, my dear, though much I wish.
    For you have tied my hands,
    For you have tied my hands."

HUNTING SONG

"Hunting Song" was contributed by Mrs. Manley, of Harris County, who said the song was sung to her by her grandmother thirty years ago. At that time the family was living in Bell County.

1 Come, all you jolly huntsmen
    Who like to chase the fox,
  And we will chase Brer Reynard
    Through all those rills and rocks.

Chorus: To my whoop, whoop, whoop and a heigho!
All in one merry train,
To my ran-tan-tan-tan-tiffy, tiffy, ta!

226   *Texas and Southwestern Lore*

  And with my royal dog and gun,
  My bugle onto my saddle—Oh!
  Dickey-di-de-oh!
  And through the woods we'll run, brave boys,
  Through the woods we'll run.

2 The first I saw was a peddler,
   A-peddling of his clocks;
  He swore he saw Brer Reynard
   Run through the rills and rocks.

3 The next I saw was a blind man
   As blind as he could be;
  He swor he saw Brer Reynard
   Run through a hollow tree.

WEAVER JOHN

The following is doubtless a very old weaving song brought over to America from Ireland. Mr. J. G. Walker, of Sherman, Texas, learned it from an Irish school dame who taught in Texas about 1875.

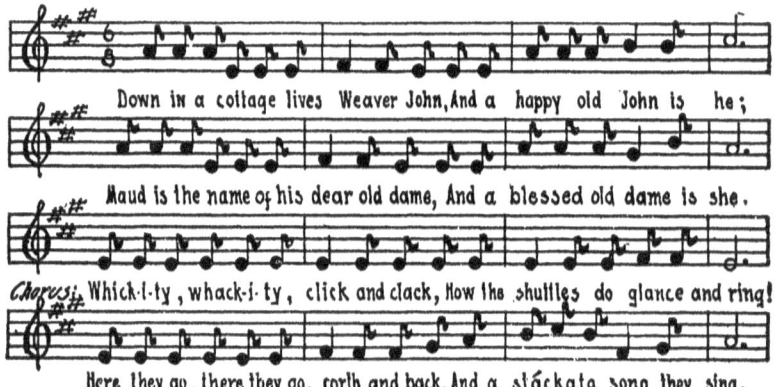

1 Down in a cottage lives Weaver John,
  And a happy old John is he;
 Maud is the name of his dear old dame,
  And a blessed old dame is she.

Chorus: *Whickity, whackity, click and clack,*
   How the shuttles do glance and ring!
  Here they go, there they go, forth and back,
   and a stackata song they sing.
  And a stackata song they sing.

2 Pussy is frisking about the room
   With her kittens, one, two, three, four;
   Towser is taking his wanton nap
   On the settle behind the door.

I LOVE SOMEBODY

The widely known "I Love Somebody" was reported by Miss Jewell Cowan, of Pecos, Texas, in 1924. In my youth I often heard this comic old song sung in Alabama. A fragment of another song of this title but with entirely different music and verse form is reported from East Tennessee mountains by E. C. Perrow, *Journal of American Folk-Lore*, Vol. 28, p. 185.

1 I love somebody, I do, Ma-ma,
  I love somebody, I do;
  I love somebody, but don't you tell Pa,
  For how can I help it, how can I, Ma-ma?

2 He wrote me a letter, he did, Ma-ma, etc.

3 He told me he loved me, he did, Ma-ma, etc.

4 He gave me a ring, he did, Ma-ma, etc.

5 We're going to be married, we are, Ma-ma, etc.

6 The parson is coming, he is, Ma-ma, etc.

7 And now we are married, we are, Ma-ma,
  And now we are married, we are;
  And now we are married, and you can tell Pa,
  For how can he help it, how can he, Ma-ma?

ALPHABET SONG

Another well known song that is familiar to me and members of my own family, having been transported from Alabama, is called "Alphabet Song." I have heard it sung in social gatherings in Alabama and have occasionally sung it to my own children here in Texas.

B-A ba, B-E be, B-I bi, ba-be-bi;
B-O bo, ba-be-bi-bo,
B-U bu, ba-be-bi-bo-bu.
Litoria, litoria, sweedledewee dum hiro sol,
Litoria, litoria, sweedledewee dum bum!

D-A da, D-E de, D-I di, da-de-di;
D-O do, da-de-di-do,
D-U du, da-de-di-do-du.
Litoria, litoria, sweedledewee dum bum!

And so forth, throughout the alphabet, omitting the consonants C and G because they do not conveniently combine with all the vowels.

BETSY BROWN

Nearly half a century ago, my eldest sister (now Mrs. C. T. Morris, of Sheffield, Alabama), taught me the song called "Betsy Brown." I remember how my sisters used to perch me up on the old square piano at our home in Auburn, Alabama, and show me off before company by making me sing the old song. The words and tune come to me perfectly even now, and I feel something of the spirit of youthful exuberance and hilarity as I sing it. It is probably a popular song-ballad of the last half of the nineteenth century. Certainly it has little of the quality of the folk song.

Songs and Ballads—Grave and Gay

1 I love a little girl, and she lives down town;
   Her daddy's a butcher and his name is Brown;
   I tell you, boys, I've got it sound,
      She's the girl for me.
   Her eyes are as bright as diamonds,
   Her teeth are as white as pearl;
   I tell you, boys, she's handsome,
   And I know she's one of the girls.

Chorus: *Oh! I love a little girl, and she lives down town,*
Her daddy is a butcher, and his name is Brown;
I tell you, boys, I've got it sound,
She's the girl for me.

2 I'm goin' to get married tomorrow night;
   I asked her daddy, and he said all right;
   I feel so awful jolly I'd like to get tight;
      But that wouldn't do.
   Her dad, you know, is a fine old chap
   And the richest man in town,
   And he's a-goin' to give me a house and lot
   Along with Betsy Brown.

COLUMBUS IS DEAD

"Columbus Is Dead" comes in from three sources and under three titles, "Old Crummy" and "Old Crumpy" being the variant names of the deceased. Miss Hassie Davis, of Haskell, Texas, learned about old Crummy in her childhood (about 1904) in Robertson County. Her parents came from near Birmingham, Alabama, and probably brought the song with them. Mrs. J. B. Jourdan, of Austin, reports "Old Crumpy" as she learned it from a cousin of hers named Anderson. The family is descended from a branch of the Livingstons from

England. Mrs. J. G. Burr, of Austin, formerly Pearl Pace, of Huntsville, Walker County, learned the "Columbus" version in the eighties. Her grandparents came from Alabama and Virginia and were among the early settlers in East Texas. The three versions are very much alike in words and tunes. Similar versions have been recorded, "Poor Robin," "Old Rover," "Poor Johnny," being some of the variants of the title character. (See Miss Pound's note on No. 114, *American Ballads and Songs*, p. 256.)

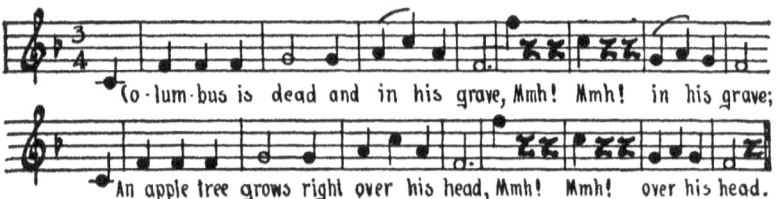

1 Columbus is dead and in his grave,
   Mmh! mmh! in his grave;
   An apple grows right over his head,
   Mmh! mmh! over his head.

2 The apples are ripe and ready to fall,
   An old woman comes to gather them all.

3 He up with his foot and kicked her down,
   And apples were scattered all over the ground.

4 The bridle and saddle are on the shelf,
   If you want any more, just sing it yourself.

KILLING OF THE SOW

When Miss Annie Ray Kiefer, of San Angelo (now Mrs. H. W. Taylor, of Austin), was teaching in the Pearsall High School in 1923-1924, she induced several of her students to make anthologies of all the old songs they knew or could collect from their relatives. Gabe Lewis, a sixteen-year-old high-school boy, brought in a set of fifteen songs. Most of them he could himself sing, and the others he copied down from the singing of his relatives and neighbors. I have selected seven of these for publication. Most of them are old songs widely known, not only in Frio County but elsewhere through the country.

 1 As I walked out one morning in the spring,
   Ding dong-billy, dong-ki-o-me,
  To hear the small birds whistle and sing,
   Ding dong-billy, dong-ki-o-me.

Chorus: *Ki-up-anow-bill-do-gaw,*
  Up jumped billydump,
  Crawled down billydump,
  Billy-lily-lingdum-ki-o-me.

 2 I spied a crow a-settin' on a yoke,
   Ding dong-billy, dong-ki-o-me,
  Watching a tailor cut out a cloak,
   Ding dong-billy, dong-ki-o-me,

 3 I told my wife to bring me the gun,
   Ding dong-billy, dong-ki-o-me,
  To shoot that crow before he run,
   Ding dong-billy, dong-ki-o-me,

 4 I blazed away and I missed my mark,
   Ding dong-billy, dong-ki-o-me,
  And I shot my old sow through the heart,
   Ding dong-billy, dong-ki-o-me.

 5 I told my wfe to run there soon,
   Ding dong-billy, dong-ki-o-me.
  For our old sow's in a helluva tune,
   Ding dong-billy, dong-ki-o-me,

 6 I told my wife to take her to the house,
   Ding dong-billy, dong-ki-o-me,
  To make some pudding hash and souse,
   Ding dong-billy, dong-ki-o-me.

 7 The saddle and bridle are hanging on the shelf,
   Ding dong-billy, dong-ki-o-me.
  If you want any more you can sing it yourself,
   Ding dong-billy, dong-ki-o-me,

THE LITTLE BLACK MUSTACHE

 1 Oh, once I had a charming young beau,
  And I loved him dear as life,
  For I thought the time would surely come
  When I would be his wife.

232 — Texas and Southwestern Lore

2 His pockets they were filled with gold,
    And oh, he had the cash,
A diamond ring, gold watch and chain,
    And a little black mustache.

3 He came to see me Sunday night
    And he stayed till half-past three;
He said he never loved a girl
    As well as he loved me.

4 He said we'd live in grand old style,
    And oh, we would cut a dash;
Then he pressed upon my lips
    The little black mustache.

5 At length there came a sorry old maid,
    She was worth her weight in gold.
She wore false hair, she wore false teeth,
    She was forty-five years old.

6 He cruelly deserted me
    For that old maiden's cash.
So you see I lost my beau
    With the little black mustache.

7 There they lived across the street
    In their gay mansion old.
She married him for his mustache;
    He married her for gold.

8 So, girls, take heed to my sad fate,
    And never be so rash;
Always shun the Pearsall boy
    With a little black mustache.

I WISH I WERE SINGLE AGAIN[2]

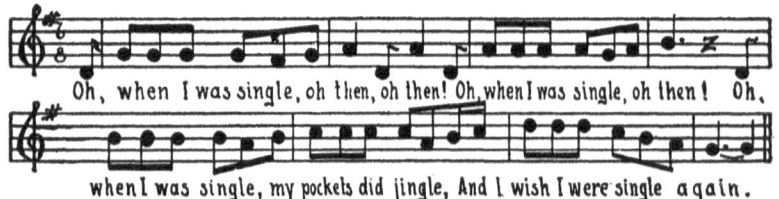

Oh, when I was single, oh then, oh then! Oh, when I was single, oh then! Oh, when I was single, my pockets did jingle, And I wish I were single again.

---

[2] Professor H. M. Belden lists "When I Was Single" as No. 48 in his **A Partial List of Song-Ballads . . . Known in Missouri** (1910). Also in an article by him, "A Study

1 Oh, when I was single, oh then, oh then!
      Oh, when I was single, oh then.
   Oh, when I was single my pockets did jingle,
      And I wish I were single again.

2 I married me a wife, oh then, oh then!
      I married me a wife, oh then!
   I married me a wife, and she led me a life,
      And I wish I were single again.

3 My wife she took fever, oh then, oh then!
      My wife she took fever, oh then!
   My wife she took fever, and I wish to never leave her,
      And I wish I were single again.

4 My wife she died, oh then, oh then!
      My wife she died, oh then!
   My wife she died, and I laughed till I cried,
      And I wish I were single again.

5 I went for a shroud, oh then, oh then!
      I went for a shroud, oh then!
   I went for a shroud, and I laughed right out loud,
      So glad I was single again.

6 I went for a coffin, oh then, oh then!
      I went for a coffin, oh then!
   I went for a coffin and nearly died laughing,
      So glad I was single again.

7 I went to her grave, oh then, oh then!
      I went to her grave, oh then!
   I went to her grave, but I couldn't behave,
      I was so happy I was single again.

8 I married me another, oh then, oh then!
      I married me another, oh then!

in Contemporary Balladry," **Midwest Quarterly**, Vol. 1, No. 2 (January, 1914), he tells the story of the quadruple murder of the Gus Meeks family by George and Bill Taylor in 1894, and gives five ballads on this subject. Incidentally in his remarks on the author of the fifth version, George Meeks, an old and decrepit ballad singer of Missouri, he says that Meeks claimed to be the author of several other songs, among them, "I Wish I Were Single Again." Professor Belden refuses to credit the authorship of the song to Meeks, saying, "I imagine he claimed the authorship of any piece that he sang or that was popular and authorless." Miss Pound prints a four-stanza version of the song (No. 98 in **American Ballads and Songs**). In my boyhood in Lee County, Alabama, I heard the piece sung frequently, though I never saw it in print. Now after forty years have intervened, I am transcribing the music as I recall it, adapting it to the full text as sent in by Gabe Lewis.

I married me another, the devil's step-mother,
And I wish I were single again.

9 She beat me, she banged me, oh then, oh then!
She beat me and banged me, oh then!
She beat me, she banged me, she swore she would hang me,
And I wished I were single again.

10 She went for the rope, oh then, oh then!
She went for the rope, oh then!
She went for the rope my neck for to choke,
And I wish I were single again.

11 Oh boys, take warning from me, from me,
Oh, boys, take warning from me!
Be good to the first, for the second is worse,
And I wish I were single again.[3]

POOR OLD BACHELOR[4]

1 I'm a poor old bachelor a-settin' around,
As sad as I can be.
The aim of my life is to get me a wife;
Won't somebody marry me?

Chorus: *I'm a poor old bachelor, poor old bachelor,*
A poor old bachelor I be.

---

[3] Mr. L. D. Moses, an instructor in English at the University of Texas, has just supplied me with another version of this song. He says that in his youth in the mountains of southeast Kentucky he used to hear his mother recite the stanzas (singing ballads was considered sinful by the strict religionists of the mountains), and he remembers hearing his mother and a neighbor argue rather strenuously as to the correct conclusion. This version of six stanzas is in its first five stanzas exactly parallel with stanzas 1, 2, 4, 8, 9 of the version given above; but the concluding, or sixth, stanza is entirely new and is given in two forms as follows:

6a I got tired of her yoke, oh then, oh then!
I got tired of her yoke, oh then!
So I bought me a rope and greased it with soap,
And now I am single again.

6b My wife she took sick, oh then, oh then!
My wife she took sick, oh then!
My wife she took sick, I sent for the devil right quick,
And now I am single again.

[4] Compare this with "A Bachelor's Lament," a different song on the same theme, reported by Phillips Barry in **Journal of American Folk-Lore**, 25:281; Belden, No. 105 in his Missouri **Song-Ballads**; Cox, No. 160 in **Folk Songs of the South**.

*Won't some lady kind, pray, make up her mind,
To marry a fellow like me?*

2 I've travelled o'er Kentucky from the east to the west,
   Ohio, and the State of Tennessee,
   But there's not a single girl whose lips wouldn't curl,
   Just even at the sight of me.

3 I've tried the widows too, but they said it wouldn't do,
   Too many—it never could be;
   Some flatly refused, others begged to be excused;
   Won't somebody marry me?

OLD BRIEN-O-LIN[4a]

1 Old Brien-o-Lin, his wife, and his wife's mother,
   They all went over the bridge together;
   The bridge it broke, and they all fell in—
   "You'll find sand on the bottom!" cried Brien-o-Lin,
   Cried Brien-o-Lin.

2 Old Brien-o-lin had no breeches for to wear,
   So he got him a sheepskin and made him a pair
   With the flesh side out and the whooly side in—
   "What a cool pair of breeches!" cried Brien-o-Lin,
   Cried Brien-o-Lin.

3 Old Brien-o-Lin had but one horse for to ride;
   He was spavined, both crippled and blind;
   His back it was broken, and his sides were caved in—
   "What a gay young colt!" cried Brien-o-Lin,
   Cried Brien-o-Lin.

KISSING ON THE SLY

1 When a boy falls in love
   With a pretty turtle dove,
   He will linger all around her underjaw.
   He will kiss her for her mother,
   For her sister and her brother,

[4a]This song is a very interesting American corruption of an ancient Scotch and North-of-England rhyme. Under the title of "Tommy Linn" it appears in **The North-Country Chorister**, "by a Bishopric Ballad Singer," Durham, 1802, pp. 3-4. **The North-Country Chorister** is reprinted in **Northern Galands**, by Joseph Ritson, London, 1810. As "Tam O' The Linn," the song appears in **Popular Rhymes of Scotland**, by Robert Chambers, London and Edinburgh, 1870, pp. 33-34, Chambers giving some discussion of the song. Halliwell included it, under the title of "Tommy Linn," in his **Nursery Rhymes and Tales of England**, fifth edition, pp. 338-339. It is not to be confused with "Tam Lin," No. 39 in Child.

Till the old man kicks him from the door.
He pulls a pistol from his pocket,
And the hammer from its socket,
And vows he'll blow away his giddy brain;
But ducky says he musn't,
So he loads it and he doesn't,
And they're kissing one another once again.

2 When a girl is seventeen
She'll think it very mean
If she ain't got something for to mash;
She'll pucker up her mouth
In a very pretty pout,
And linger round some man's moustache;
She'll make your heart quiver,
She'll send you o'er the river,
She'll stick as tight as granulated glue.
And you need not try to tell her,
That you're some other girlie's feller,
For she'll masticate your smeller if you do.

YOUNG FOLKS' DISPOSITIONS[5]

1 Come on, all ye good people,
I pray you draw near,
A comical ditty that you may hear.
The boys about here, they think they're advanced
By courting the ladies and learning to dance.
Li-o-fa-diddle-di-da.

2 The boys about here make it a plan,
Whenever they hear anything, they tell it again,
And add as much to it as ever they can;
There's many a little boy set out for a man.
Li-o-fa-diddle-di-da.

3 But it is now high time we're leaving the lads,
And turning to the ladies, who are ten times as bad;
They primp their mouth and curl their hair,
Just like an owl in bush appear.
Li-o-fa-diddle-di-da.

4 They dress very fine, to a quilting they go,
There expecting to catch a beau,
And when they get there, they laugh and play,

---

[5] Compare with "A Comical Ditty," Cox, **Folk-Songs of the South,** 253; "Arizona Boys and Girls," Lomax, 211.

Do anything else but work away.
Li-o-fa-diddle-di-da.

5 Their old snuff boxes—they'll take them out,
And give them a rub and look about,
Then pass them around from one to two,
"Oh, won't you have snuff? Oh, madam, won't you?"
Li-o-fa-diddle-di-da.

AN OLD PROHIBITION SONG

1 While wandering through the woodlands
One lovely morn I strayed,
The merry, merry song birds
Their sweetest music made.
I asked a bright-eyed linnet
That boldly ventured near:
"What is it makes your heart so light?
What makes your voice so clear?"

Chorus: "*Water, water, water, water, water, water, water, water,*"
So the sweet bird sang,
"*Water, water, water, water, water, water, water, water,*"
Through the fiery spring.

2 A streamlet rippled onward
And o'er each burdened bank
Gave many a fragrant blossom,
And grasses tall and rank.
Oh, could they speak, then surely
They, like the birds, would [say]:
"'Tis water—sparkling water,
That makes us young and gay."

3 Oh, shun the tempting wine cup,
For want and shame are there;
Touch not the drunkard's poison,
Nor once to taste it dare.
But drink the pure, cold water
That heaven so freely gives,
For strength and health and beauty,
To everything that lives.

R. C. H.

"When I lay dis body down"

In the death, May 5, 1927, of Richard Clarence Harrison, the Texas Folk-Lore Society has lost one of its most interested and useful members. For the year 1925-1926 he was president of the Society, and an outstanding contribution to the *Publications* for 1926 was his article, "The Negro as Interpreter of His Own Folk-Songs." As near noon, May 8, his body was being lowered into the ground of an Austin cemetery, there sounded on the quiet Sabbath air the chorus of an old-time negro spiritual, sung by negroes in a church not far away. The blowing of taps over a soldier's grave could not have been more appropriate. No man ever had a deeper spiritual appreciation of the negro spirituals than Harrison had.

Richard Clarence Harrison was born at Alvarado, Texas, February 13, 1884. He spent his boyhood on a farm and was 18 years old before he entered high school, where he had "considerable Greek and Latin." Interspersing his undergraduate work with teaching, he took his B.A. degree from the University of Texas, 1912. Just after graduating he married Miss Sallie May Lauderdale of Austin, and from this union was born a son, Richard. For a brief time he held a position in the State Department of Education. He took his M.A. in the University of Texas in 1917, after which he taught English in Southwestern Texas State Teachers College at San Marcos. For the year 1921-1922 he did graduate work in Harvard University, and in 1924-1925 he did graduate work in the University of Texas, where he began what was to have been his Doctor's thesis on Whitman. In the fall of 1925 he went to Texas Technological College, which was just opening at Lubbock, as head of the Department of English. When apoplexy struck him on the night of Thursday, May 5, he had just completed a full day of work. He liked tnat spiritual,

Steal away, steal away home.

J. F. D.

PROCEEDINGS OF THE TWELFTH ANNUAL SESSION (1926) OF THE TEXAS FOLK-LORE SOCIETY

The Society met the evening of April 23 and the afternoon and evening of April 24, 1926, in the Y.M.C.A. Auditorium of the University of Texas at Austin.
The programs were as follows:

FRIDAY EVENING, APRIL 23, 8 O'CLOCK

South Texas Negro Work Songs: Collected and Uncollected, Professor Gates Thomas, Southwest Texas State Teachers College, San Marcos.
The Pictographs and Petroglyphs of the El Paso District (illustrated), Colonel M. L. Crimmins, Fort Sam Houston, San Antonio.

SATURDAY AFTERNOON, APRIL 24, 2 O'CLOCK

President's address: **The Negro as Interpreter of His Own Folk-Songs,** Professor R. C. Harrison, Texas Technological College, Lubbock.
Legend of the Mission Bells of San Augustine at Mission Nuestra Señora de los Dolores de los Ais and **The Legendary Origin of the Head Spring, or Ojo de Agua, of the San Marcos River,** Miss Adina De Zavala, San Antonio.
Foundation for Legends of Lost Mines on the Nueces, Mr. Henry Yelvington, Three Rivers.
The Enchanted Moat, or Irish Fairies in Texas, Miss Louise von Blittersdorf, Austin.
The Legend of Caddo Lake, Mr. G. T. Bludwort, State Department of Education, Austin.
The Making of Legends, Miss Fannie Ratchford, University of Texas, Austin.
Folk Tales of the Kentucky Mountaineers, Mr. Leon Denny Moses, University of Texas, Austin.
The White Mustang; A Legend of the American Frontier, Mr. J. Frank Dobie, University of Texas, Austin.
The following papers were read by title: **The Piney Woods Folk: Their Superstitions and Remedies,** Dr. William P. Barron, New York City; **Reptiles of the South and Southwest in Folk-Lore,** Mr. John K. Strecker, Baylor University, Waco; **Negro Treasure Lore,** Mr. R. R. Smith, Jourdanton; **Uncle Remus in the Brazos Bottoms,** Mr. A. W. Eddins, San Antonio; **The Sources of Some Texas Place Names,** Mr. Paul Morgan, Clarendon; **Familiar Sayings of Old-Time Texas Settlers,** Miss Mary Jourdan, Austin; **Superstitions of Bexar County,** Mr. E. R. Bogusch, San Antonio.

SATURDAY EVENING, APRIL 24, 8 O'CLOCK

Paul Bunyan in the Oil Fields, Mr. John Lee Brooks, Southern Methodist University, Dallas.

Music of the "Holy-Rollers," Mr. Samuel E. Asbury, College Station, Texas.

Old-time frontier songs, dance calls, and fiddling by J. E. Newcomer and Jim Edwards, of Bandera County. With Dean T. U. Taylor of the University of Texas leading the dancers, genuine old-time square (ances were demonstrated.

The following resolution presented by J. Frank Dobie, Secretary of the Society, was adopted:

WHEREAS, The old-time Texas longhorn was, with cotton, the basis of the commercial prosperity of the State;

WHEREAS, In song, romance, and sentiment the old Texas longhorn is forever linked with the human and soil background of the State; and

WHEREAS, The Texas longhorn is now bellowing his last bellow and is nearer extinction than the American buffalo ever was,

Therefore, we of the Texas Folk-Lore Society recommend that the Legislature of the State of Texas appropriate sufficient funds and provide adequate means for preserving in its original purity the longhorn breed—the most history-making breed of cattle the world has ever known.

Officers for the year 1926-1927 were elected as follows:

President, Professor Gates Thomas, Southwest Texas State Teachers College, San Marcos.

Vice-Presidents, Miss Adina De Zavala, San Antonio; Mrs. A. B. Looscan, Houston; Colonel M. L. Crimmins, Fort Sam Houston, San Antonio.

Councillors, Dr. L. W. Payne, Jr., University of Texas; Mr. Victor J. Smith, Sul Ross State Teachers College, Alpine; Miss Julia Estill, Fredericksburg.

Recording Secretary and Treasurer, Miss Fannie Ratchford, University of Texas, Austin.

Secretary and Editor, Mr. J. Frank Dobie, University of Texas, Austin.

The report of the Recording Secretary and Treasurer showed that, counting $125 on hand May 9, 1925, the Society had received during the year $1,644.45 and had paid out $1,189.08, leaving a balance of $455.37. As part compensation for her work as financial officer, the Society voted Miss Fannie Ratchford $75.

The Texas State Historical Association met on Friday afternoon, April 23, thus allowing several members from out of town to attend in one trip the meetings of both the Historical and Folk-Lore organizations.

CONTRIBUTORS

Julia Beazley, of Houston, Texas, contributed one of the outstanding legends, "The Uneasy Ghost of Lafitte," to **Legends of Texas.** She teaches in the Houston schools.

Mody C. Boatright, a familiar of Texas all his life, teaches English in Sul Ross State Teachers College, Alpine; for the year 1926-1927 he instructed in English and did graduate work in the University of Texas. He has been in charge of "folk-lore research" for the West Texas Historical and Scientific Society.

John R. Craddock is a frequent contributor to the **Publications** of the Texas Folk-Lore Society. In 1923 he contributed **"The Cowboy Dance."** His "Legend of Stampede Mesa" is becoming one of the best known of all range traditions.

Hartman Dignowity, now connected with the Extension Department of the University of Texas, contributed a vivid article on "Superstitions of the Northern Seas" to the **Publications** of 1925.

Bertha McKee Dobie, ex-officio co-editor of the **Publications** of the Texas Folk-Lore Society, contributed several legends of the coast country to **Legends of Texas.** She has taught in the University of Texas.

Jovita Gonzâlez, whose article on the Texas-Mexican vaqueror is perhaps the freshest thing that the members of the Society have been treated to in some time, was born at Roma on the Texas border and has spent a great deal of time on the ranch of her ancestors. Grants of border land to her forefathers run back as far as 1745, when her great-great-grandfather, who lived to be 125 years old, was by the king of Spain patented a large body of land along the Rio Grande. Her great-grandfather was the richest land owner of the Texas border. Thus she has an unusual heritage of intimacy with her subject. At present she is teaching Spanish in St. Mary's Hall, San Antonio.

J. Evetts Haley has not yet altogether reformed from being a Plains cowboy. His people are cattle people. As Field Secretary of the Panhandle-Plains Historical Society, he spends his days, his nights and his gasoline in talking with old-time ranchmen of the Llano Estacado. He took his M. A. degree in History at the University of Texas last year, writing his thesis on "A Survey of Texas Cattle Drives to the North, 1866-1895." He is still working on the subject, preparing to expand it into a book.

George E. Hastings is a member of the English faculty of the University of Arkansas, Fayetteville. He has done special work on the ballad and lectures on that subject.

Mattie Austin Hatcher, descended from a cousin of Stephen F. Austin, is Archivist in the Library of the University of Texas. She contributed to the **Publications** for 1926, and her book, **The Opening of Texas to Foreign Immigrants, 1801-1821,** is now being issued by the University of Texas Press, Austin. She is specializing in the lore of Texas Indians.

Robert Adger Law, Professor of English in the University of Texas, was president of the Texas Folk-Lore Society 1912-1913, and for **Publications Number I** (1916), now out of print and much sought after, he wrote a "History of the Folk-Lore Society of Texas."

Arbie Moore lives at Alpine, Texas, with the cowboys of which country he is familiar.

L. W. Payne, Jr., was one of the founders of the Texas Folk-Lore Society, 1909, and in addition to serving it as president for the first two years has contributed to every number of the **Publications** and is a permanent councillor. He is always in search of songs and ballads of the folk.

Ina Sires, as she explains in her article, has long been on the trail of cowboy songs. She was born in the Texas Panhandle, near Lamesa. Her book, **Songs of the Open Range,** is to appear shortly. She has lectured on subjects pertaining to the range; at present she is teaching in the Dallas, Texas, schools. Her address is 727 North Madison Avenue, Dallas.

Della I. Young, Secretary of the Oklahoma Folk-Lore Society and also of the Old Timers of Cheyenne and Arapahoe, lives at Cheyenne, Okla. As her interesting article would indicate, she, like all successful folklorists, is very intimately acquainted with the soil.

INDEX OF BALLADS, RHYMES, AND SONGS

Titles are given in quotation marks; first lines, without quotation marks. Asterisks indicate that the titles so marked are merely referred to.

	PAGE
A man whose name was Johnny Sands	224
A nice young ma-wa-wan	211
*"Adieu to Old El-lum"	198
Along about the time old Eve she did climb	199
"Alphabet Song"	227
An old white hen with yellow legs	65
"Annie Breen from Old Kaintuck"	207
*"Arizona Boys and Girls"	n236
As I walked out one morning in the spring	231
As I was going to Strawberry Fair	68
As I went up the hill today	67
At the foot of yon mountain	158
"Away Here in Texas"	140
Away here in Texas the bright sunny South	140
Ay, mi querida Nicolasa	21
B-A ba, B-E be, B-I bi, ba-be-bi	228
*"Bachelor's Lament, A"	n234
"Backward, Turn Backward"	203
Backward, turn backward, oh time on your wheels	204
Bacon in the pan	136
"Barney Payne"	147
*"Battle of Shiloh Hills, The"	144
*"Beggars of Coldingham Fair, The"	68
"Beggars of Ratcliffe Fair, The"	68
"Betsy Brown"	228
*"Boggus Creek"	201
*"Bonnie Black Bess"	157
Born high up on the Guadalupe	149
"Bow-Legged Ike"	163
Bow-Legged Ike on horseback was sent	164
"Bring Me out My Bottle"	220
Bring me out my bottle	220
"Brown-eyed Lee"	216
"Bud Ballew's Last Draw"	145
"Buffalo Hunters' Song, The"	198, 202
*"Buffalo Skinners, The"	201
*"Burial of Sir John Moore, The"	157

"Californian's Lament, The" 131
"Columbus Is Dead" 229
Columbus is dead and in his grave 230
Come, all my young companions, wherever you may be 187
Come, all who will, and listen 122
Come, all ye good people 236
Come, all ye men of Arkansas, a tale to you I'll sing 207
Come, all you girls of fashion, to you these lines I'll write ... 203
Come, all you jolly huntsmen 225
Come, all you 3 L buceros 160
*"Comical Ditty, A" n236
*"Como Los Rayos del Sol" 198
"Cowboy's Dream, The." See "Cowboy's Hymn."
"Cowboy's Hymn, The" 166
*"Cruel Miller, The" 213
"Custer's Last Fight" 132
Cynically smile the scoffers and say 146

"Davy Crockett" 205
*"Days of Forty-nine, The" 171
"Death of Little Joe, The" 222
"Don't Grow Weary, Boys" 157
Down in a cottage lives Weaver John 226
Down in the Lowlands a poor boy did wander 30
Down in the mill-pond eating up moss 157
Draw near, my gallant comrades, and a story to you I'll sing .. 144
*"Drummer Boy of Shiloh, The" 144
"Drunkard's Dream, The" 125
"Dying Cowboy, The" 173
*"Dying Ranger, The" 150

"Factor's Garland, The." See "The Turkish Factor."
*"Fair Charlotte" 215
"Fox and the Hen, The" 65

Governor Culberson, from among the rest 152
"Grass of Uncle Sam, The" 193

"Haunted Wood, The" 129
Hickey, pickey, zickey, zan 68
"Hills of Mexico, The" 201
"Home, Sweet Home" 165
"Honest Tramp, The" 124
"Hunting Song" 225
*"Husband's Dream, The" 126

Index

I am a wandering cowboy 190
I found myself in Griffin in the spring of '83 201
I got a little girl 190
I love a little girl, and she lives down town 229
"I Love Somebody" 227
I love somebody, I do, Ma-ma 227
"I Must Not Work on Sunday" 135
I must not work on Sunday, Sunday, Sunday 135
"I Wish I Were Single Again" 232
"I'd Like to Be in Texas When They Roundup in the Spring" 161
*"Idle Girl, The" 71
*"If All the Waters in the World Were Made into One Water" 71
*"If Ever I Cease to Love" 157
If you can't get up, there are men in Dodge that can 136
I'll buy fer you fine ribbins 157
I'll tell you a ditty, a truth and no jest 59
*"I'm a Good Old Rebel" n143
I'm a poor old bachelor a-settin' around 234
In a little rosewood casket 221
In a lonely spot by an old, old mill 213
In an olden time a river ran 129
In the lobby of a big hotel, in New York town one day 162
In the Lone Star State of Texas 187
It was just before George Custer's last fight 133
It was on last Monday morning, all troubled in mind 123
It was way down in lower Texas 169

*"James Bird" 215
*"Joe Bowers" 143
"Johnnie Cox" 145
Johnnie Cox he live in Albuquer-ky 145
"Johnny Sands" 223
*"Jolly Cowboy, The" n188
"Juice of the Forbidden Fruit, The" 199

"Killing of the Sow" 230
Kind friends, if you will listen 217
"Kissing on the Sly" 235

*"Lackey Bill" n185
"Leave It! Ah No! The Land Is Our Own" 141
Leave it! Ah no! The land is our own 142
Let me sleep in your barn just tonight, sir 124
Let's go huntin', says Robbin to Bobbin 70
"Little Black Moustache, The" 231
*"Little Joe, the Wrangler" 158, 184
*"Lone Prairie, The" 173
*"Lone Star Trail, The" 198, 200

"Mañanitas de San Juan, Las" ... 20
"Mi Caballo Bayo" ... 21
"Mi Querida Nicolasa" ... 21
"My Lover Is a Cowboy" ... 189
My lover is a cowboy ... 189
*"My Parents Reared Me Tenderly" ... n185
My parents reared me ten-der-lee ... 185

"Not Long Since a Young Girl and I Fell in Love" ... 128
Not long since a young girl and I fell in love ... 128
Now don't you want to know something concernin' ... 206
Now pay attention unto me ... 131
Now, people of the Eastern towns ... n193

O bury me not in the deep, deep sea ... 180
O I'm wild and woolly ... 189
"Ocean Burial, The" ... 173
Ofttimes I get to thinking ... 171
Oh, a trapper lay at the point of death ... 174
"Oh, Bury Me Not on the Lone Prairie" ... 158, 173-183
Oh, bury me not on the lone prairie ... 181
Oh, I am a Texas cowboy ... 196
Oh, I came to the river ... 189
Oh, I just kept a-running ... 190
Oh, once I had a charming young beau ... 231
*"Oh, Listen to the Crickets" ... 154
"Oh, Susan, Quit Your Fooling" ... 134
Oh, Susan, quit your fooling ... 134
Oh, the day seems long and dreary ... 148
Oh, when I was single, oh then, oh then ... 233
"Old Brien-O-Lin" ... 235
Old Brien-o-Lin, his wife, and his wife's mother ... 235
*"Old Chisholm Trail, The" ... 155, 201
*"Old Crummy" ... 229
*"Old Crumpy" ... 229
*"Old Gray Horse, The" ... n189
"Old Grey" ... 123
"Old Mill, The" ... 213
"Old Prohibition Song, An" ... 237
*"Old Rover" ... 230
*"Old Scout's Lament, The" ... 131
*"Old Shawnee, The" ... 213
On Springfield mountains there did dwell ... 210
*"Old Time Cowboy" ... 171
"Old Time Cowboy" ... 171
*"Old Woman of Slapsadam" ... 223
"On Red River Shore" ... 158
*"On the Banks of the Old Pedee" ... 213

One-ery, two-ery	69
*"Orphant Girl, The"	133
Our pack mule Balaam took a tare	152
*"Over the Wall"	157
"Package of Old Letters, A"	221
*"Polly Vaughn"	215
*"Pompey Smash"	n205
"Poor Little Fisherman Boy So Far Away from Home"	29
*"Poor Johnny"	230
"Poor Old Bachelor"	234
*"Poor Robin"	230
*"Pretty Fair Maiden, A"	n194
"Pretty Little Maiden"	194
Pretty little maid out in the garden	194
*"Quantrell's Call"	198
Que bonitas mañanitas	20
Raised in a canebrake	149
"Rattlesnake"	209
"Robbin to Bobbin"	69
*"Rock Me to Sleep"	204
*"Rye Whiskey"	157
*"Sailor's Return, The"	n194
*"Sam Bass"	158, 202
"See, Saw, Margery Daw"	69
See, saw, saddle the old goose	69
*"Shiloh"	144
"Shiloh: A Confederate Song"	143
*"Sing Polly Wolly Doodle All Day"	189
*"Sing, Sing, What Shall We Sing?"	71
"Sister Mary"	215
"Song of the Happy Hunters"	122
"Springfield Mountain"	210
*"Tam O' The Linn"	n235
*"Tam Lin"	n235
"Texas Cowboy, The"	196
"Texas Heroes"	137
*"Texas Lullaby"	156
"Texas Rangers After the Mob"	152
"Three Gay Punchers"	184
"Three L [3 L] Buceros, The"	160
*"Tommy Linn"	n235
"Tonight My Heart's in Texas"	187
"Turkish Factor, The"	56
'Twas a stormy night in winter	215

*"Utah Carl" 184

"Wake up, Jacob" 135
Wake up, Jacob 135
*"Wake up, Snakes, and Bite A Biskit" 135
"Wandering Cowboy, The" 190
We are out on the roundup to brand the sucking calves 194
We are three gray punchers from Yellowstone Flat 184
We lay the crown of memory 139
We are lying on a prairie 165
"Weaver John" 226
*"Wexford Girl, The" 213
What will the birds do, Mother, next spring 222
When a boy falls in love 235
When I think of the last great roundup 167
*"When Work Is Done This Fall" 143
While wandering through the woodlands 237
Why, Durmont, you look healthy now 126
"Wild Boy, The" 185
"William a-Trimbletoe" 66
William a-Trimbletoe 67
"With Three Thousand Texas Steers" 168

Ya no vuelve a su palenque 21
"Young Companions, The" 186
"Young Folks' Dispositions" 236

*"Z Bar Dun, The" 184

GENERAL INDEX

This index is not "complete." To put down the names of all titles and writers cited, all geographic points mentioned, all persons credited as informants, all folkloristic items touched upon would be redundant. Every index, even the fullest, must draw the line somewhere. The purpose of this one is to afford convenient reference to the lore and personalities of the Southwest, not altogether neglecting the comparative relationships that exist everywhere.

Adams, Andy, 161
Agua Corriente, 74
Agua Dulce, 75, 76
Agua Fria, 75
Alabama, 129, 227, 228
Alamocitos, Los, 75
Alamogordo Creek, 75-76
Allan, Francis D., **Lone Star Ballads**, 141, 144
Amarillo, 76
Anderson, William A., 174
Angling Lake, 86
Arapahoe. See Cheyenne
Arkansas, reputation of, expressed in nicknames, 101; song from, 207
Arrington, Capt. G. W., ranger, 74
Arroyo de Gallinas, 75
Arroyo Piedra, 75
Asbjörnsen, 45

Ballew, Bud, bad man, 145-147
Barry, Phillips, 173, 174, 234
Barnes, Will C., **Tales from the X-Bar Horse Camp**, 167-168n.
Bean, Judge Roy, 83
Bear grass, 23
Beazley, Julia, 241; "The Ballad of 'Davy Crockett,'" 205-206:
  Note on the song, 205; singing of it, 205; verses, 206
Belden, H. M., **A Partial List of Song Ballads and Other Popular Poetry Known in Missouri**, 205, 223, 232-233n., 234.
Bell County, Texas, 216, 217, 225
Bitter Creek, 189
Black House, 74

Blanco Canyon, 75
Blanco County, Texas, 147
Boatright, Mody C., 241; "The Devil's Grotto," 102-106:
  The Rio Grande valley between Presidio, Texas, and Ojinaga, Mexico, 102; early exploration of the region, 102-103; Mountain of the Holy Cross and the Devil's Grotto, 103; the habitation of the devil as proved by supernatural phenomena, 103; Pedro's story of how the devil got holed up, 104-105; the Mexican commemoration of the event, 105-106; explanation of the ceremony, 106.
Boggy Creek, 201, 202
Bois d'Arc Creek, 93
Bolte und Polívka, 34, 42, 45, 53, 55
Bolton, H. C., **The Counting-out Rhymes of Children**, 66
Bonham, Texas, 132
Bosque River, 143
Brady, Texas, 175
Brands, cattle, 79, 83, 85, 154, 185, 190, 197, 203
Brightman, Emiline. See Russell
Brightman, Geo. Claver, and family, 23-24
Brazos River, 74
Bugbee, T. S., 84; Canyon, 84
Buffalo Bayou, 134
Buffalo chips, 78-80
Buffalo fat, in rites, 111-112
Buffalo hunters, in Texas Panhandle, 72, 79-83; in Okla., 154
Bull, 35, 36, 43, 44
Burro, tailless, 103

Burton, W. W. and family, representative frontier folk, 121 ff.

Cache Creek, 73
Cadodachos country, 110
Calls to breakfast, 135-136
Canadian River, 73, 74, 75, 78, 84, 136; North and South, 90-97, **passim**
Cañoncito Blanco, 75
Canyon, Texas, 5, 132
Cardo santo. See Thistle
Casa Prieta, 74
Casas Amarillas, 74
Cat, 35, 36, 37, 39-41
Catfish, 84-85
Cattle Ranch to College, by Russell Doubleday, 163, 193
Cattle thieves, 76-78
Catsclaw, 12, 14
Causey Hill, 81
Cenizo **(leucophyllum texanum),** legend of, 9-10.
Ceremonies: of Tejas Indians, 108-118; of Mexicans, 105-106; of hunting the wren, 69
Chambers, Robert, **Popular Rhymes of Scotland,** 28n., 31, 42-43, 55, 68, 69, 235n.
Cherokee Strip, 154, 157, 169
Cheyenne and Arapahoe Territory, 90-97, **passim**
Chihuahua Trail, 102
Chimeneas Ranch, legend about, 14-17
Chinati Mts., 102, 104
Chisholm Trail, 142, 149
Chisum, Jim, 83; John, 83; Canyon, 83
Civil War, 134, 143
Clapp, Sarah, "Peele's Use of Folk-lore in **The Old Wives' Tale,"** 43
Clear Fork, 82
Colorado River, 74, 82
Colt, magic, 45-47
Coma tree, 8
Comanche, Texas, 24
Comanches, 73, 77

Conchos, 74
Confederates, 141-143
Cortina, border bandit, 22
Cow, 39-41, **passim**
Cowboy Life in Texas, by W. S. James, 167
Cowboys(s) American and Texas, 17, 72, 83-86, 90-97, 154-204; Mexican, 7-22
Cowboy Songs, 154-204; see Note 15, p. 154
Cow people, influence on Plains lore, 83-86, 90-97
Cow Punchers' Association of the Cherokee Strip, 169
Cox, J. H., **Folk-Songs of the South,** 125, 133, 143n., 173, 185n., 194n., 205n., 213, 234n., 236n.
Corpus Christi, Texas, 23
Craddock, John R., 174, 181n., 241; "Songs the Cowboys Sing," 184-191:
  Locale of the songs, 184: "Three Gay Punchers," 184-185; "The Wild Boy," 185; "The Young Companions," 186-187; "Tonight My Heart's in Texas," 187-188; fragments, 188-190; making a cowboy song ("The Wandering Cowboy"), 190-191
Cricket, 47-48
Crockett, "Davy," 205
Crosby County, Texas, 88, 89
Crosbyton, Texas, 88, 89
Crow, 69
Custer, General George, 90, 132

Dagger Hollow, 5
Davidson Draw, 81
Davis Mts., 199
Dead Indian Creek, Okla., 93-94
Deep Creek, 81
Deep Lake, yarn about how it was stocked with catfish, 84-85
Deer, buck, 48-51
Devil, holed up in cave, 102-106; in form of giant, 109
Devil's Grotto, 102-106

Dialectical and local words and expressions: brotus, 120; bucero, 160; buckra, 119; bullwhacker, 136; cayuse, 164; cenizo, 9-10; coma, 8; cooter, 119; cresote, 102; crib, 26; cut-back, 168; drag, 203; dry camp, 122; Frazier saddle, 185; gal, 26; gaucho, 7; goober, 120; groundnut, 120; javelin, 122; jinglebob ear mark, 83; johnny cake, 26, 30-33; lazy bench, 100; lechuguilla, 102; Mexican strawberry, 12; mimosa, 102; nester, 86-87; niam, 120; ocotillo, 102; pinder, 119-120; powerful, 26; puncheons, (to noon), 207; raising hair, 203; rooster, 26; rope choker, 99; saddle-broke, 23; scalawag, 160; scatter lead, 147; shindig, 171; sleeper, 168; slick, 168; sotol, 102; swivel neck, 99; tailing, 168; vara, 112. See Mexicanisms.

Dickens County, Texas, 184

Dignowity, Hartman, 241; "Nicknames in Texas Oil Fields," 98-101:

The real workers in oil fields much misrepresented, 98, 101; conditions conducive to nicknames among oil men, 98-99; examples of nicknames, their fitness and unfitness, how they originate, 99-101.

Dilworth spelling book, 25, 71

Dixon, Billie, 82

Dixon Creek, 82

Dobie, Bertha McKee, 6, 241; "Tales and Rhymes of a Texas Household," 23-71:

Introduction, 23-29: The Russell family, from whom the tales have come down, 23-24; frontier home life, 24-25, 28-29; Mrs. Russell's folk inheritance, her manner of telling the stories, 25-28; John C. Duval, 29; Mr. Russell and "The Poor Little Fisherman Boy So Far Away from Home," 29-30.

I. The English Folk Tales, 30-48: "The Johnny Cake," 30-33; "How Jack Went to Seek His Fortune," 33-38; "The Little Long Tail," 38-41; "The Silver Toe," 41-42; "The Bad Gal and the Good Gal," 42-45; "Nor'west Wind and Jack," 45-47; "The Cricket's Supper," 47-48.

II. The Incidents of Pioneer Life, 48-53: "Uncle Billy and the Buck," 48-51; "The Crane's Drumstick," 51-53.

III. Manuscript Tales Not Printed, 53-56: "The Vinegar Bottle," 53-54; "The Peck and a Half," 54; "Count Li-without," 55; "The Old Woman and Her Pig," 55; "Kid Won't Go," 55; "Old Blackbeard the Robber and Murderer," 55; "Simon," 55-56; "Monkeys and Redcaps," 56; "The Young Lion," 56.

IV. "The Turkish Factor," 56-65: Discussion, 56-59; the ballad, 59-65.

V. "The Fox and the Hen," 65-66.

VI. Nursery Jingles, 66-71; "William a-Trimbletoe," 66-67; "As I went up the hill today," 67; "The Beggars of Ratcliffe Fair," 68; "Limpin' Joe" and "Jumpin' Joe," 68-69; "See, saw, Margery Daw," 69; "Robbin to Bobbin," 69-71.

Dobie, J. Frank, "Ballads and Songs of the Frontier Folk," 121-183:

The literary effect of crude frontier ballads, 121.

I. Songs from Frontier Homes and Domestic Camps, 121-135; The Burton family, 121; "Song of the Happy Hunters," 122-123; "Old Grey," 123-124; "The Honest Tramp," 124-125; "The Drunkard's Dream," 125-127; "Not Long Since A Young Girl and I Fell in Love," 128-129; "The Haunted Wood," 129-130; "The Californian's Lament," 131; "Sandy" Morris, singer, 132; "Custer's Last Fight," 132-134; R. J. Dobie, as singer, 134, 135; "Oh, Susan, Quit Your Fooling," 134-135; "I Must Not Work on Sunday," 135.

II. Breakfast Calls, 135-136: "Wake Up, Jacob," 135; morning refrain of bullwhackers, 136; trail cooks' singing, 136.

III. Texas Patriotic Songs, 137-142: Character of the patriotic songs, 137; "Texas Heroes," 137-140; San Jacinto Day celebrations, 137-139; "Away Here in Texas," 140; "Leave It! Ah No! The Land Is Our Own," 141-142.

IV. Confederate Songs, 142-144: Confederates as frontiersmen, 142; singing in Confederate camps, 143; "Shiloh: A Confederate Song," 143-144.

V. American-Mexican songs, 144-145: Bi-lingual speech in the Southwest, 114-145; "Johnnie Cox," 145.

VI. Songs of the Bad Men, 145-150: The bad man Bud Ballew, 145-146; "Bud Ballew's Last Draw," 146-147; "Barney Payne," 147-149; Bad Man Yells, 149-150.

VII. Ranger Songs, 150-153: **Esprit de corps** of the Texas rangers, 150; account of their morning chants, 150-151; Sowell's "sample of the poetical genius of a Texas ranger," 151-152; "Texas Rangers After the Mob," 152-153.

VIII. Cowboy Songs, 154-183: Cowboys sing humanly as well as professionally, 154-155; singing a part of their social life, 155; printable and unprintable cowboy songs, 155-158; address to the dance hall "lady," 156-157; "Don't Grow Weary, Boys," 157; "On Red River Shore," 158-159; "The 3 L Buceros," 160-161; Andy Adams and Lon Fishback, 161; "I'd Like to Be in Texas When They Roundup in the Spring," 161-163; "Bow-Legged Ike," 163-164; "Home, Sweet Home," a Slaughter Ranch song, 165-166; "The Cowboy's Hymn," 166-168; Ben Thorne, cowboy singer, 168-169; "With Three Thousand Texas Steers," 168-170; "Old-Time Cowboy," 171-173; discussion of "Oh, Bury Me Not on the Lone Prairie" as compared with its source, "The Ocean Burial," 173-176; "The Ocean Burial," 177-181; "Oh, Bury Me Not on the Lone Prairie," 181-183.

Dobie, R. J. 134, 135.
Dodge City, 136
Dog, 35, 36, 37, 49, 51
Donley County, Texas, 82
Dove, call of interpreted, 8
Drannan, W. F., **Thirty-one Years on the Plains,** 131
Drouth, 9-10
Duval, John C., 29, 47

Eagle, 40, 41, 48
Early Times in Texas, by John C. Duval, 29
Eddy. See Tolman
English Fairy Tales. See Jacobs
Emmons, Martha, 5
Escobas, legend of the Ranch of, 18

Farming element on the Plains, 87-89, 95-97
Ferry boat, 23

Index   253

Finger, Chas. J., 207
Fire, Indian fear of, 114
Flintlock, rifle and equipment described, 49-50
Folk-lore, plea for, 5; uses of, 6; fresh field of, 72, 89
Folk tales. (In the list that follows, those tales merely referred to in the present volume—such being related to tales under discussion—are marked with an asterisk.)
*"Ass, The, the Table, and the Stick," 45
"Bad Gal, The, and the Good Gal," 42
*"Blue Beard," 55
*"Cat, The, and the Mouse," 38, 39
"Crane's Drumstick, The," 29, 51-53
"Cricket's Supper, The," 29, 47-48
"Count Li-without," 55
*"Forgetful Boy, The," 54
*"Frederick and Catherine," 34
*"Gingerbread Boy, The," 31
*"Golden Arm, The," 41
*"Grim White Woman, The," 53
*"Hereinafterthis," 34
"How Jack went to Seek His Fortune," 26, 30, 33-38
"Johnny Cake, The," 26, 30-33
*"Juniper [Almond] Tree, The," 53
*"Katherine Nipsy," 28n.
"Kid Won't Go," 55
*"Lad Who Went to the North Wind, The," 45
"Lion, The Young," 56
*"Little Cakeen, The," 31
"Little Long Tail, The," 38-41
"Monkeys and Redcaps," 56
*"Murderous Mother, The," 53
"Nor'west Wind and Jack," 45-47

"Old Blackbeard the Robber," 55
*"Old Foster," 55
"Old Woman and Her Pig, The," 55
"Peck and a Half, The," 54
*"Robber Bridegroom, The," 55
*"Rose Tree, The," 53
"Silver Toe, The," 41-42
"Simon," 55-56
*"Singing Bones, The," 53
*"Spióla, The Story of," 43
*"Stupid's Mistaken Cries," 54
*"Tablecloth, D o n k e y, and Club," 45
*"Teeny-Tiny," 41
*"Three Heads of the Well, The," 42
*"Toads and Diamonds," 42, 43
*"Town Musicians of Bremen, The," 34
"Uncle Billy and the Buck," 29, 48-51
*"Vinegar, Mr.," 34, 54
"Vinegar Bottle, The," 53-54
*"Wal at the Warld's End,, The," 42
*"Wee Bannock, The," 26, 31
*"Wife and Her Bush of Berries, The," 55
*"Wishing Table, The," etc., 45
(See tales under González, Jovita.)
Fort Concho, 82
Fort Elliott, 83, 94
Fort Griffin, 201, 202
Fort Reno, 94
Fort Stockton, 145
Fox, 65-66
Frog, 48
Frying Pan Ranch, 76
Gallinas Creek, N. M., 77
Galveston, 23, 24
Gander, 35, 36
Garrett, Buck, sheriff, 146
Ghosts, 14-18, 19-20, 41-42, 87-89, 94
Giant, 109-110

Goliad, 23-29 **passim**
Goliad County, 48
González, Jovita, 241; "Folk-lore of the Texas-Mexican Vaquero," 7-22:
   I. The vaquero as Texan and man, 7-8.
   II. His attitude towards nature, 8-14: Interpretation of cries of birds (dove and killdee), 8; legend of the cenizo bush, 9-10; legend of the mocking bird, 10-11; legend of the **cardo santo** (thistle), 12-13; of the guadalupana vine, 13-14.
   III. Legends of ghosts and treasures, 14-20: Legend of Chimeneas Ranch, 14-18; of Las Escovas Ranch, 18; of Las Víboras Ranch, 18-20.
   IV. The vaquero's love for music and his songs, 20-22: "Las Mañanitas de San Juan," 20; "Mi Querida Nicolasa," 21; "Mi Cabayo Bayo," 21; the **tragedia** as a form of literature, 22.
   V. Possibilities of a distinct vaquero literature.
Goodnight, Charles, 73, 74n., 75n., 76n., 77, 78, 79n., 82n., 92
Goodnight-Loving Trail, 198, 201
Grimm brothers, 25, 26, 34, 45, 53, 55
Guadalupana vine, legend of, 13-14
Guadalupe River, 28

Haley, J. Evetts, 5, 241; "Lore of the Llano Estacado," 72-79:
   Introduction, 72: Geographical location of the Llano Estacado, 72; the five social groups that have contributed to the lore of the Plains, 72.
   I. Indian contribution as seen in place names, 72-73: Kiowa Creek, 73; Prairie-dog-town River, 73; Tahoka, 73; Miami, 73; Quanah, 73. See also Mobeetie, 76.
   II. Spanish and Mexican contribution in nomenclature, all important streams bearing Spanish names, 73-79: Conchos, 74; Casas Amarillas (Yellow Houses), 74; Casa Prieta (Black House), 74; Agua Corriente (Running Water), 74-75; Blanco Canyon, 75; Tule, 75; Agua Fria, 75; Cañoncita Blanca, 75; Tierra Blanca, 75; Palo Duro, 75; Agua Dulce, 75, 76; Venado Colorado (Red Deer), 75; Arroyo Piedra, 75; Arroyo de Gallinas, 75; Rios Amarillos, 75; Sierrita de la Cruz, 75; Los Alamocitos, 75; Alamogordo, 75; Las Tecovas, account of trade in stolen stock at, 76-78; Las Lenguas, 77; Sierrita de la Cruz, story of how it got its name, 78-79.
   III. Buffalo hunter contribution, 79-83: Lore about buffalo chips, 79-80; nicknames among buffalo hunters, 80; place names derived from, 81-83.
   IV. Cattle people most distinct social group in Plains history, 83-86: Chisum Canyon, 83-84; Bugbee Canyon, 84; cowboy boot, catfish, and Deep Lake, 84-85; cowboys and rangers fight against Indians at Angling Lake, 85-86; sheepmen, 86.
   V. Farmng element, 86-89: Toadloop Draw, 86-87; legend of the haunted WIL S Ranch in Crosby County, 87-89.
Haley, J. Evetts, "Cowboy Songs Again," 198-204:
   Searching for cowboy songs, 198; "Honey Jim" Mullens, the prince of singers, 198; "The Juice of the Forbidden Fruit," 199-200; "The Hills of Mexico," 201-202; "The Buffalo Hunters' Song," 202-203; "Backward, Turn Backward," 203-204.

Hall County, Texas, 84
Halliwell, **Nursery Rhymes and Tales,** 38, 55, 56, 57, 58, 66, 68, 68, 71, 235
Harrisburg, Texas, 134
Harrison, Richard Clarence, 238
Hastings, George E., 241; "Annie Breen from Old Kaintuck," 207-208:
  The Arkansas minstrel, 207; the ballad, 207-208.
Hatcher, Mattie Austin, 241; "Myths of the Tejas Indians," 107-118:
  Sam Houston's plea, his belief in omens, 107; the Tejas Indians of the Southwest, 108; their customs, myths, etc., described by Spanish chroniclers, 108-109.
  The Tejas god, 109; origin of heaven, 109; first people of earth, 109; the devil giant, 109-110; the after-world, 110-11; fire-worship, 111; the **coninici,** 111-112; the grand **Xinesí** and his tricks with the **coninici,** 112-113; seasonal ceremonies, 113-117; war ceremony, 117; May fëte, 117-118.
Haunted wood, 129-130
Helena, Texas, 25, 28
Headlton, Okla., 145, 146
Hell Roaring Hollow, 82
Hen, 65-66
Horse, theme of song, 21, 123; 43, 44
Houston, Sam, belief in omens, 107
Houston, True Stories of Old, by S. O. Young, 138n.
Hoxie, Jane, **Kindergarten Story Book,** 39.

Indians, 7, 8, 72, 73, 75, 128, 129; geographical nomenclature in Texas and Oklahoma derived from, 72-73, 76, 90; fights and raids, 28, 51-52, 82-83, 85-86, 130; Tejas, 107-118

Jacobs, Joseph, 25, 26, 30, 31, 33-34, 38, 39, 41, 42, 43, 45, 53, 54, 55
James, W. S., **Cowboy Life in Texas,** 167
Jennings, N. A., **A Texas Ranger,** 150 ff.
Jones and Plummer Trail, 83
"Jumpin' Joan," 68
"Jumpin' Joe," 68

Ke-che-a-que-ho-no, 73
Kennedy, Ruth, 41
Kent County, Texas, 184
Killdee, call of, interpreted, 8
Kiowa Creek, 73, 90
Kiowas, 73, 77
Kittredge, Professor George Lyman, 57-58, 224

La Bahia. See Goliad
Lang, Andrew, 25
Las Vegas, N. M., 77
Law, Robert Adger, 242; "A note on Four Negro Words," 119-120: "Buckra," 119; "pinder," 119-120; "niam," 120; "brotus," 120.
Legend of Sour Lake, Young, 141
Legends, 7-20, **passim;** 87-89. See Folk tales.
Lelia Lake, 82
Lenguas, Las, 76-77
Leucophyllum texanum. See Cenizo.
Lewis, Gabe, 230, 233
"Liberty Pole," 138-139, 140
"Limpin, Joan," 68
"Limpin' Joe," 68
Linnet, 69
Little Cottonwoods, 75
Live Oak County, Texas, 134
Lizard, 47, 48
Llano Estacado, 72-89. See Haley, "Lore of the Llano Estacado." See also Panhandle.
Lomax, John A., **Cowboy Songs and Other Frontier Ballads,"** 131n., 154, 171, 175, 184, 185n., 186n., 188n., 192, 196n., 201, 202n., 209, 236n.

Los Vegas, legendary legacy of, 16-17
Lubbock, Texas, 74, 228
Lubbock County, Texas, 81
Lynn County, Texas, 73

Marcy, R. B., 72-73, 75-76
Maverick County, Texas, 14
May Day among Tejas Indians, 117-118
McClellan Creek, 75-76
McCulloch County, Texas, 175
McKenzie Trail, 82
McNelly, Capt. L. H., ranger, 150
Mexicans, lore of, 7-22; raids by, 28; in Panhandle, 72, 78-79
Mexicanisms common to Texas and the Southwest: **carretas,** 77; **Chata,** 7; **compadre,** 12; **escopeta,** 29; **guaraches,** 15; **jacal,** 16; **javelina,** 122; **laguna,** 12; **lagueneño,** 10; **nopal,** 15; **pastor,** 14-18; **pitahaya (pitalla),** 12; **potrero,** 12; **uña de gato,** 12, 14; **vaquero,** 7-22.
Miami, Texas, 73
Midland, Texas, 86, 87
Midland County, Texas, 85
"Minometer," for finding trasure, 5
Mocking bird, legend of, 10-11
Mobeetie, 76
Mooar's Creek, 82
Mooar's Draw, 82
Moore, Arbie, 242; "The Texas Cowboy," 196-197:
Reports of the song, 196n.; music and words, 196-197.
More English Fairy Tales. See Jacobs.
Morris, "Sandy," singer, 132
Mouse, 39-41
Mullens, "Honey Jim," 198
Musical instruments: of Mexican vaquero, 20; of Tejas Indians, 112, 117
Myths, of Tejas Indians, 107 ff. See Hatcher, Mattie Austin.

Napkin, magic, 46-47
Navajo sheepherder, 78
Nealy Flats on South Canadian changed to Pie Flat, a folk tale, 95-97
Negro songs, 5; words, 119-120
Newell, W. W., **Songs and Games of American Children,** 39, 55, 66, 69
New Mexico, New Mexican, 74, 132
Nicknames among buffalo hunters, 80-81; among cowboys, 172, 198, 199; among oil men, 98-101
North Carolina, 57
Nueces (in Panhandle), 76
Nueces River, 122

Oil men, their reputation, 98; their real nature, 98, 101; nicknames among, 98-101
Oklahoma, lore of western part, 90-98
Omens. See Houston, Sam
Ox Bow Crossing, 84

Pack Saddle Creek, Okla., 90
Palo Duro, 75, 78
Panhandle, Panhandle-Plains, 72-89, **passim;** 90-97, **passim**
Panhandle-Plains Historical Society, 5, 204
Parker, Cynthia Ann, 73. See Quanah Parker
"Passover Song of the Kid, The," 39, 55
Payne, Barney, outlaw, 147-149
Payne, L. W., Jr., 5, 242; "Songs and Ballads—Grave and Gray," 209-237:
How the songs were collected, 209; "Rattlesnake," 209-212; "The Old Mill," 213-214; "Sister Mary," 215-216; "Brown-eyed Lee," a Bell County ballad, 216-220; "Bring Me Out My Bottle," 220-221; "A Package of Old Letters," 221-222; "The Death of Little Joe," 222-223; "Johnny

Sands," 223-225; "Hunting Song," 225-226; "Weaver John," 226-227; "I Love Somebody," 227; "Alphabet Song," 227-228; "Betsy Brown," 228-229; "Columbus Is Dead," 229-230; Gabe Lewis, the singer, 230; "Killing of the Sow," 230-231; "The Little Black Mustache," 231-232; "I Wish I Were Single Again," 232-234; "Poor Old Bachelor," 234-235; "Old Brien-O-Lin," 235; "Kissing on the Sly," 235-236; "Young Folks' Dispositions," 236-237; "An Old Prohibition Song," 237.
Pearsall, Texas, 230, 232
Pease River, 76
Peck's Spring, 86
Perrault, 42, 45n., 55
Perrow, E. C., 189, 221, 223, 227
Pie Flat, Okla., 95-97
Pig, 40, 41
Pitcher Creek, 82
Plains. For lore of, see Haley, J. Evetts, also Young, Della I.
"Plains children," 72
Platte River, 131
Point Comfort, Texas, 24
Pot, magic, 46-47
Pound, Louise, **American Ballads and Songs**, 70, 175, 210n., 213, 224, 230, 233n.
Prairie-dog-town River, 73
Presidio, Texas, 102, 106
Proverbs, Mexican, 7, 8; old English, 54.
Provincialisms. See Dialect.

Quanah, Texas, 73
Quanah Parker, his name interpreted, 73

Rabbit, without forefeet, 103
Ram, 35, 36. See Sheep.
Rangers and Pioneers of Texas, Sowell, 149, 151
Rangers, Texas, 146, 150-153; fight with Indians, 85-86

Rath Trail, 83
Red Deer, 75
Red River, 73, 84; song involving, 158
Remedies, folk, 11n., 14n.
Rigby, John, 155
Rincón de Las Piedras, N. M., 78
Rios Amarillos, 75
Robber's Roost, Okla., 91-92
Roberts, Capt. Dan W., ranger, 166
Rooster, 34, 36, 37
Running Water Creek, 75
Russell, Charles, 23-30, **passim**
Russell, Emeline Brightman, 23-30; 58
Russell, L. B., 24-30, 34, 58

S M S Ranch, 190
San Jacinto, omen at, 107; celebration of San Jacinto Day, 137-139
San Marcos River, 108
San Patricio, Texas, 23
Sanborn Spring, 76-77
Santa Fe, N. M., 77, 145
Scarborough, Dorothy, **The Wind,** 6
Schimerhorn Mt., 81
Scott, Roy S., 155
Scurry County, Texas, 81
Sergeant Major Creek, Okla., 90
Sharps rifles, 72, 203
Sheep, 43, 44; trouble over, 78-79. See Ram.
Sierrita de la Cruz, 75, 78-79
Sires, Ina, 242; "Songs of the Open Range," 192-195:
  Significance of the cowboy songs, 192; importance of melodies, 192; how songs were procured, 192-193; "The Grass of Uncle Sam," 193-194; "Pretty Little Maiden," 194-195.
Siringo, Chas. A., **Riata and Spurs,** 121, 188
Slaughter family in Texas, 165
Slaughter, Will, 87
Smith, Victor J., 5, 196n.
Snake, 48
Snyder, Pete, 81-82

258   *Texas and Southwestern Lore*

Snyder, Texas, 81
Soap maker, 26, 32, 33
Songs. See pp. 121-237
Sour Dough Creek, Okla., 92-93
South Carolina, 25, 28, 51
Sow, 40, 41
Sowell, A. J., **Rangers and Pioneers of Texas,** 149, 151-152
Spaniards, among Tejas Indians, 108-110; influence on Plains country, 72, 73-79; traditions connected with, 14-20; also, 5, 7, 72
Sparrow, 69
Springer's Ranch, a story about, 94
Spur, Texas, 188
Starr County, Texas, 18
Starvation Creek, Okla., 95
Stonewall County, Texas, 184
Studebaker wagon, 25
Sullivan, W. J. L., ranger and author of **Twelve years, etc.,** 152 166
Sweetwater Creek, 75, 76

T Anchor Ranch, 79; Roundup, 132
Tahoka, Texas, 73, 88
Tales. See Folk tales
Tarrant County, Texas, 167
Tascosa, Texas, 78-76
Tecovas, Las, a trading point, 75-76
Tejas Indians. See Hatcher, Mattie Austin
Texas—Paradise, 108
Texas Folk-Lore Society, 5-6, 24
Texas Gems, Kyger, 137
Texas Jo, 207
Texas, Poetry and Poets of, Dixon, 137
Texas Poetry Society, 6
Texas Prairie Flower, Winkler, 138
Texas Ranger, A, Jennings, 150-151
Texino—devil, 110
Thistle **(cardo santo),** legend of, 12
Thorne, Ben, 168-169

Thorp, N. H., **Songs of the Cowboys,** 166, 175, 188n., 192
Tierra Blanca, 75
Toadloop Draw, 86-87
Tobacco, 124; rites of, 111-112, 115
Tolman and Eddy, **Traditional Texts and Tunes,** 29n., 223, 224
Tongue River, 76-77
Tragedia, the, as a genre, 20-22
Trail drivers, 142
Treasure, robber, 37, 38; buried 14-20; Spanish, 5, 14-20
Trunk Creek, Okla., 91
Tule Canyon, 75
"Turkish Factor, The," 56-65
Twelve Years in the Saddle for Law and Order on the Frontiers of Texas, Sullivan, 152.

Uvalde, Texas, 173

Vaquero, Mexican cowboy, 7-22, 160
Venado Colorado, El, 75
Víboras Ranch, legend of, 18
Virgin, a, attacked by devil, 109
Virgin, Holy, belief in, 9-10, 13-14, 15, 18

Wagon Creek, Okla., 90
Wagon Sheet Creek, Okla., 91
Wateree River, 52
Webb, W. P., 201
West Texas Historcal and Scientific Society, 5, 196n.
Wichita Falls, Texas, 146
WIL S Ranch, ghosts of, 87-89
Williams, Judge O. W., 145
Wolf, eats up johnny cake, 32, 33
Wolf Creek, Okla., 155
Woll, Mexican general, 28
Worley Lake, 82
Wren, ceremony connected with, 69

X I T Ranch, 74

Young, Della I., 242; "Names in the Old Cheyenne and Arapahoe

Territory and the Panhandle of Texas, 90-97:
The turtle back between Red River and the South Canadian, 90; names of this region generally applied by cowboys, 90; few Indian names, 90; Custer's influence in names of Wagon, Pack Saddle, and Sergeant Major creeks, 90; influences determining cowboy application of names, 90-91; Wagon Sheet Creek, 91; Trunk Creek, 91; Robber's Roost, 91-92; Sour Dough Creek, 91; Home Ranch Creek, 93; Bois d'Arc Creek, 93; Dead Indian Creek, 93-94; Springer's ghost, 94; Starvation Creek, 95; how Nealy Flats became Pie Flats, 95-97.

Young, Dr. S. O., **True Stories of Old Houston and Houstonians,** 138

Zenzontle. See Mocking bird.

www.ingramcontent.com/pod-product-compliance
Lightning Source LLC
Chambersburg PA
CBHW030313080526
44584CB00012B/547